| | | | | | | |
|---|---|---|---|---|---|---|
| GREAT JOB! | WAY TO GO! | I'M A STAR! | A+! | RIGHT ON! | GREAT WORK! | KEEP IT UP! |
| GREAT JOB! | WAY TO GO! | I'M A STAR! | A+! | RIGHT ON! | GREAT WORK! | KEEP IT UP! |
| GREAT JOB! | WAY TO GO! | I'M A STAR! | A+! | RIGHT ON! | GREAT WORK! | KEEP IT UP! |
| GREAT JOB! | WAY TO GO! | I'M A STAR! | A+! | RIGHT ON! | GREAT WORK! | KEEP IT UP! |
| GREAT JOB! | WAY TO GO! | I'M A STAR! | A+! | RIGHT ON! | GREAT WORK! | KEEP IT UP! |
| GREAT JOB! | WAY TO GO! | I'M A STAR! | A+! | RIGHT ON! | GREAT WORK! | KEEP IT UP! |
| GREAT JOB! | WAY TO GO! | I'M A STAR! | A+! | RIGHT ON! | GREAT WORK! | KEEP IT UP! |
| GREAT JOB! | WAY TO GO! | I'M A STAR! | A+! | RIGHT ON! | GREAT WORK! | KEEP IT UP! |
| GREAT JOB! | WAY TO GO! | I'M A STAR! | A+! | RIGHT ON! | GREAT WORK! | KEEP IT UP! |
| GREAT JOB! | | I'M A STAR! | A+! | RIGHT ON! | | KEEP IT UP! |

GIANT BASIC SKILLS™

# Getting Ready For KINDERGARTEN

**Modern Publishing**
A Division of Unisystems, Inc.
New York, New York 10022
Series UPC: 49130

This book

belongs to:

..................................

Illustrated by Arthur Friedman
Educational Consultants: Shereen Gertel Rutman, M.S.
Mary Mclean Hely, M.A. in Education, Design and Evaluation of Educational Programs
Colorization and page design by quadrum www.quadrumltd.com



Printed in Canada

# To the Parents

## Dear Parents,

As your child's first and most important teacher, you can encourage your child's love of learning by participating in educational activities at home. Working together on the activities in this workbook will help your child build confidence, learn to reason, and develop skills necessary for early childhood education.

The following are some suggestions to help make your time together enjoyable and rewarding.

- Choose a time when you and your child are relaxed.
- Provide a writing tool that your child is familiar with.
- Don't attempt to do too many pages at one time or expect that every page be completed. Move on if your child is frustrated or loses interest.
- Don't attempt to do too many pages at one time or expect that every page be completed. Move on if your child is frustrated or loses interest. Discuss each page. Help your child relate the concepts in this book to everyday experiences.
- Encourage your child to use the practice pages provided at the end of many of the sections to work independently and reinforce skills.
- Use the Achievement Checklist to keep track of the pages you need to revisit. When the "Mastered" column is full, your child has earned the diploma at the back of the book!

**Happy Learning!**

# Essential Skills

The repetitive activities within each chapter have been designed to help children learn the skills necessary for learning and thinking.

## CHAPTER 1 HANDWRITING SKILLS

Learning to control the small muscles of the hand **(fine motor skill development)** allows a child to make the precise movements necessary for forming letters. **Writing from left to right, tracing,** and **forming lines** help to refine eye/hand coordination. Making associations enables a child to recognize that an uppercase "A" and a lowercase "a" go together.

## CHAPTER 2 COLORS, SHAPES, AND NUMBERS

Looking at familiar shapes helps children notice similarities and differences. Reproducing and matching shapes to words encourages **sight vocabulary recognition** and the ability to make **associations between words and objects. Classification activities** encourage development of a child's ability to reason and make logical connections. **Recognizing number words,** writing numerals, and **forming sets of objects** all prepare a child for basic math skills.

## CHAPTER 3 COUNTING AND MATH SKILLS

Becoming familiar with the **order of numbers from 1 to 10, learning to write those numbers**, and **understanding the connection between a set of objects and its corresponding numeral** all prepare a child to understand the concepts of addition and subtraction.

## CHAPTER 4 MEASURING

Children develop logical reasoning skills as they compare the size and length of objects. They use a variety of measurement systems to learn **basic measurement skills**. Children estimate the **weight and capacity** of various containers.

## CHAPTER 5 TIME AND MONEY

In this chapter children learn about the **numbers on the clock** and how to **tell time to the hour and half hour**. Children also explore **money concepts** and use **pennies, nickels, and dimes**.

## CHAPTER 6 READING READINESS

Determining which items in a group "go together" **(making associations)** and learning to group things according to common attributes **(classification skills)** prepare a child to notice details. These skills enable children to distinguish between the letters of the alphabet.

## VOCABULARY AND MATH SKILL BUILDER

This entertaining story revolves around math with money, illustrating the value of math in a real-world context. It also lends itself to creative language activities outlined at the end of the section.

## CHAPTER 7 PHONICS SKILLS I

This chapter focuses on teaching a child to **recognize the initial and final consonant sounds, learn to write letters and words using these sounds**, and **understand the association between sounds, symbols, and words.**

## CHAPTER 8 PHONICS SKILLS II

Phonics II focuses on training a child to **hear and reproduce the long and short vowel sounds**, as well as the sounds made by combining two letters to make **consonant blends** and **consonant digraphs**.

## CHAPTER 9 PUTTING WORDS TOGETHER

The activities in this chapter help children learn commonly used words. Children **read, spell**, and **write words** that form a basic sight vocabulary. The words learned in previous chapters are used to form **sentences**. Children **spell and write words in complete sentences**.

# Table of Contents

# Handwriting Skills

Start at the dots. Trace the broken lines. Then finish the page.

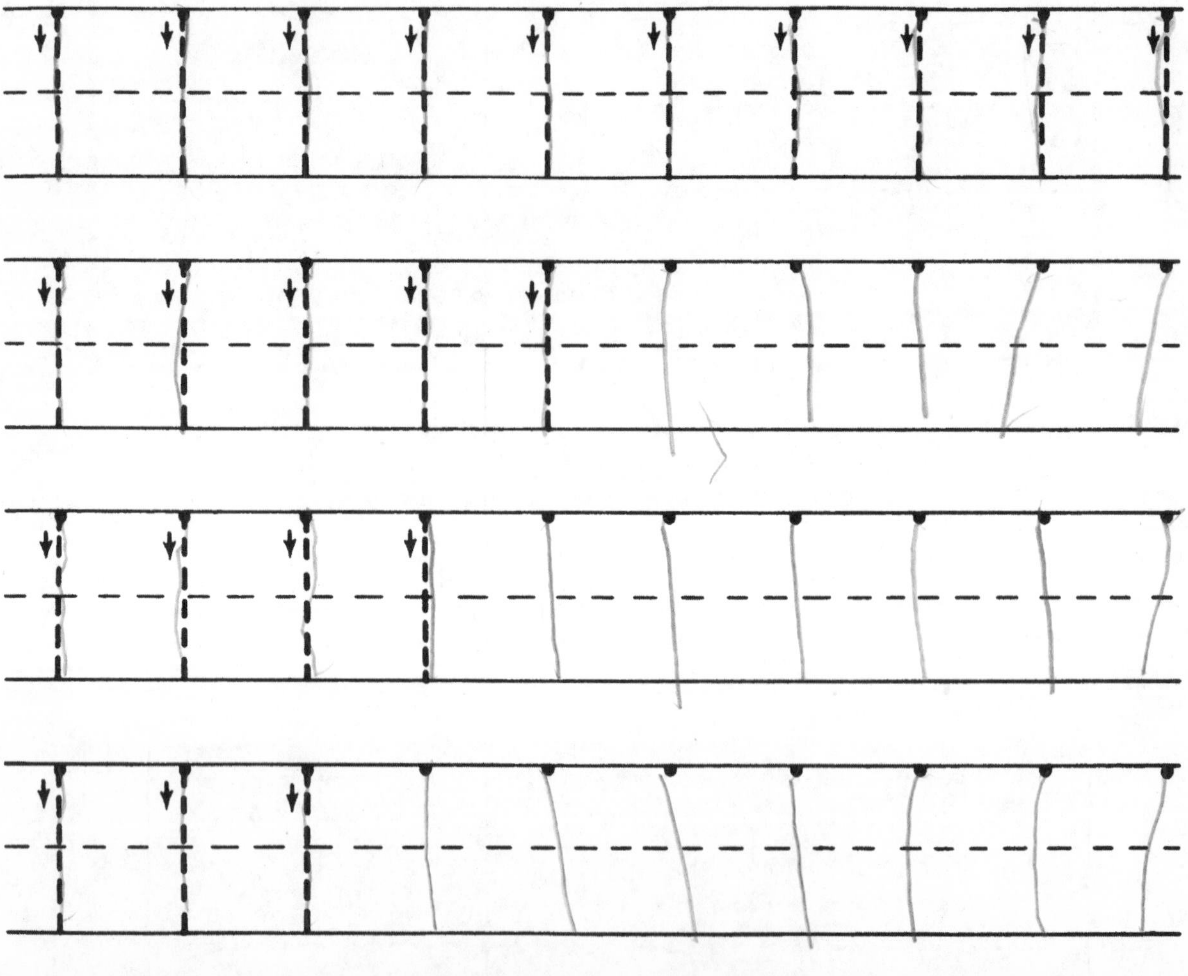

**Skills:** Fine motor skill development; Eye/hand coordination; Forming vertical lines

Start at the dots. Trace the broken lines. Then finish the page.

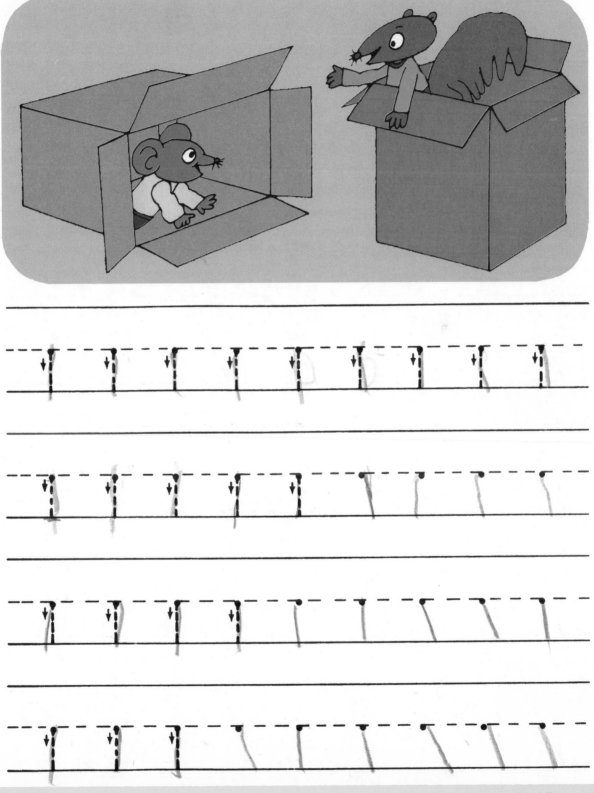

**Skills:** Fine motor skill development; Eye/hand coordination; Forming vertical lines

Start at the dots. Trace the broken lines. Then finish the page.

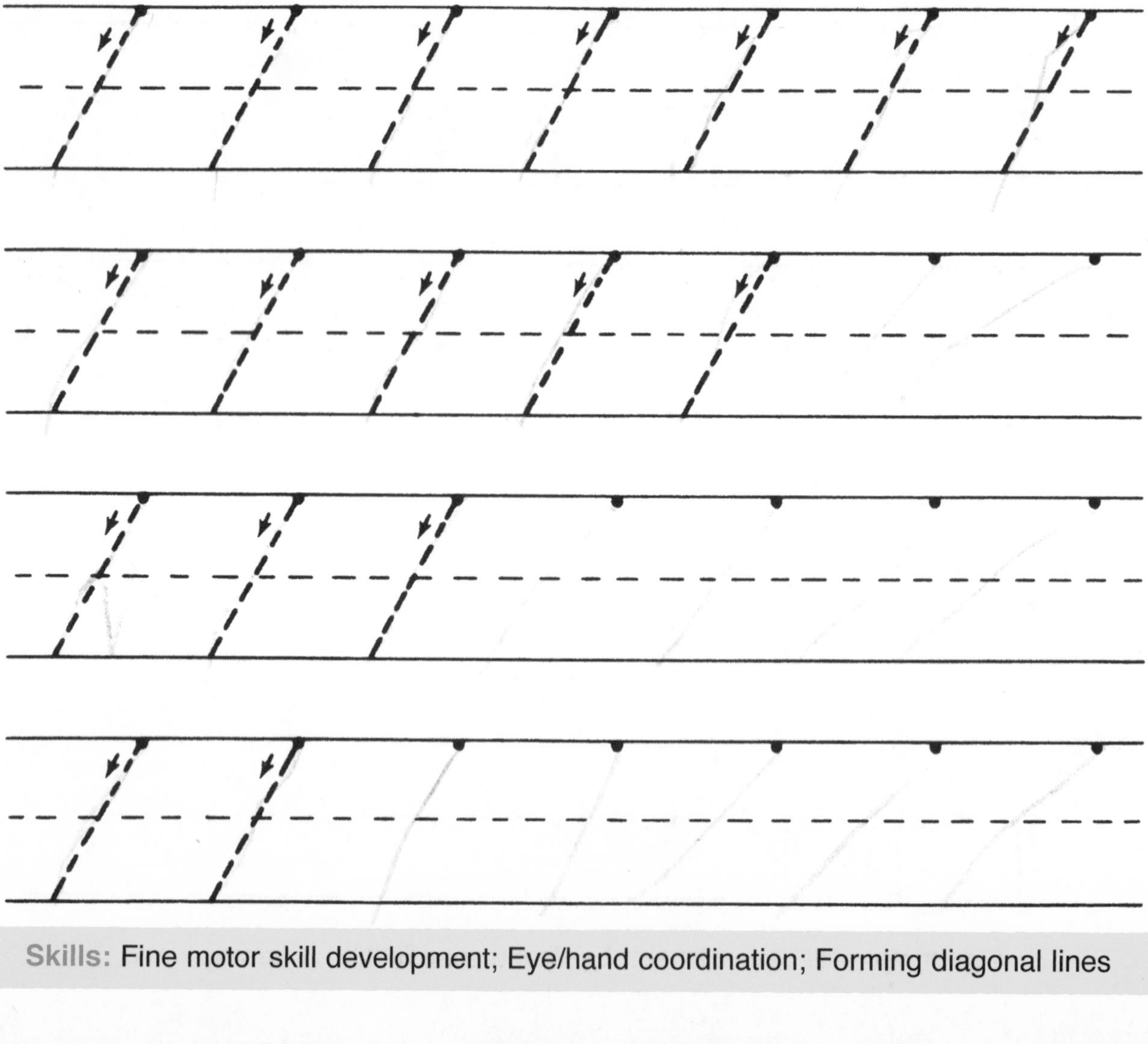

Skills: Fine motor skill development; Eye/hand coordination; Forming diagonal lines

Start at the dots. Trace the broken lines. Then finish the page.

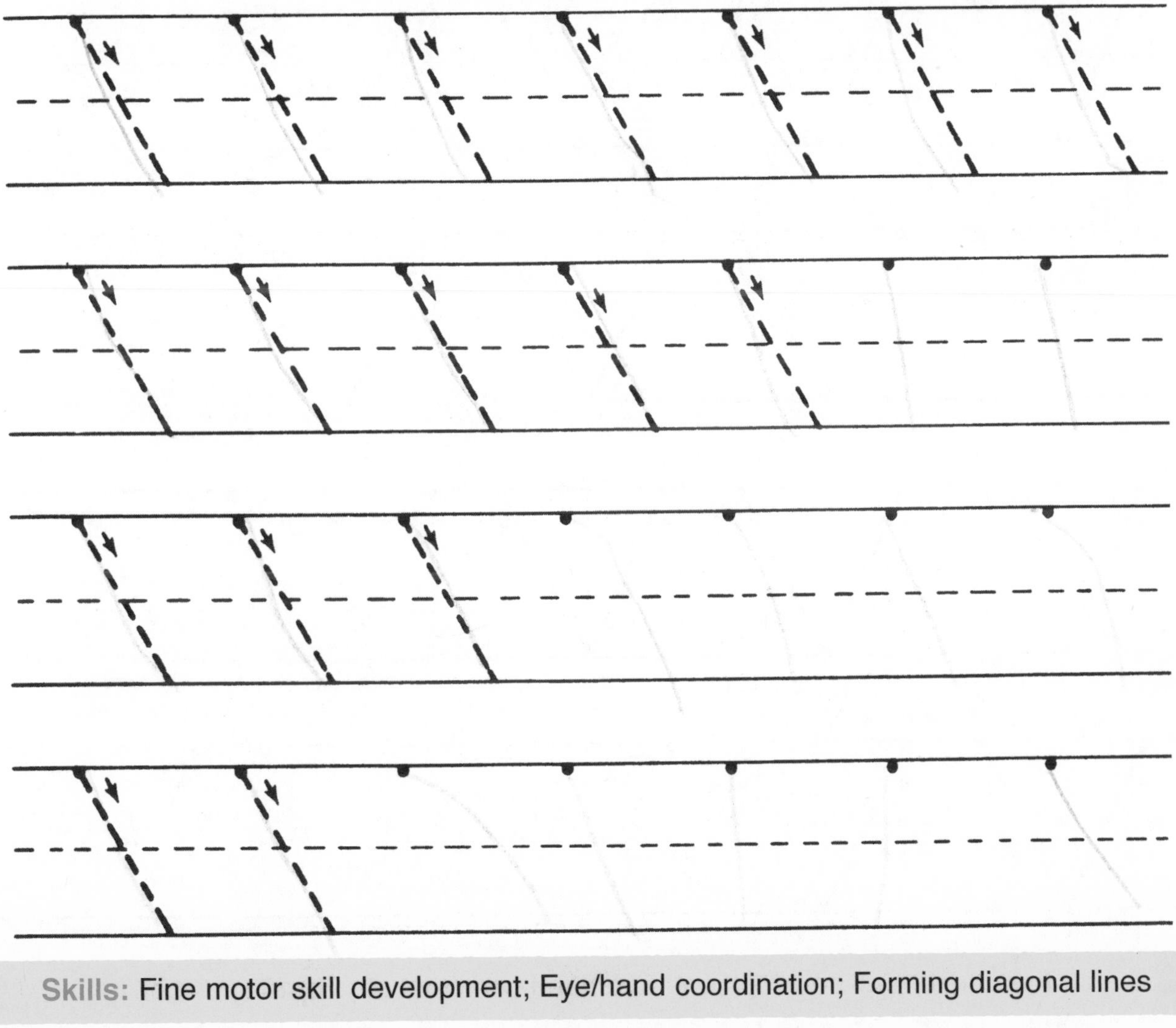

**Skills:** Fine motor skill development; Eye/hand coordination; Forming diagonal lines

Start at the dots. Trace the broken lines. Then finish the page.

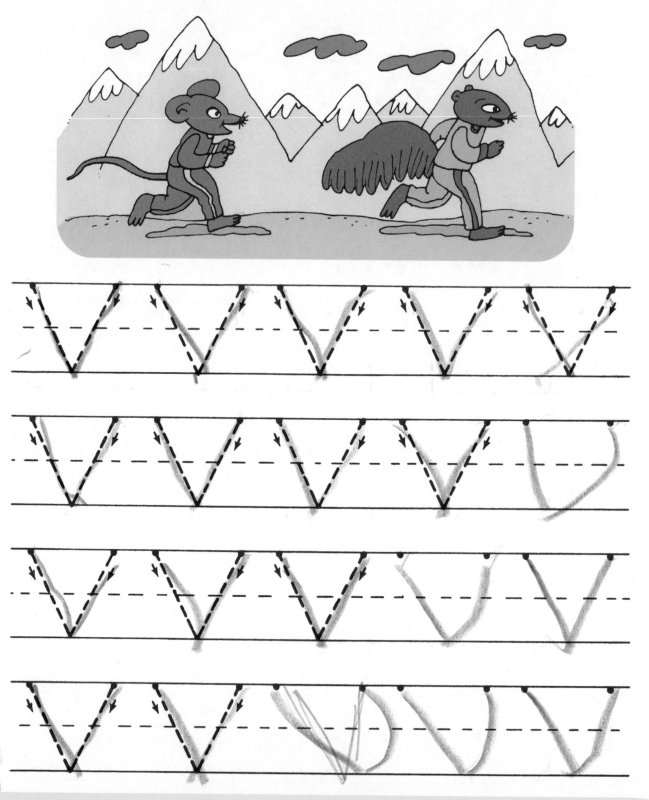

Skills: Fine motor skill development; Eye/hand coordination; Forming diagonal lines

# Handwriting Skills

Start at the dots. Trace the broken lines.

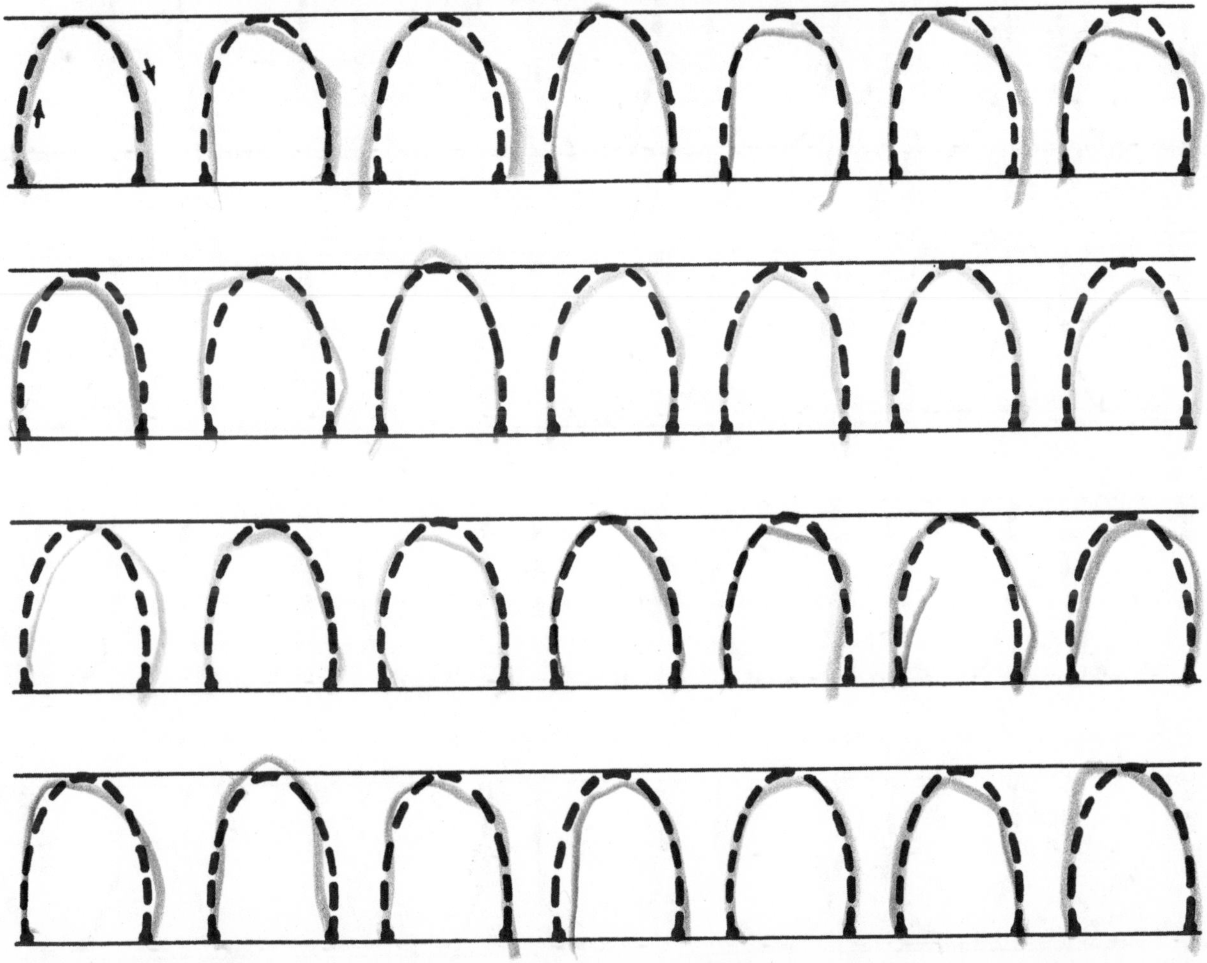

**Skills:** Fine motor skill development; Eye/hand coordination; Forming open curves

# Handwriting Skills

Start at the dots. Trace the broken lines.

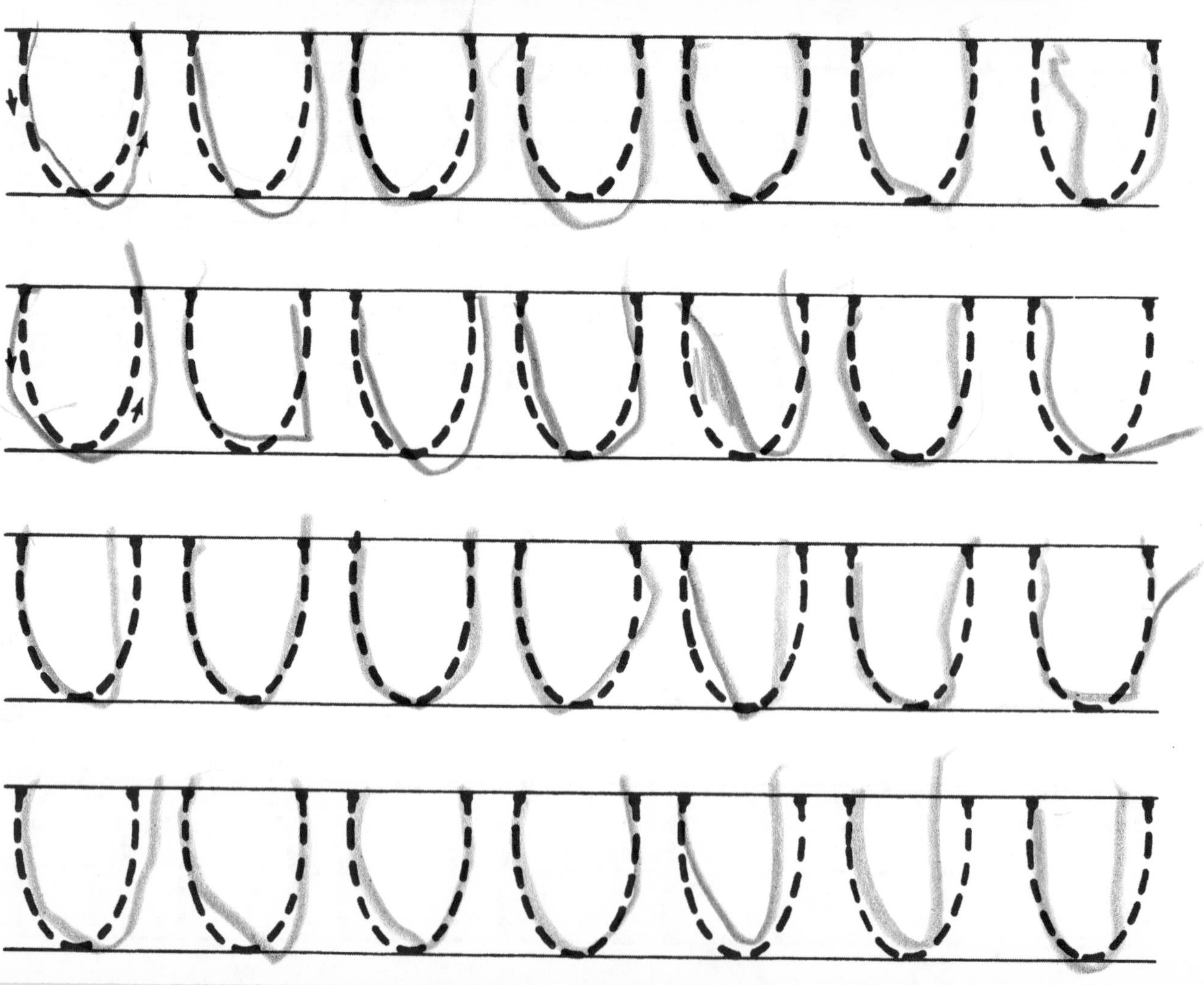

**Skills:** Fine motor skill development; Eye/hand coordination; Forming open curves

Start at the dots. Trace the broken lines. Then finish the page.

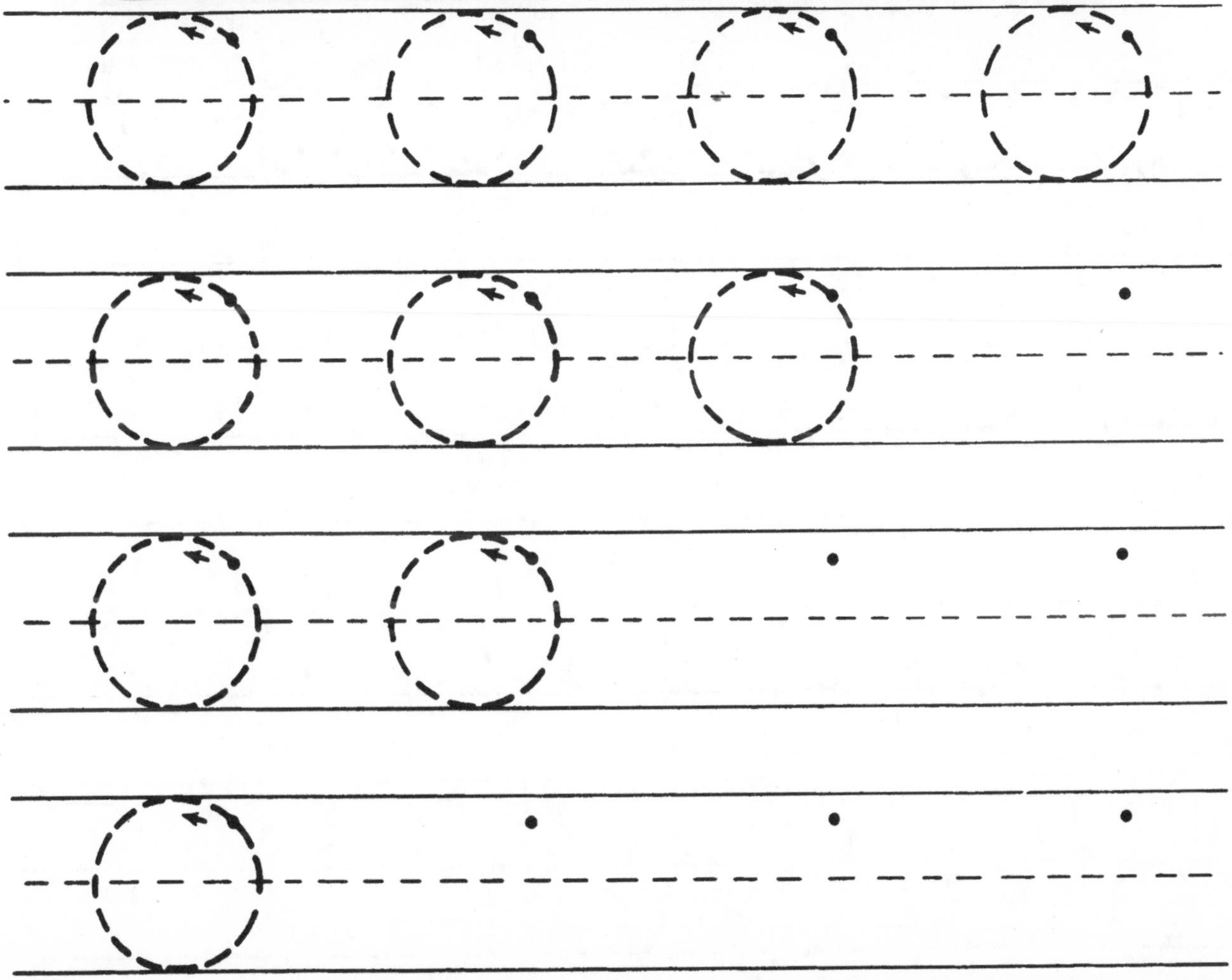

**Skills:** Fine motor skill development; Eye/hand coordination; Forming closed curves

## Handwriting Skills

Start at the dots. Trace the broken lines. Then finish the page.

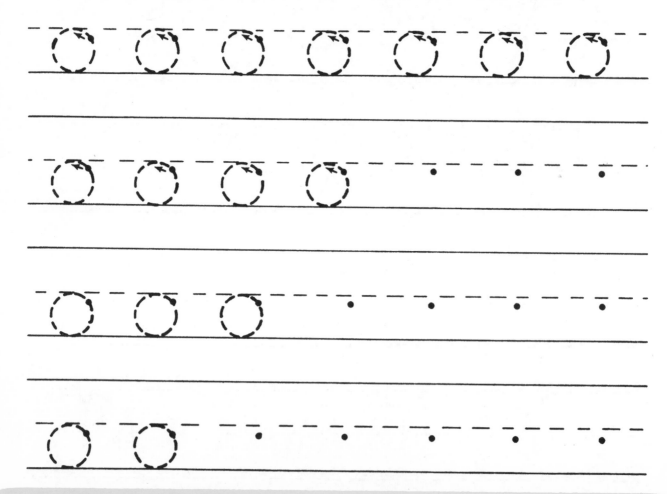

**Skills:** Fine motor skill development; Eye/hand coordination; Forming closed curves

## Handwriting Skills

Start at the dots. Trace the broken lines.

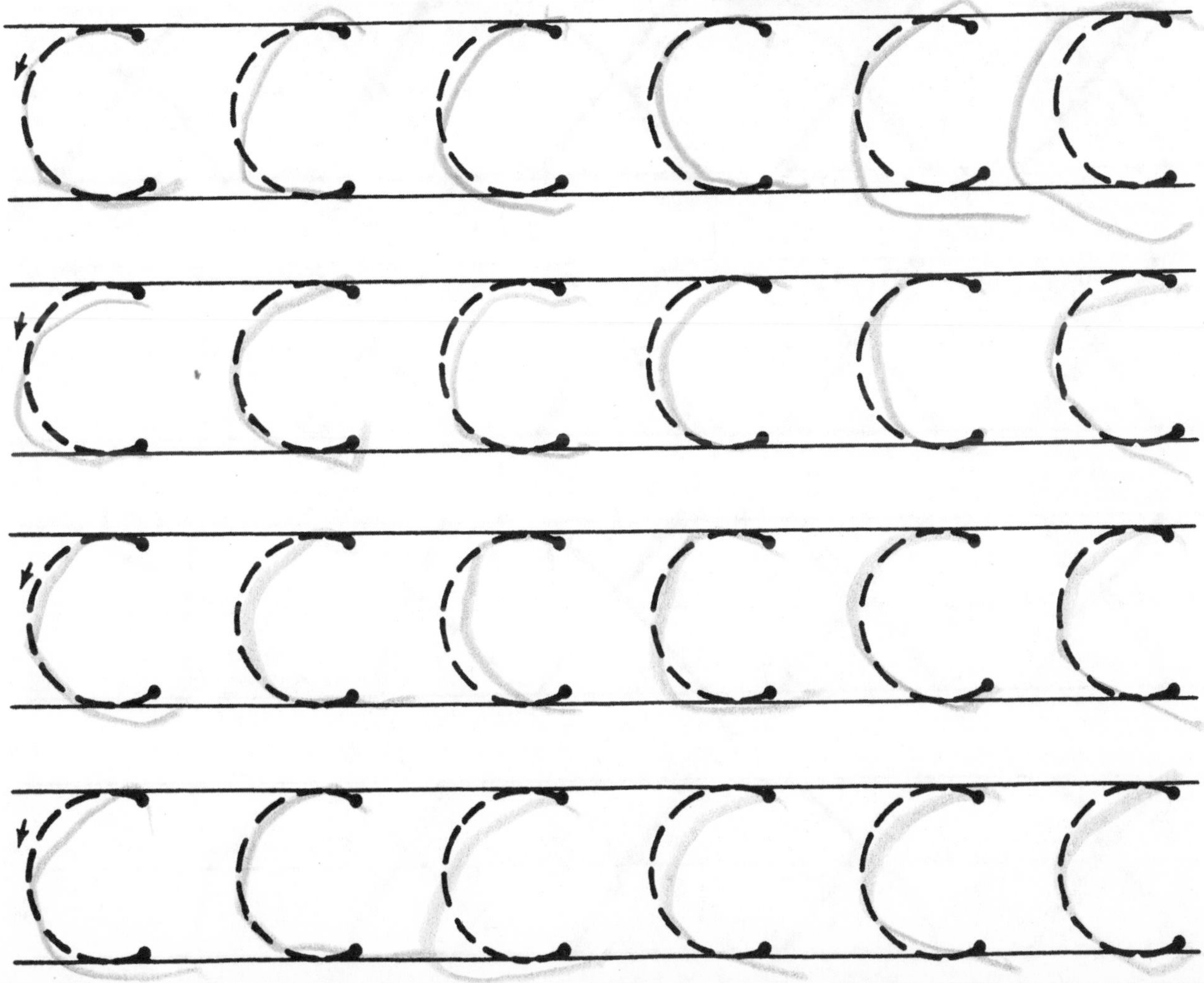

**Skills:** Fine motor skill development; Eye/hand coordination; Forming open curves

## Handwriting Skills

Start at the dots. Trace the broken lines. Then finish the page.

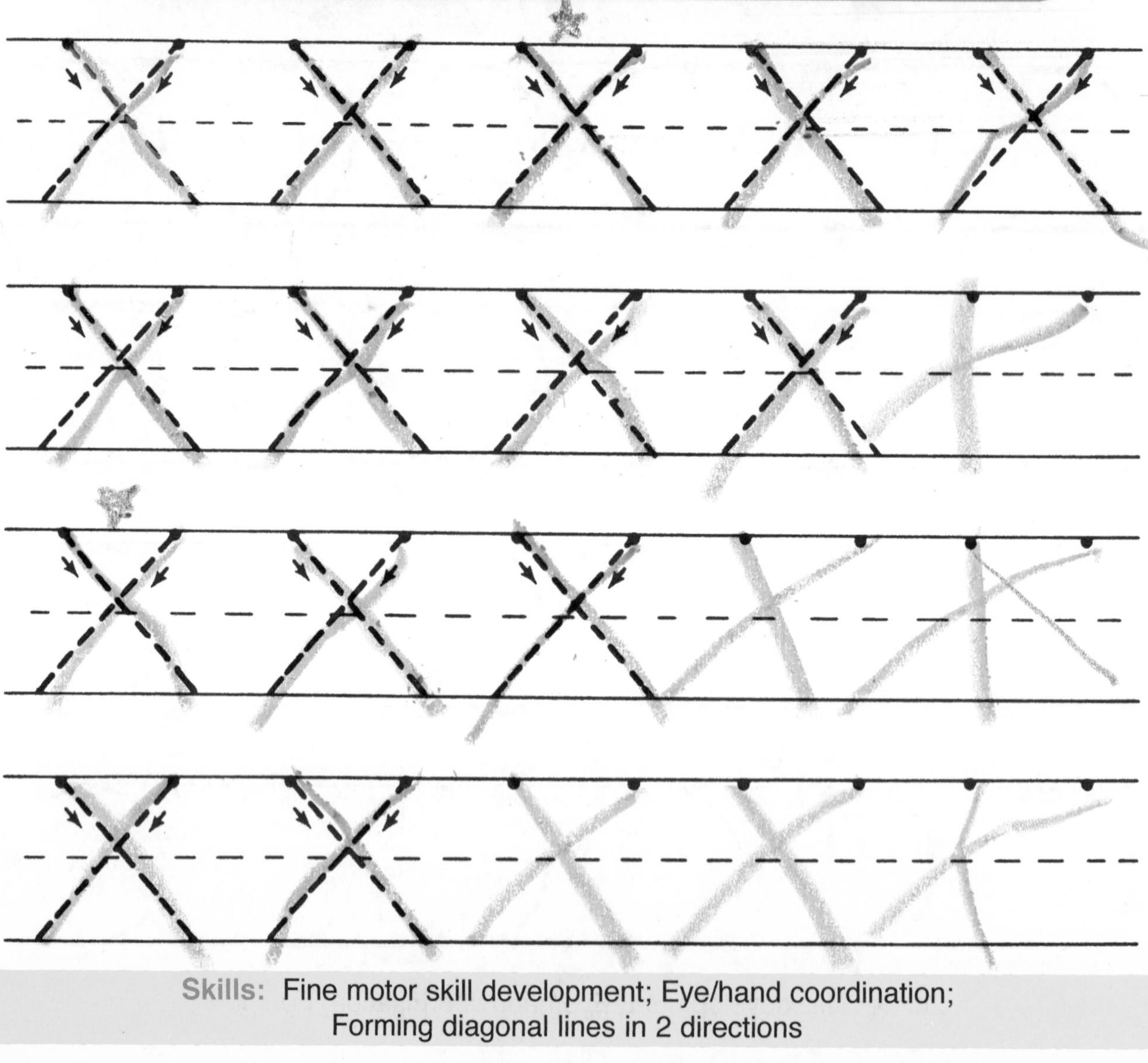

Skills: Fine motor skill development; Eye/hand coordination; Forming diagonal lines in 2 directions

Start at the dots. Trace the broken lines. Then finish the page.

**Skills:** Fine motor skill development; Eye/hand coordination; Forming horizontal lines

## Handwriting Skills

Follow the direction of each arrow. Point to something in the picture that begins with A. Then practice writing each letter.

# Aa

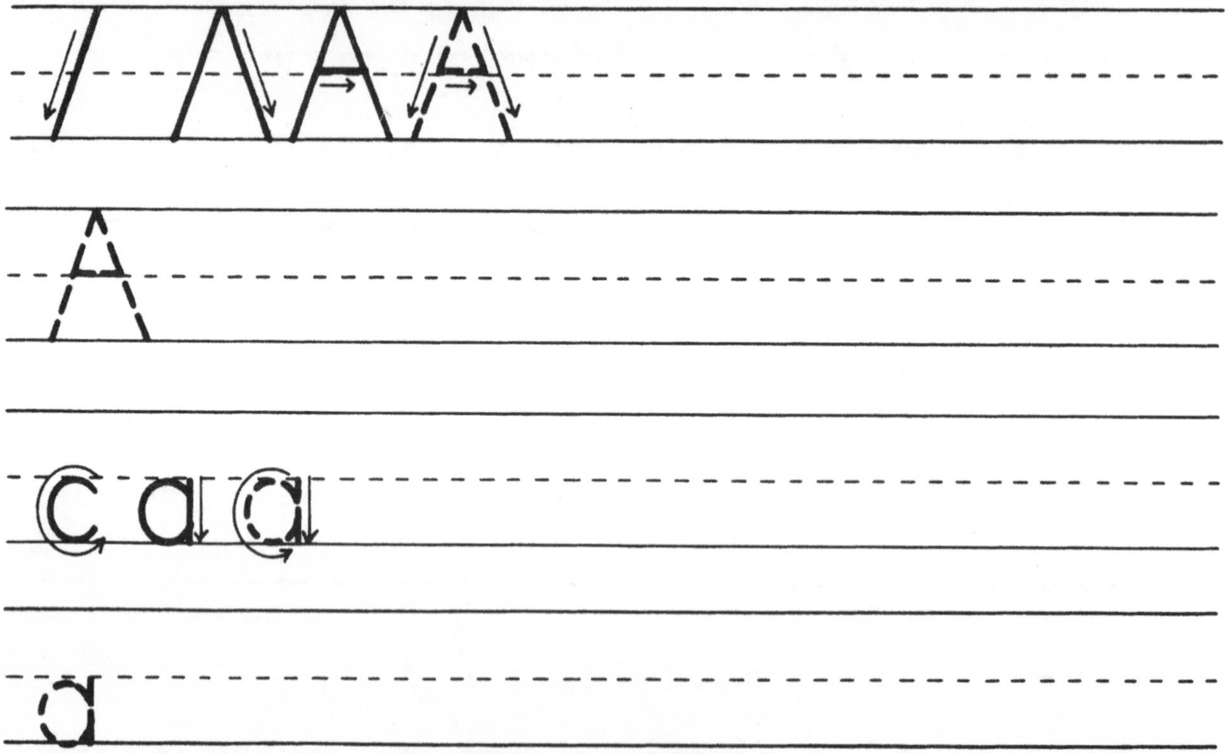

**Skills:** Forming upper/lowercase "a"; Writing left to right

Follow the direction of each arrow. Point to something in the picture that begins with B. Then practice writing each letter.

# Bb

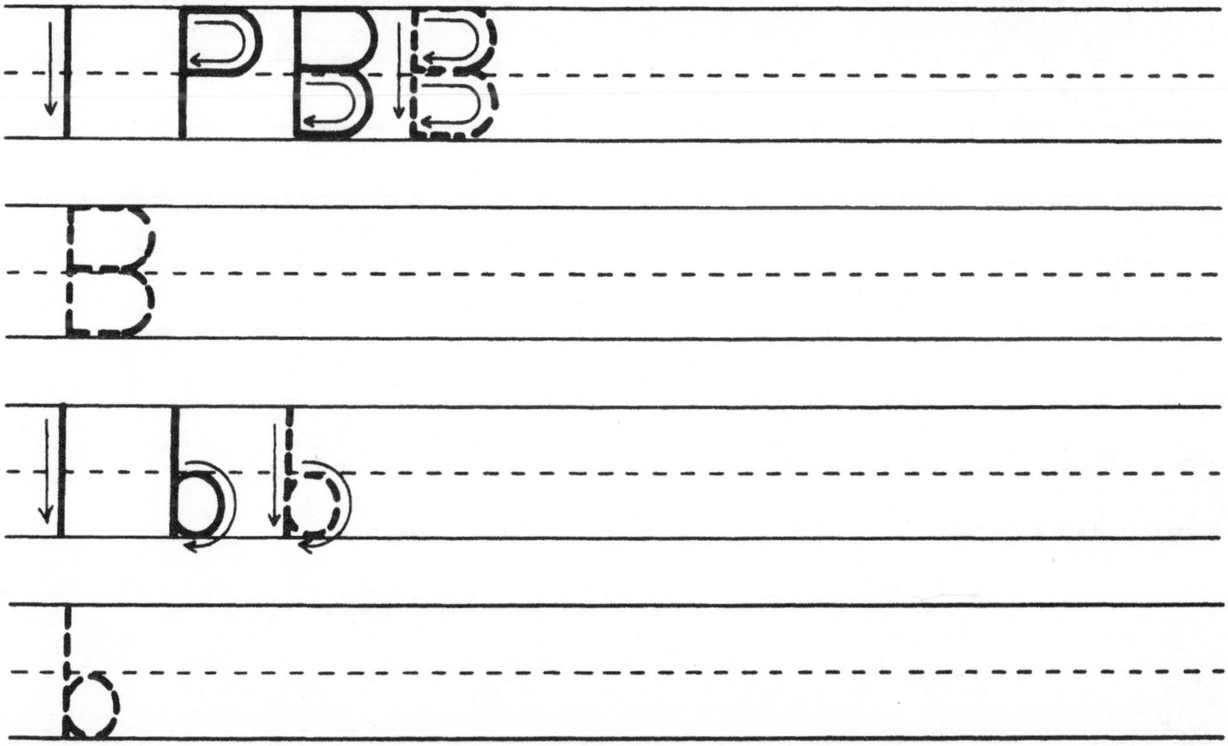

Skills: Forming upper/lowercase "b"; Writing left to right

Follow the direction of each arrow. Point to something in the picture that begins with C. Then practice writing each letter.

# Cc

Skills: Forming upper/lowercase "c"; Writing left to right

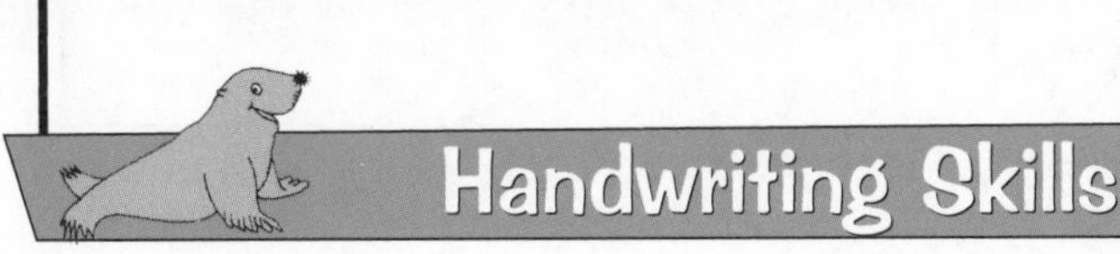


Follow the direction of each arrow. Point to something in the picture that begins with D. Then practice writing each letter.

# Dd

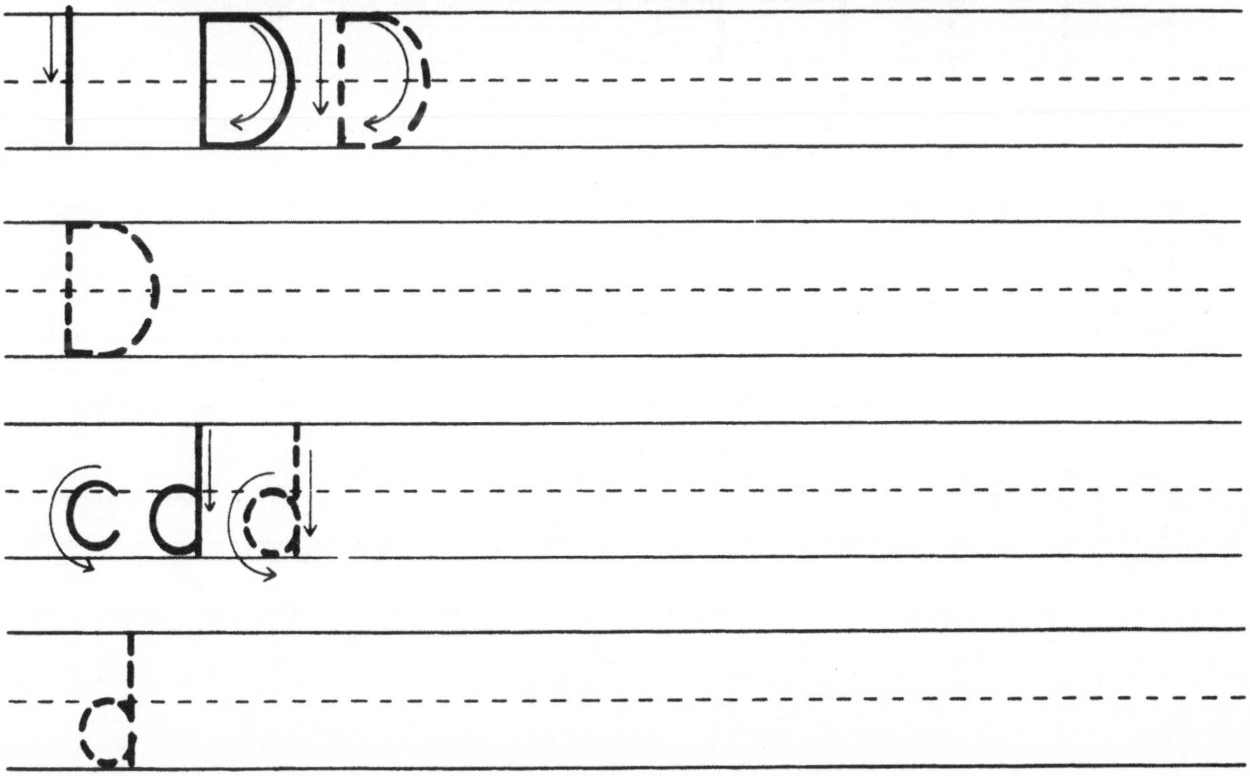

**Skills:** Forming upper/lowercase "d"; Writing left to right

Follow the direction of each arrow. Point to something in the picture that begins with E. Then practice writing each letter.

# Ee

**Skills:** Forming upper/lowercase "e"; Writing left to right

Follow the direction of each arrow. Point to something in the picture that begins with F. Then practice writing each letter.

# Ff

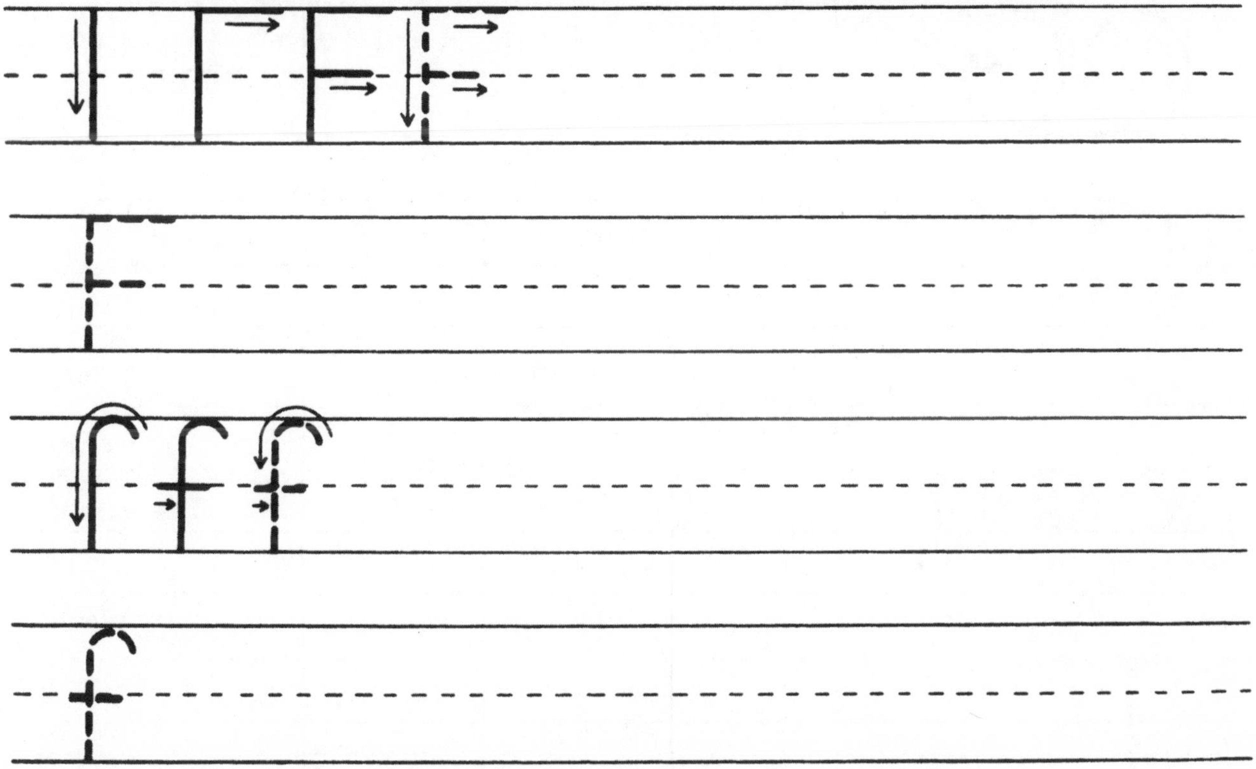

Skills: Forming upper/lowercase “f”; Writing left to right

Follow the direction of each arrow. Point to something in the picture that begins with G. Then practice writing each letter.

# Gg

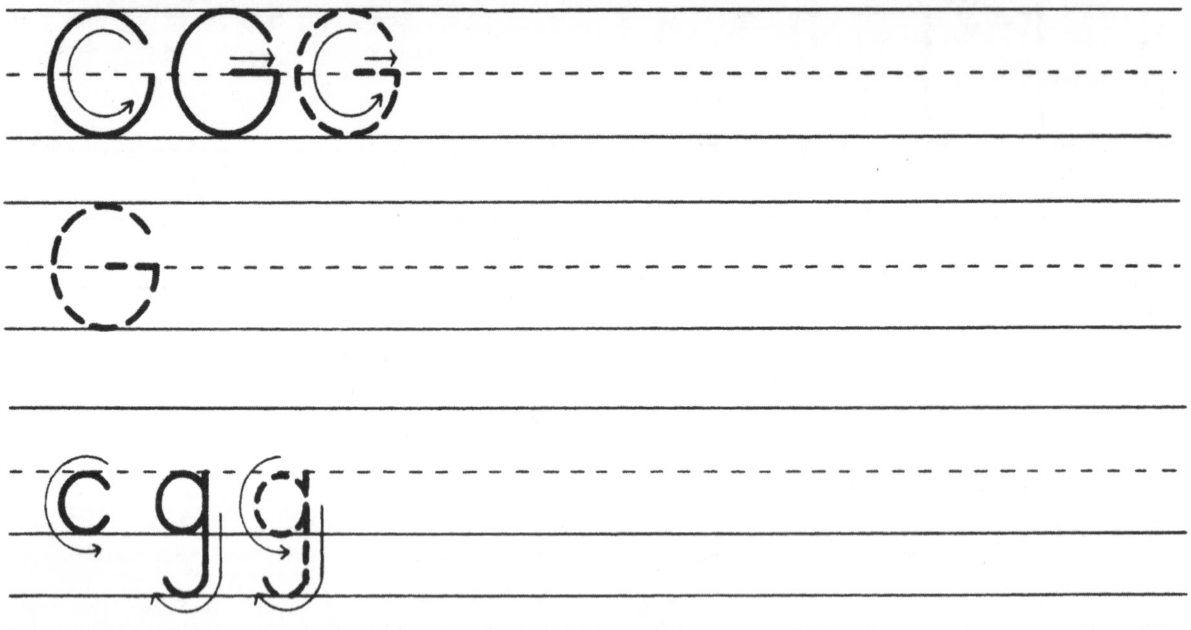

G G G

G

c g g

g

**Skills:** Forming upper/lowercase "g"; Writing left to right

Follow the direction of each arrow. Point to something in the picture that begins with H. Then practice writing each letter.

# Hh

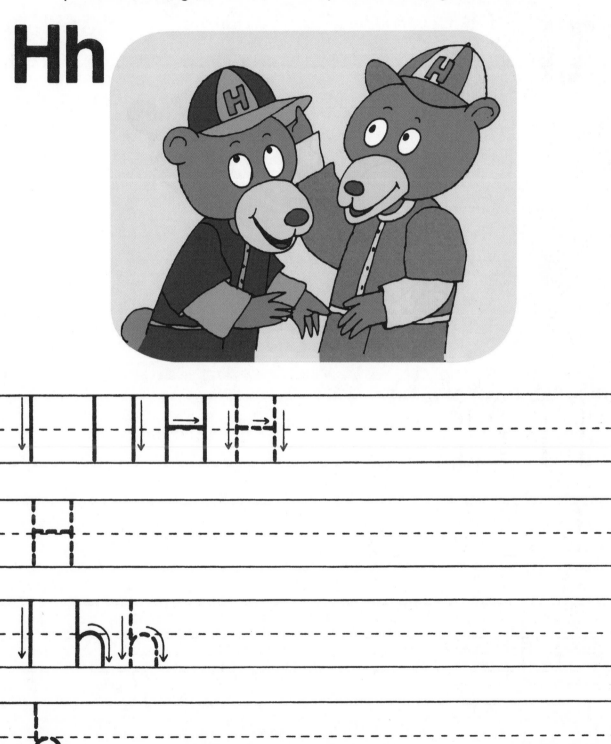

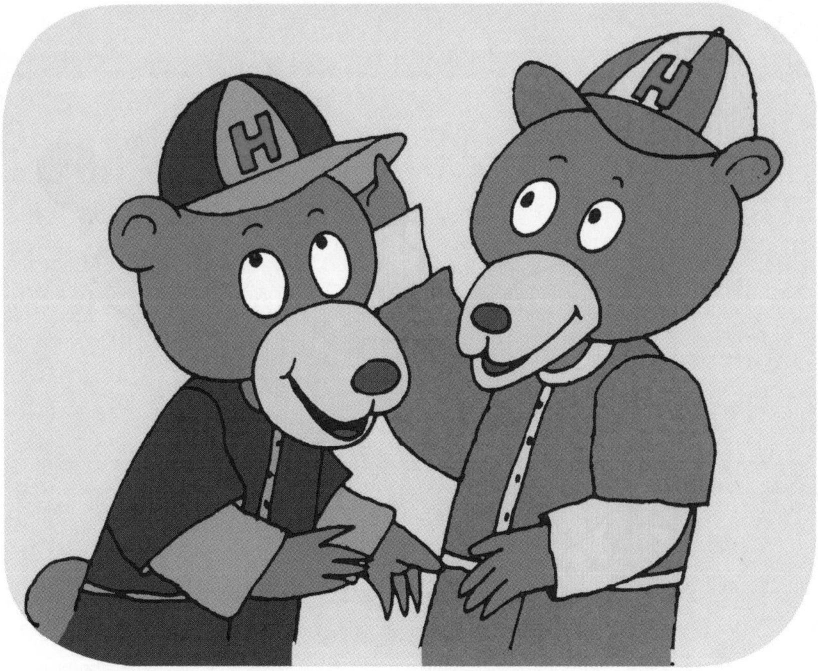

Skills: Forming upper/lowercase "h"; Writing left to right

Follow the direction of each arrow. Point to something in the picture that begins with I. Then practice writing each letter.

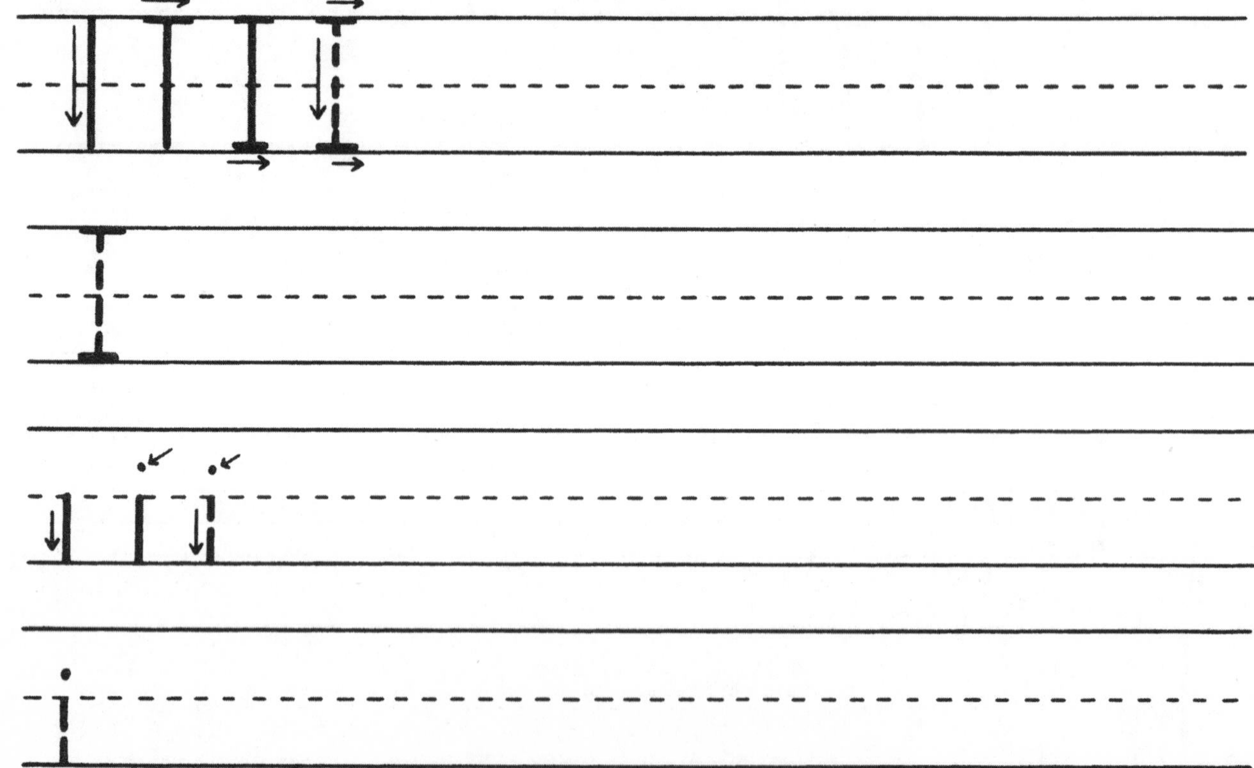

**Skills:** Forming upper/lowercase "i"; Writing left to right

Follow the direction of each arrow. Point to something in the picture that begins with J. Then practice writing each letter.

# Jj

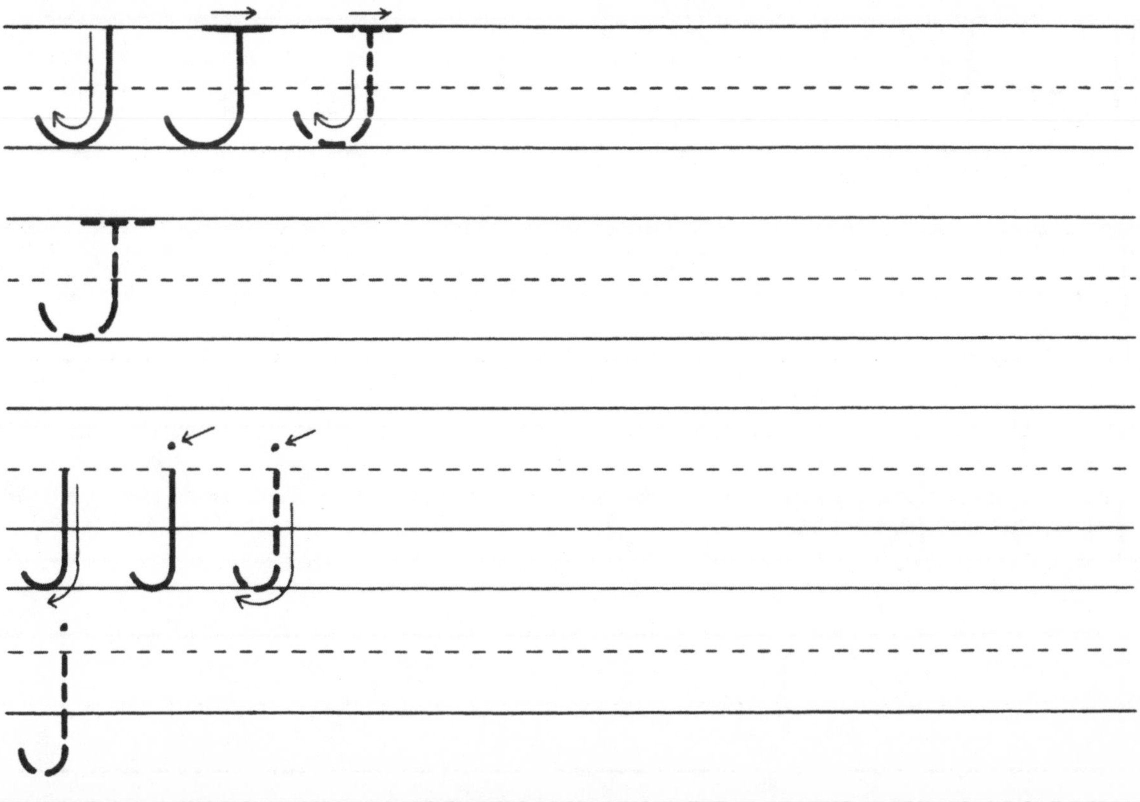

J J J

J

j j j

j

Skills: Forming upper/lowercase "j"; Writing left to right

Follow the direction of each arrow. Point to something in the picture that begins with K. Then practice writing each letter.

# Kk

Skills: Forming upper/lowercase "k"; Writing left to right

Follow the direction of each arrow. Point to something in the picture that begins with L. Then practice writing each letter.

# Ll

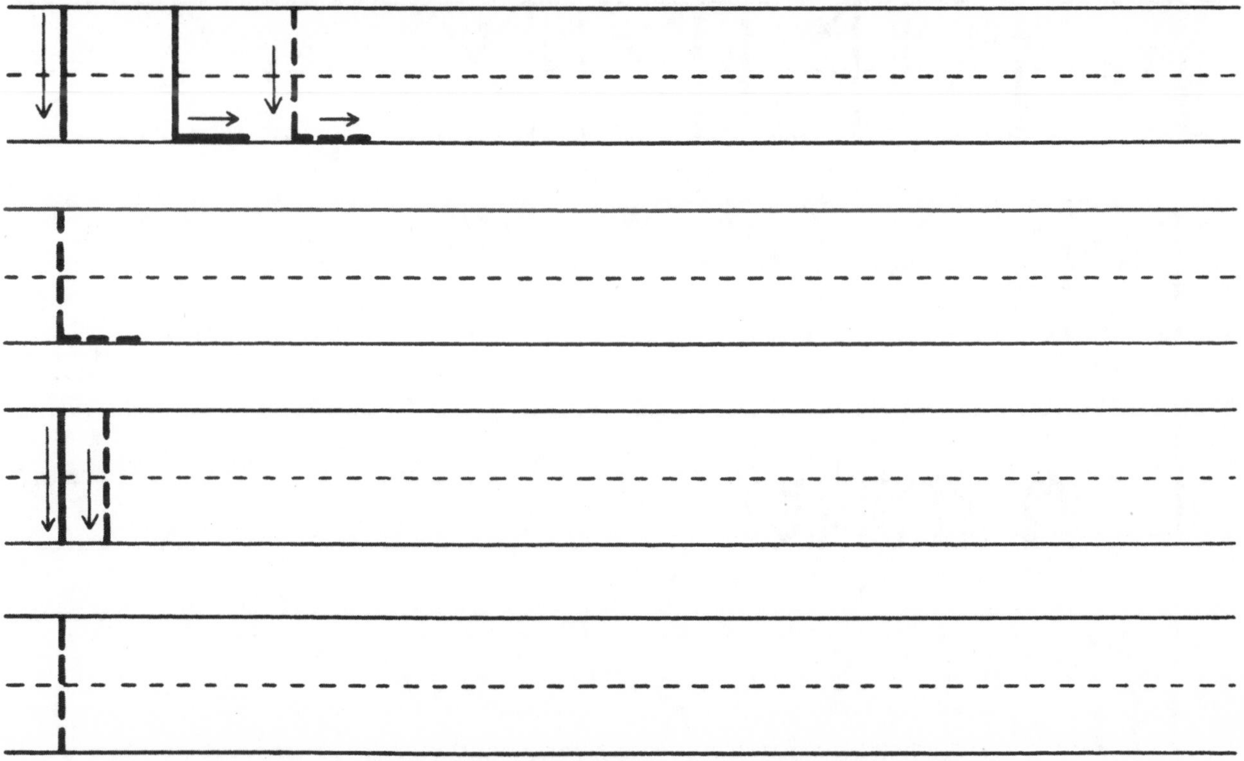

Skills: Forming upper/lowercase "l"; Writing left to right

Follow the direction of each arrow. Point to something in the picture that begins with M. Then practice writing each letter.

# Mm

MILK

**Skills:** Forming upper/lowercase “m”; Writing left to right

Follow the direction of each arrow. Point to something in the picture that begins with N. Then practice writing each letter.

# Nn

N

n

**Skills:** Forming upper/lowercase "n"; Writing left to right

Follow the direction of each arrow. Point to something in the picture that begins with O. Then practice writing each letter.

# Oo

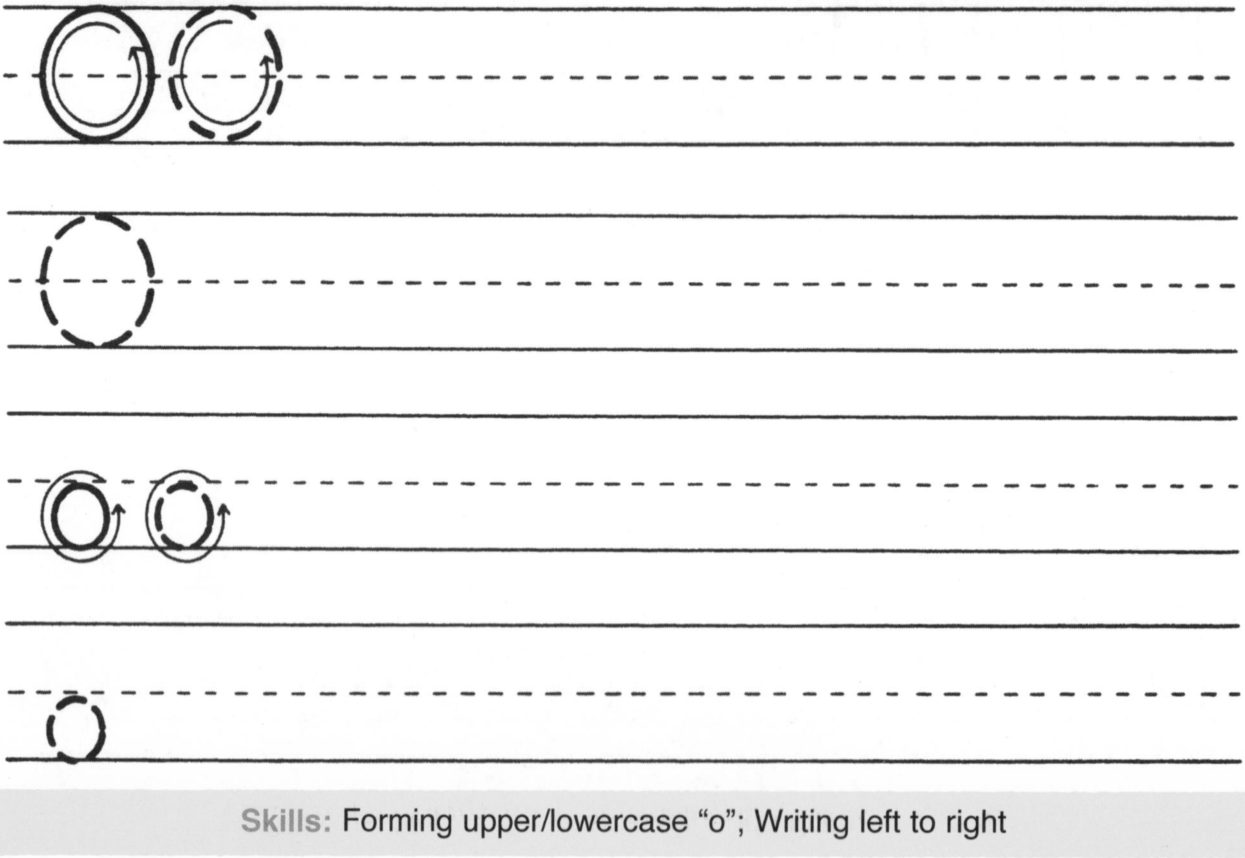

**Skills:** Forming upper/lowercase "o"; Writing left to right

Follow the direction of each arrow. Point to something in the picture that begins with P. Then practice writing each letter.

# Pp

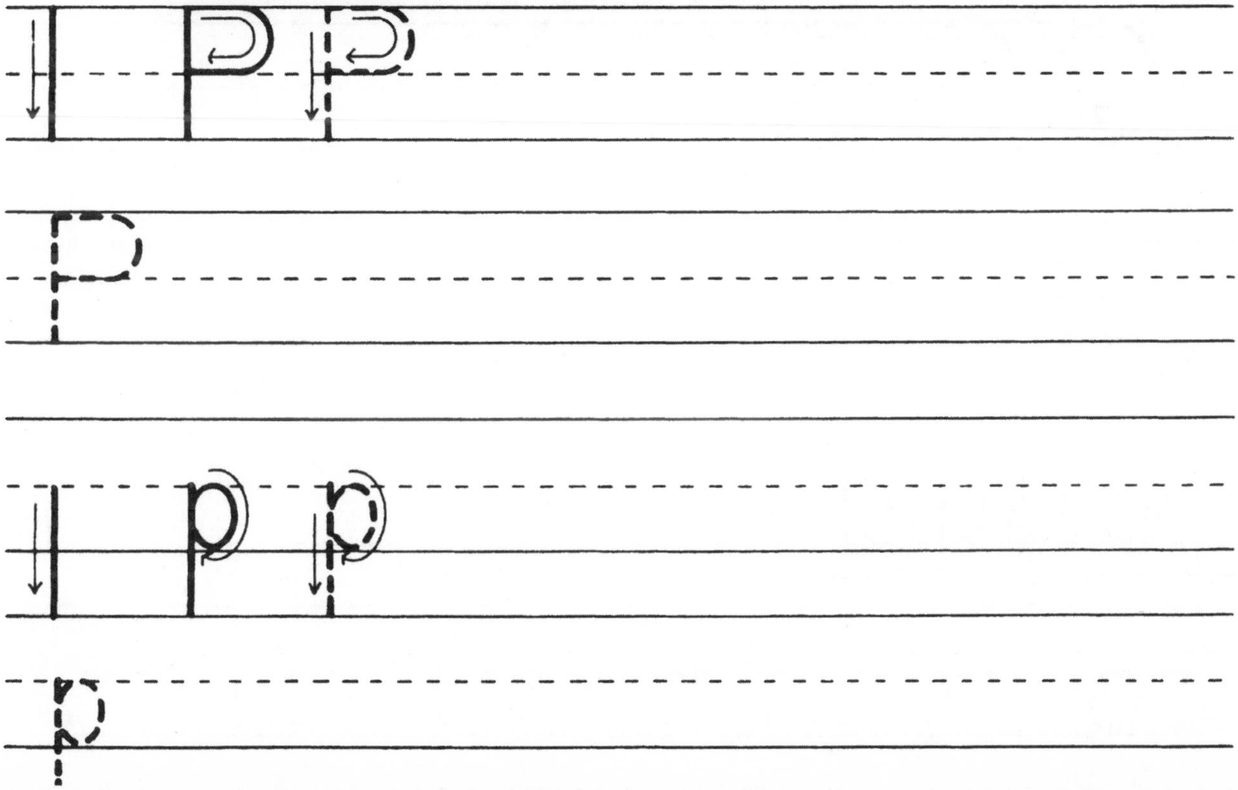

Skills: Forming upper/lowercase "p"; Writing left to right

Follow the direction of each arrow. Point to something in the picture that begins with Q. Then practice writing each letter.

# Qq

Skills: Forming upper/lowercase "q"; Writing left to right

Follow the direction of each arrow. Point to something in the picture that begins with R. Then practice writing each letter.

# Rr

Skills: Forming upper/lowercase "r"; Writing left to right

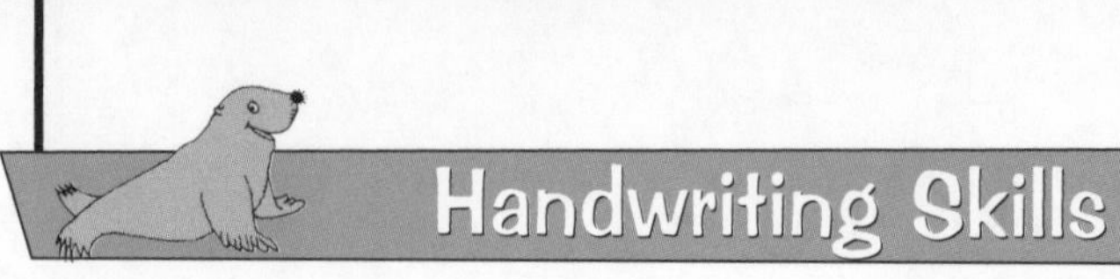


Follow the direction of each arrow. Point to something in the picture that begins with S. Then practice writing each letter.

# Ss

Skills: Forming upper/lowercase "s"; Writing left to right

Follow the direction of each arrow. Point to something in the picture that begins with T. Then practice writing each letter.

# Tt

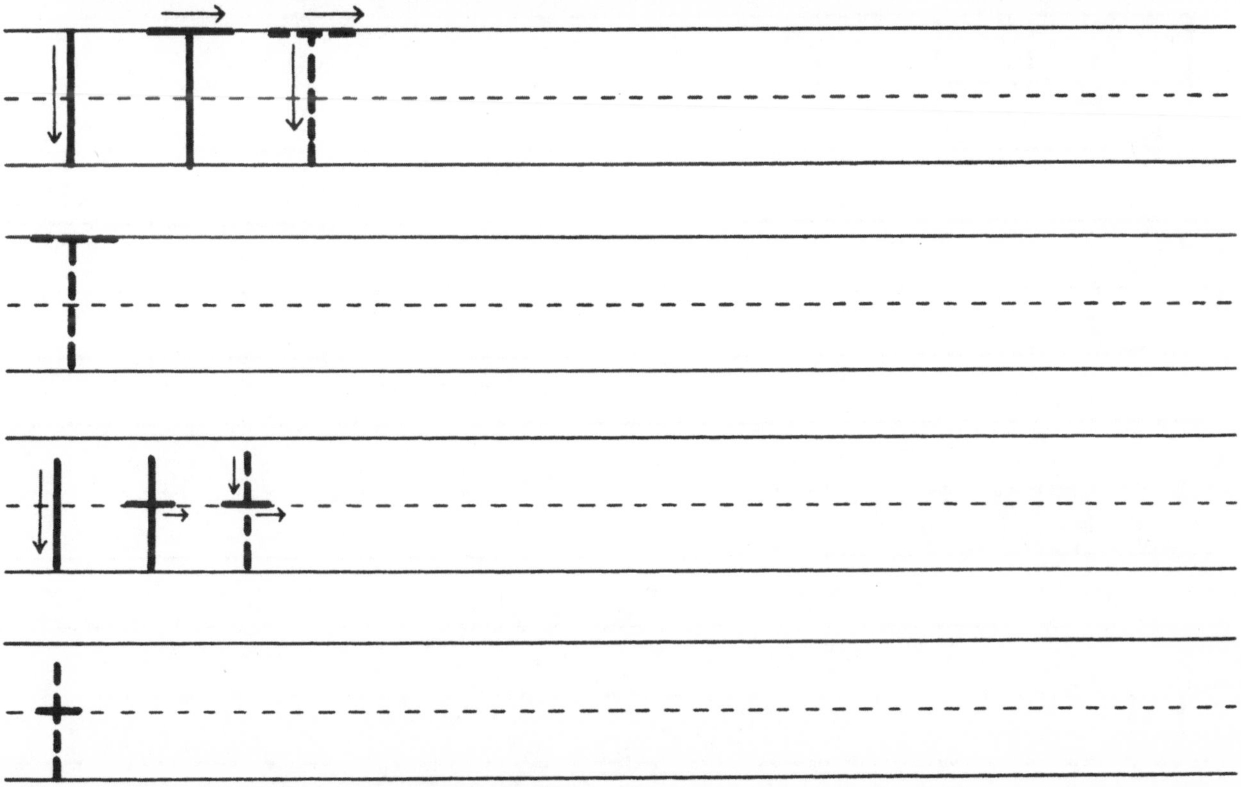

Skills: Forming upper/lowercase “t”; Writing left to right

Follow the direction of each arrow. Point to something in the picture that begins with U. Then practice writing each letter.

# Uu

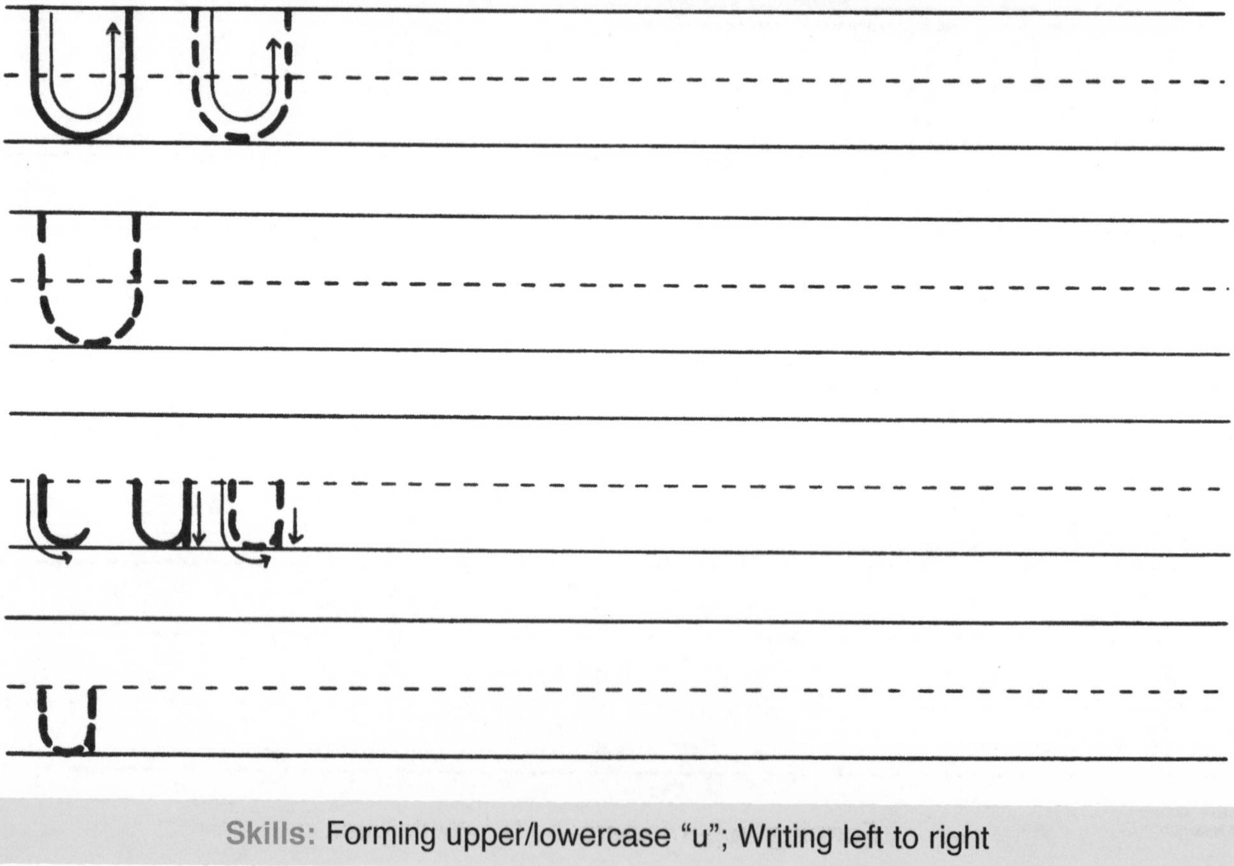

Skills: Forming upper/lowercase "u"; Writing left to right

Follow the direction of each arrow. Point to something in the picture that begins with V. Then practice writing each letter.

# Vv

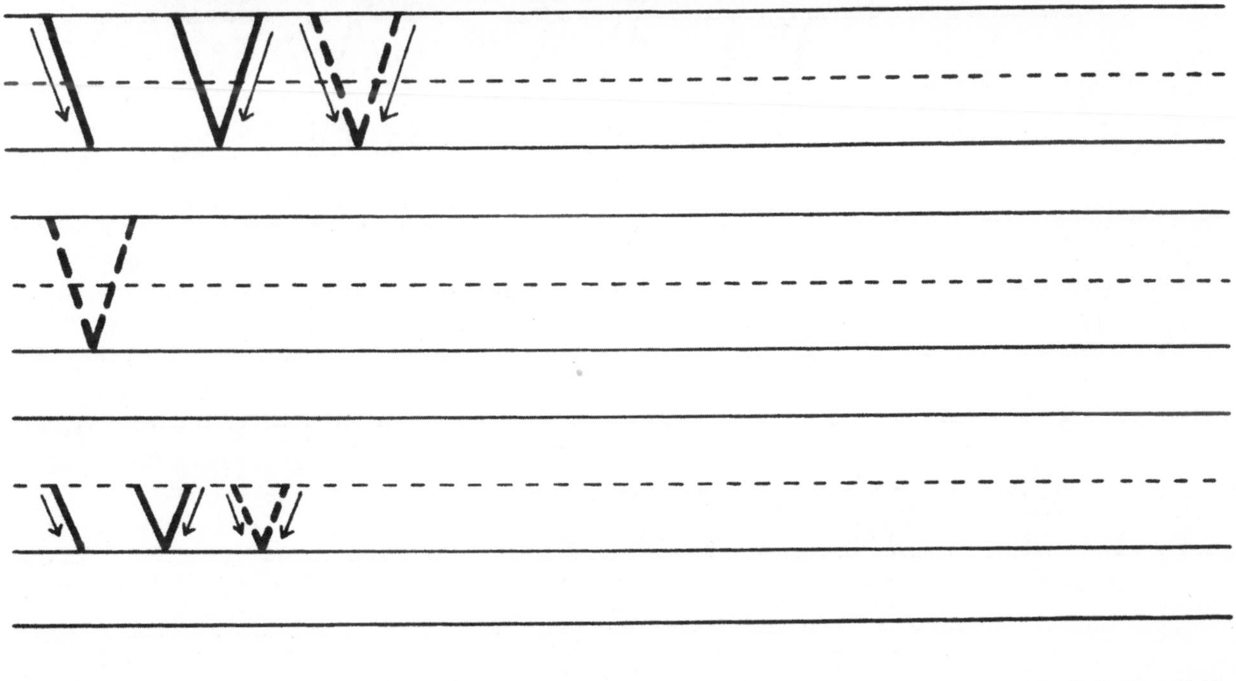

V V V

V

v v v

v

**Skills:** Forming upper/lowercase "v"; Writing left to right

## Handwriting Skills

Follow the direction of each arrow. Point to something in the picture that begins with W. Then practice writing each letter.

# Ww

**Skills:** Forming upper/lowercase "w"; Writing left to right

Follow the direction of each arrow. Point to something in the picture that begins with X. Then practice writing each letter.

# Xx

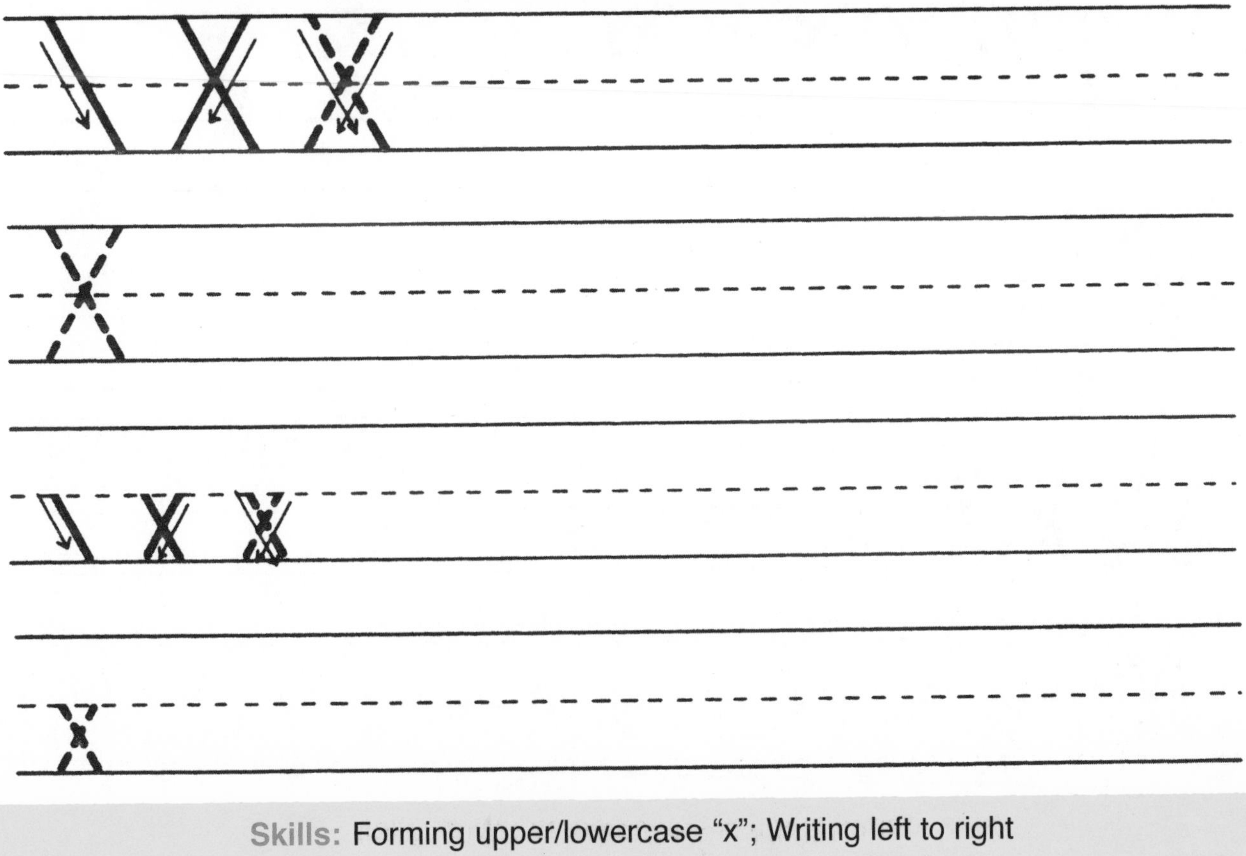

**Skills:** Forming upper/lowercase "x"; Writing left to right

Follow the direction of each arrow. Point to something in the picture that begins with Y. Then practice writing each letter.

# Yy

**Skills:** Forming upper/lowercase "y"; Writing left to right

Follow the direction of each arrow. Point to something in the picture that begins with Z. Then practice writing each letter.

# Zz

Skills: Forming upper/lowercase "z"; Writing left to right

# Handwriting Skills

Trace each letter.

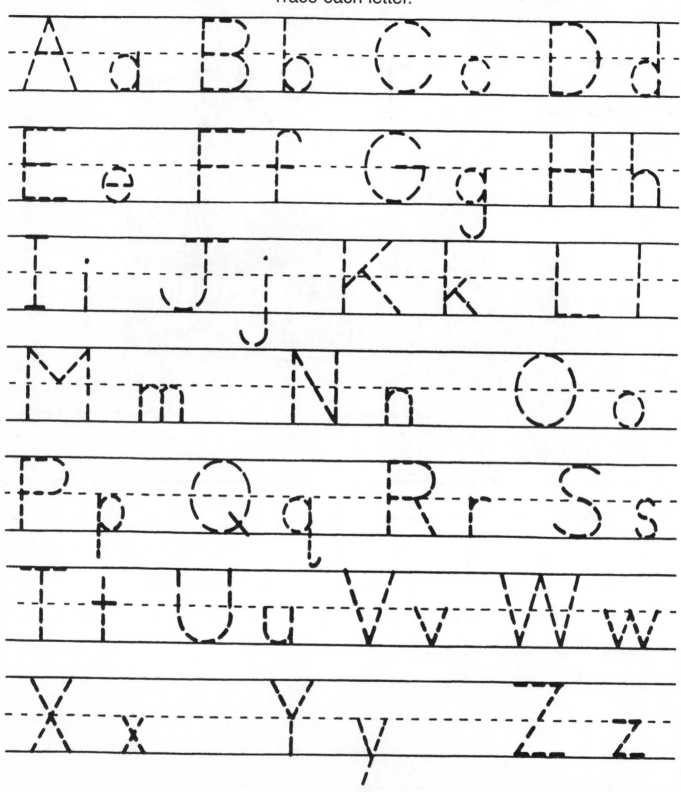

A a B b C c D d

E e F f G g H h

I i J j K k L l

M m N n O o

P p Q q R r S s

T t U u V v W w

X x Y y Z z

**Skills:** Forming upper/lowercase letters; Writing the alphabet

# Excellent!

Give
yourself
a star!

# Colors, Shapes and Numbers

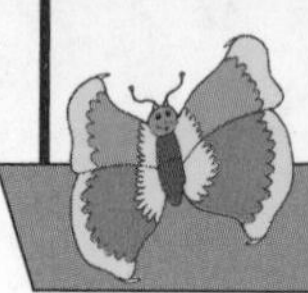



Trace and print the word.

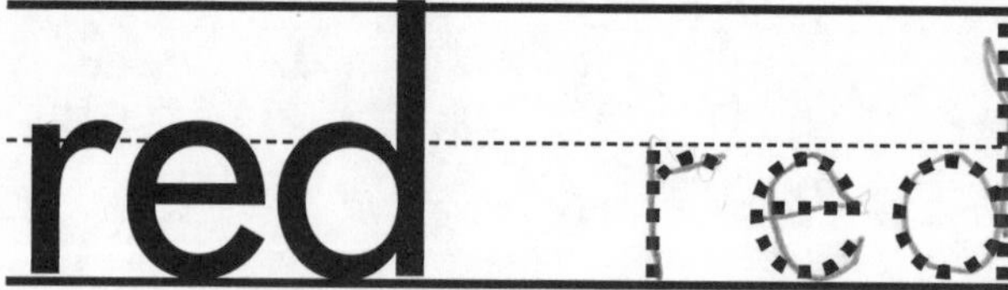


Color these things that are red.

**fire truck**

**strawberries**

**heart**

**watermelon**

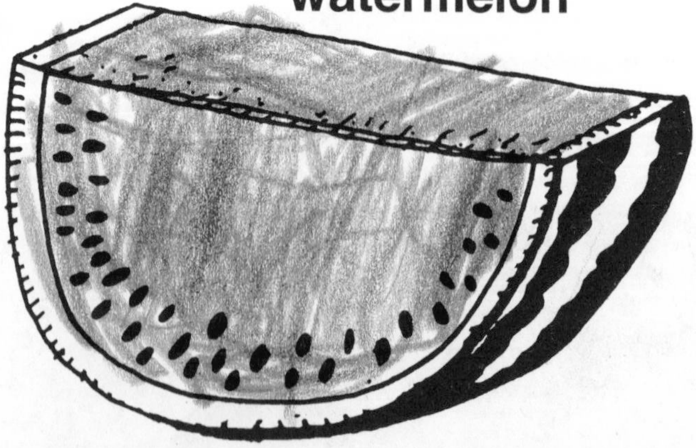

**Skills:** Distinguishing color; Classification; Word recognition

Trace and print the word.

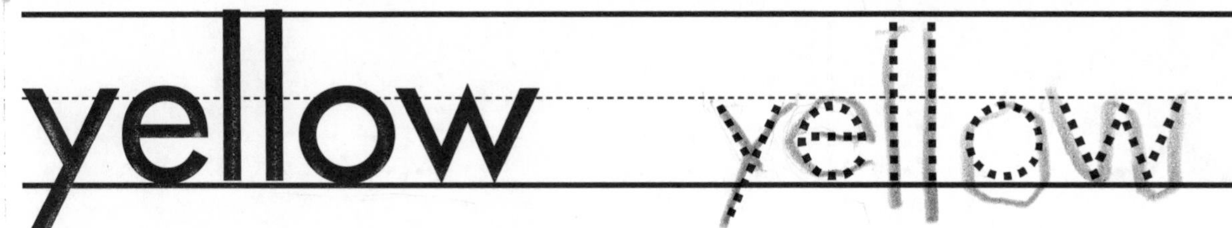


Color these things that are yellow.

**cheese**

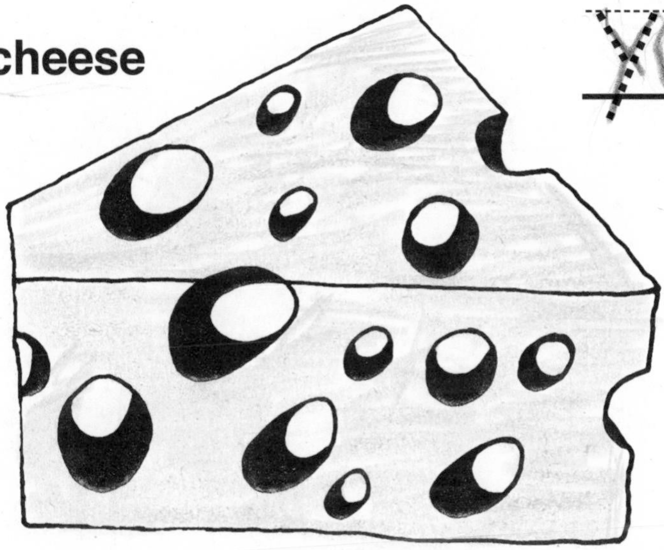

**sun**

**daffodil**

**Skills:** Distinguishing color; Classification; Word recognition

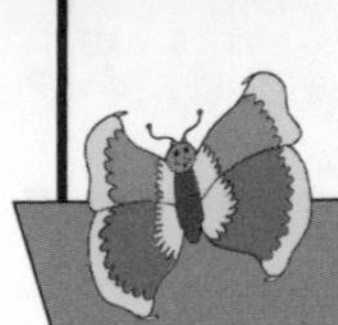



Trace and print the word.

Color these things that are blue.

**pool**

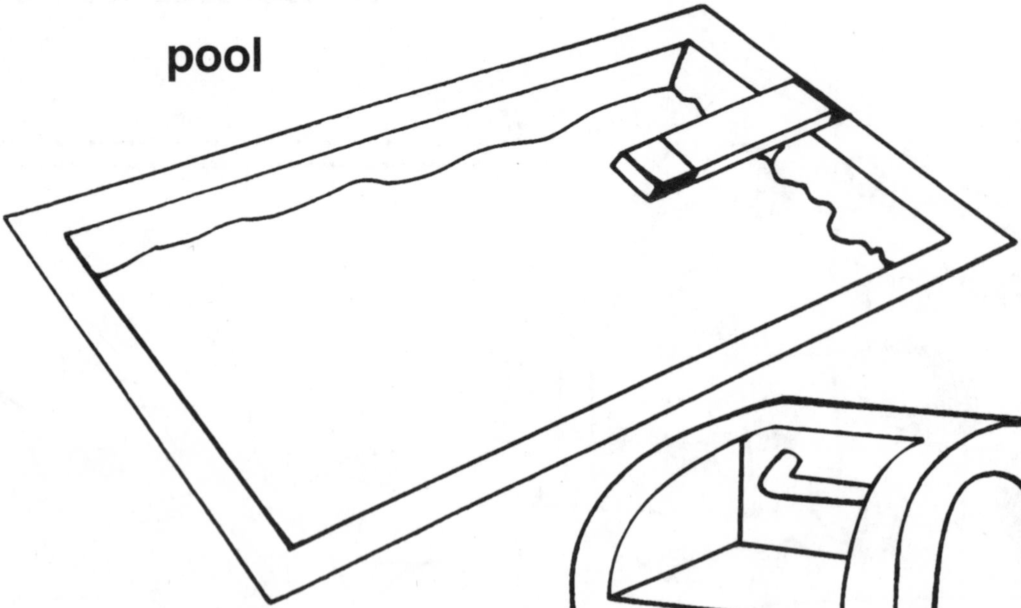

**mailbox**

**blueberries**

**Skills:** Distinguishing color; Classification; Word recognition

Trace and print the word.

Color these things that are orange.

pumpkin

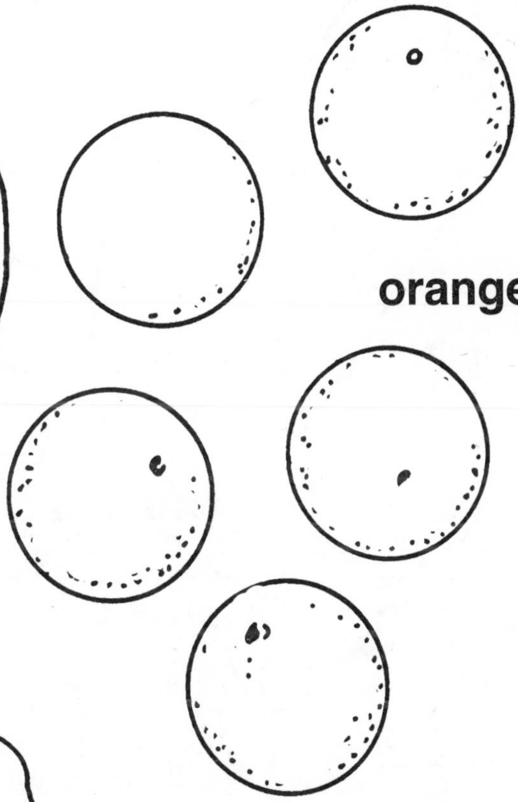

oranges

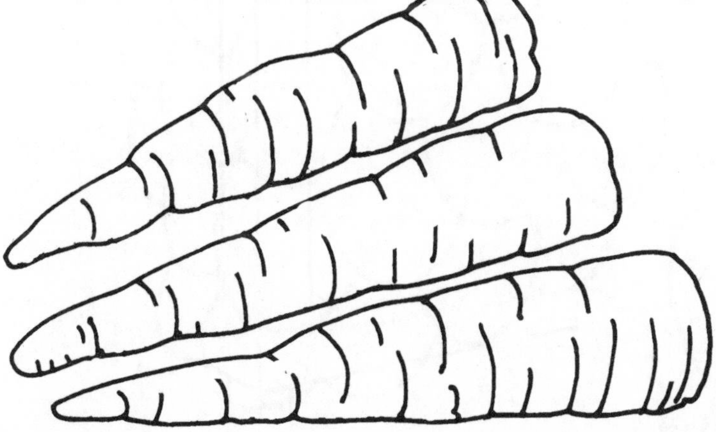

carrots

**Skills:** Distinguishing color; Classification; Word recognition

Trace and print the word.

# purple

purple

Color these things that are purple.

p

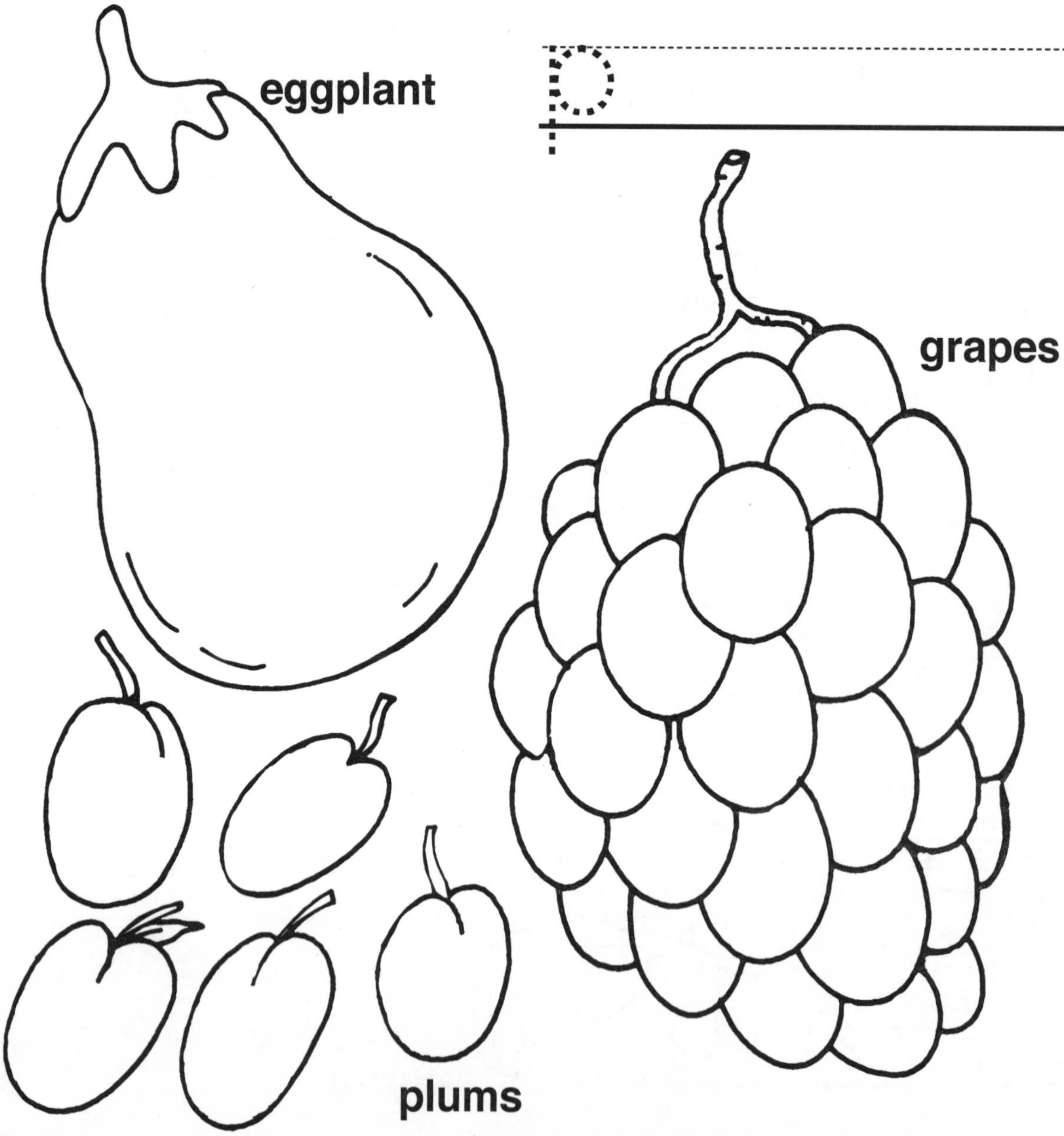

eggplant

grapes

plums

**Skills:** Distinguishing color; Classification; Word recognition

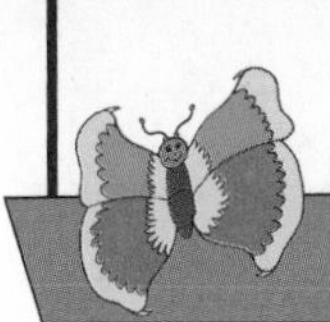

Trace and print the word.

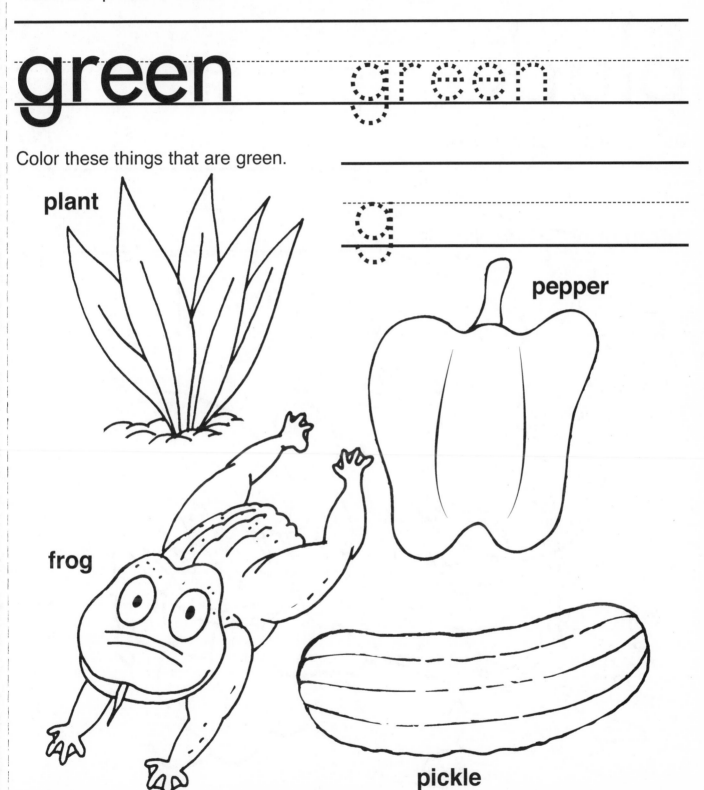

green green

g

Color these things that are green.

plant

pepper

frog

pickle

**Skills:** Distinguishing color; Classification; Word recognition

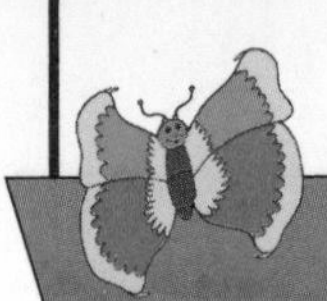



Trace and print the word.

black black

Color these things that are black.

b

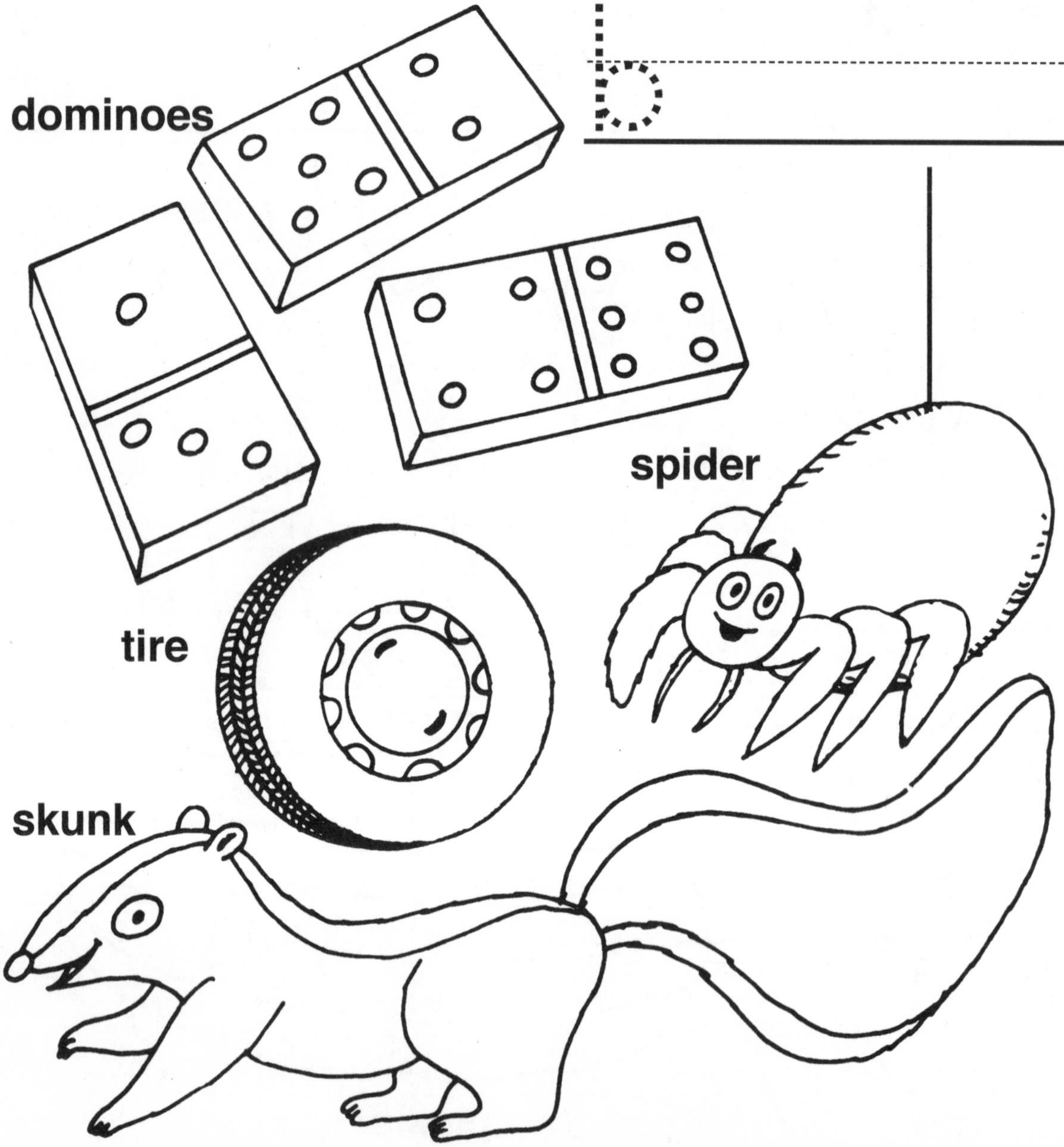

dominoes

spider

tire

skunk

Skills: Distinguishing color; Classification; Word recognition

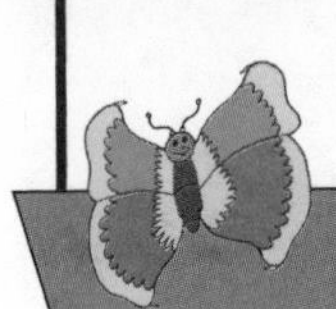



Trace and print the word.

brown brown

Color these things that are brown.

b

rope

shoes

deer

**Skills:** Distinguishing color; Classification; Word recognition

Look at the boats in the lake.
Color each boat to match the color word.
Then color the lake blue.

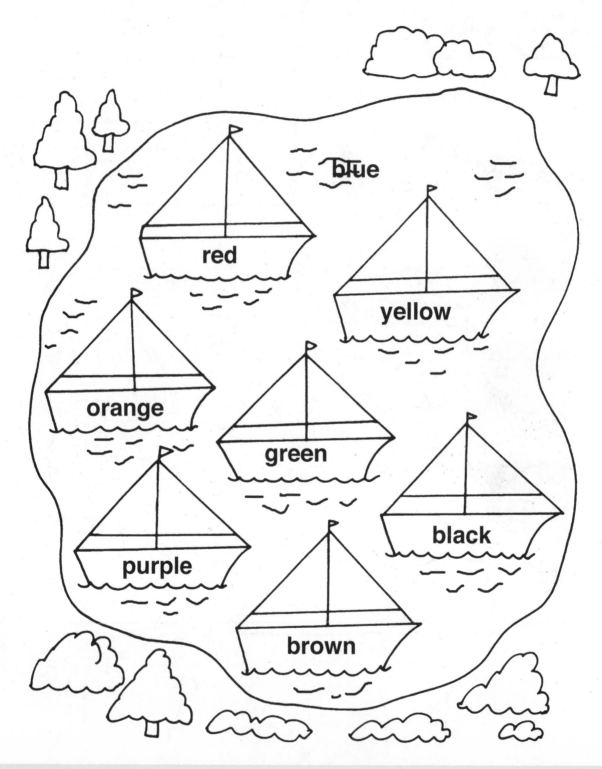

blue

red

yellow

orange

green

purple

black

brown

**Skills:** Distinguishing color; Word recognition; Fine motor skill development

What is hiding
Follow these di ns to find out.

Color the A spaces red.
Color the B spaces blue.
Color the C spaces yellow.
Color the D spaces green.
Color the E spaces brown.

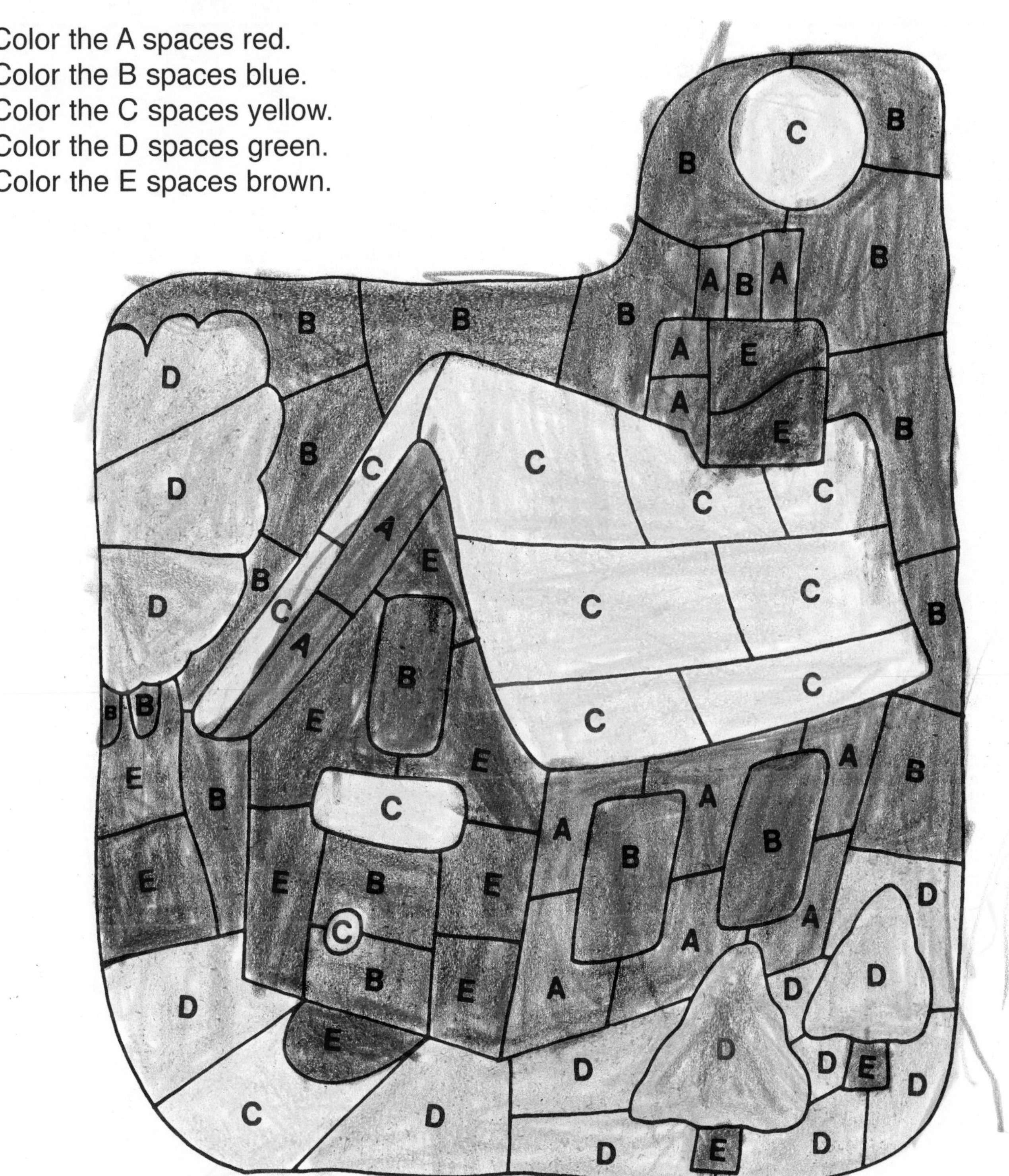

**Skills:** Distinguishing color; Matching letters to color codes

# Colors, Shapes and Numbers

Trace the circles at the top of the page.
Draw your own circles at the bottom. Then color the shapes.

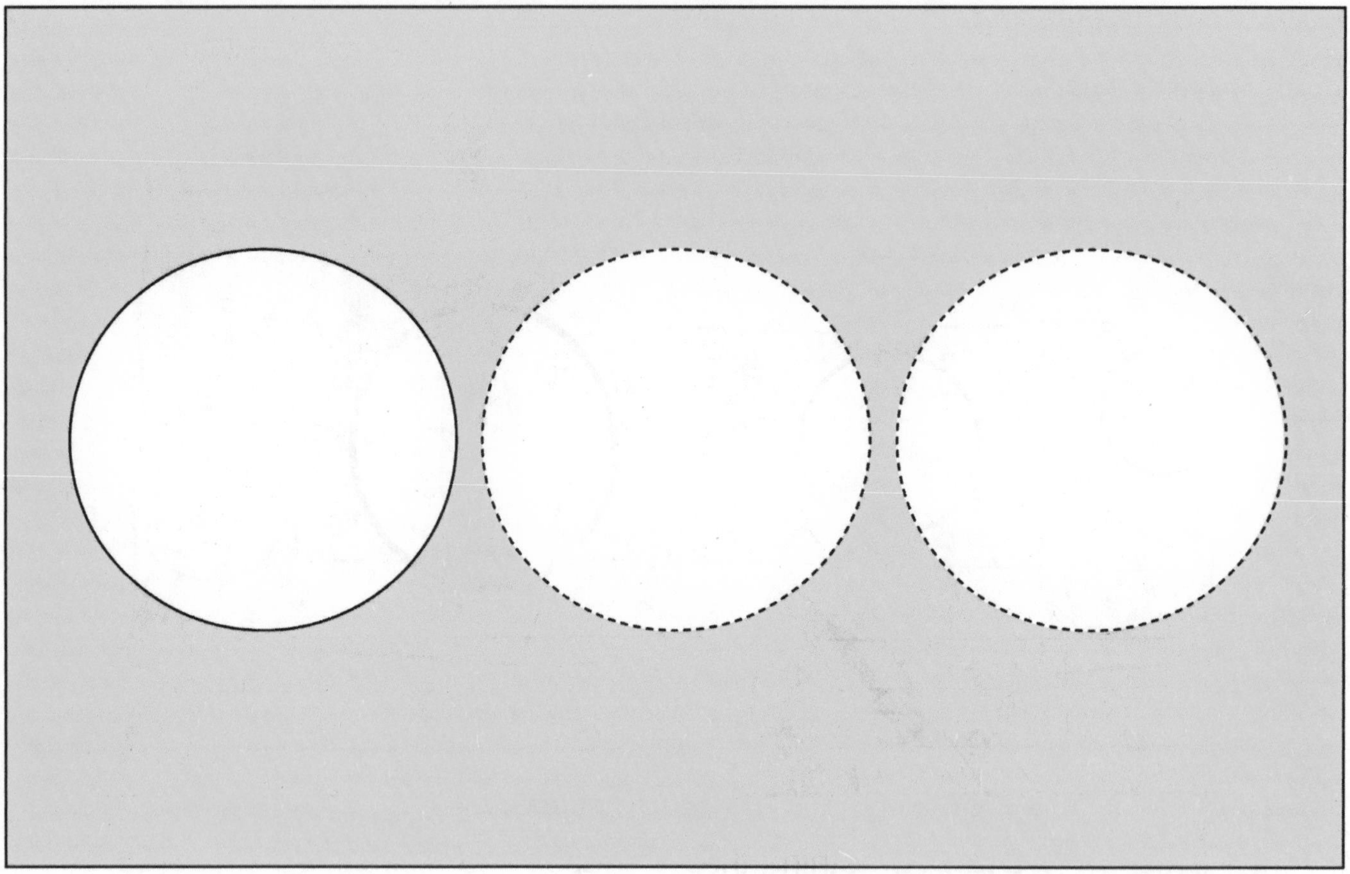

**Skills:** Recognizing shapes; Forming geometric shapes

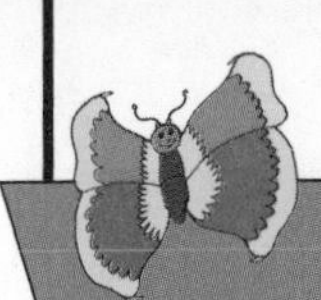

# Colors, Shapes and Numbers

Look at the circles at the top of the page.
Write the word. Then color the circles.

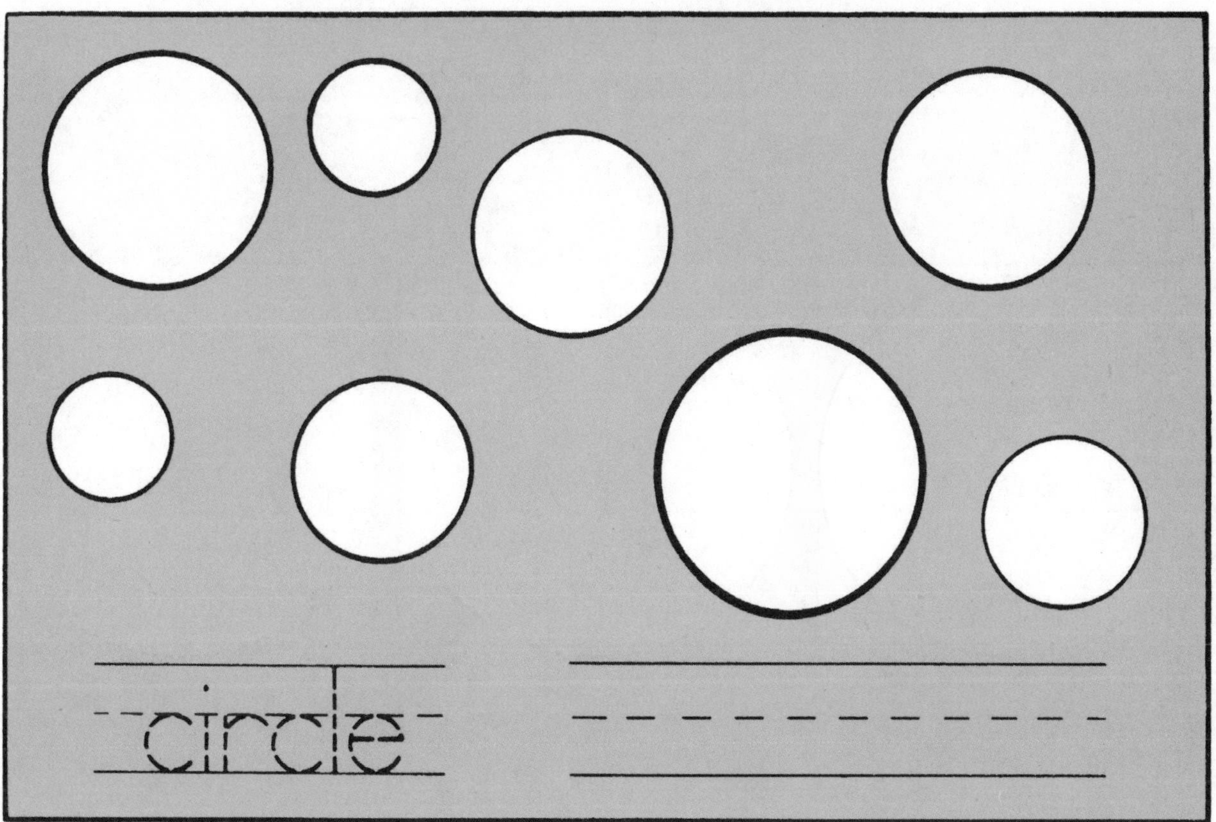


Draw something that is shaped like a circle.

**Skills:** Fine motor skill development; Sight vocabulary recognition; Association between sight vocabulary and shapes

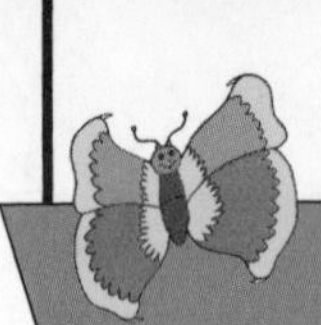

# Colors, Shapes and Numbers

Trace the squares at the top of the page.
Draw your own squares at the bottom. Then color the shapes.

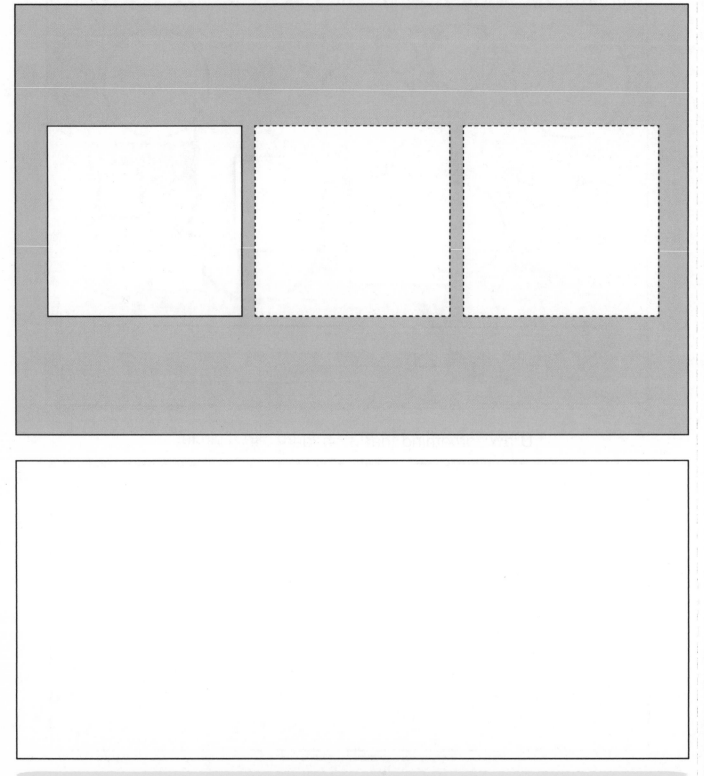

**Skills:** Recognizing shapes; Forming geometric shapes

# Colors, Shapes and Numbers

Look at the squares at the top of the page.
Write the word. Then color the squares.

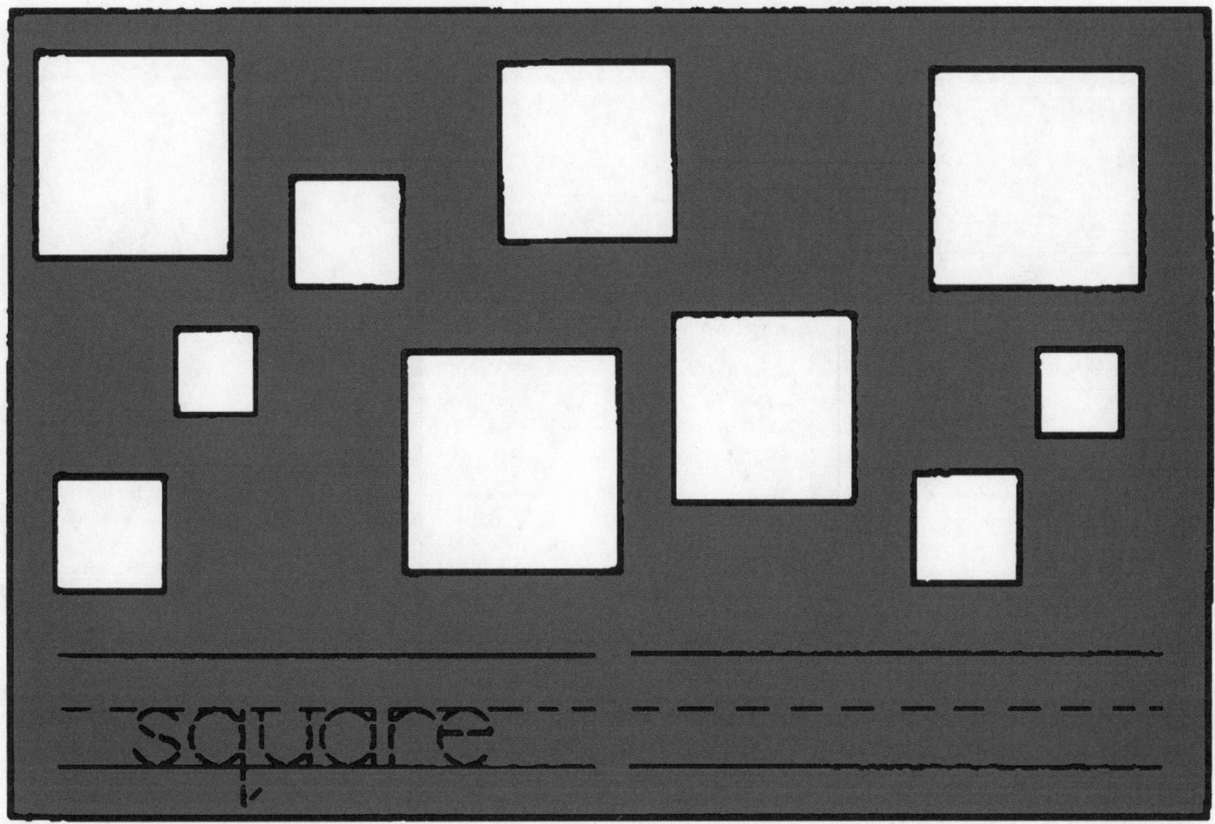


Draw something that is shaped like a square.

**Skills:** Fine motor skill development; Sight vocabulary recognition; Association between sight vocabulary and shapes

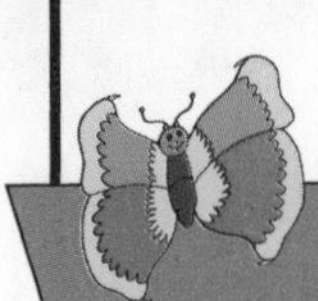

# Colors, Shapes and Numbers

Trace the triangles at the top of the page.
Draw your own triangles at the bottom. Then color the shapes.

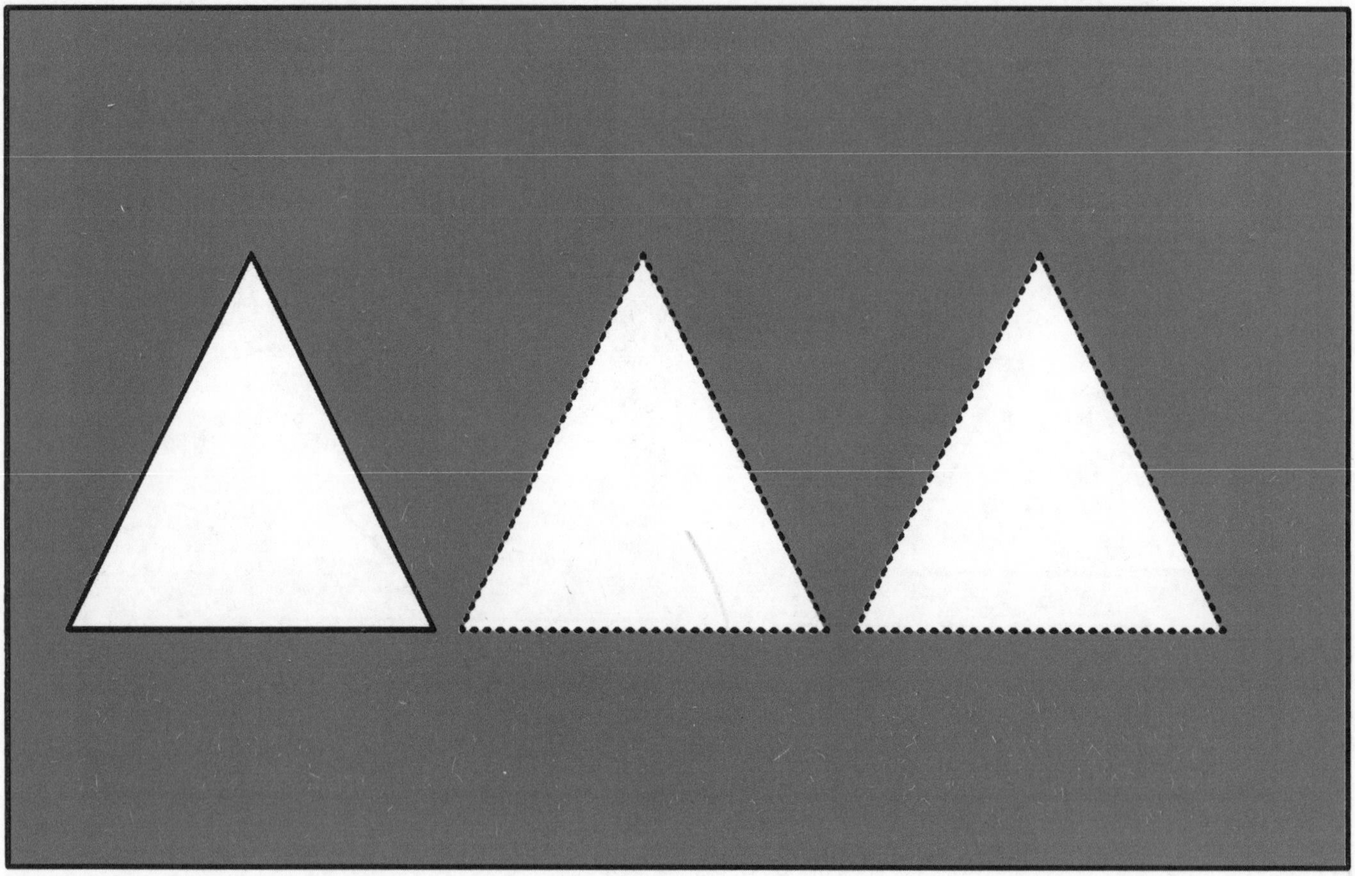

**Skills:** Recognizing shapes; Forming geometric shapes

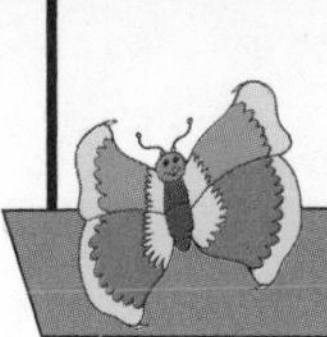

# Colors, Shapes and Numbers

Look at the triangles at the top of the page.
Write the word. Then color the triangles.

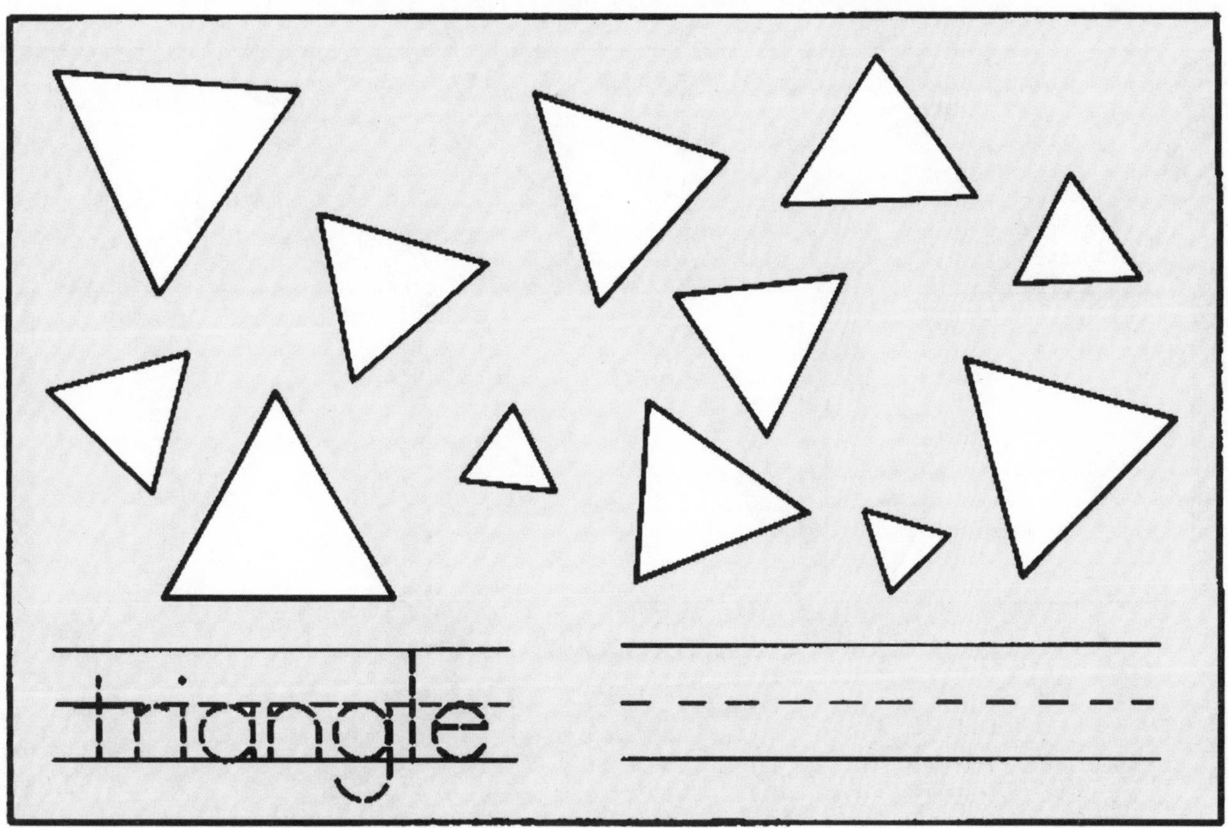


Draw something that is shaped like a triangle.

**Skills:** Fine motor skill development; Sight vocabulary recognition; Association between sight vocabulary and shapes

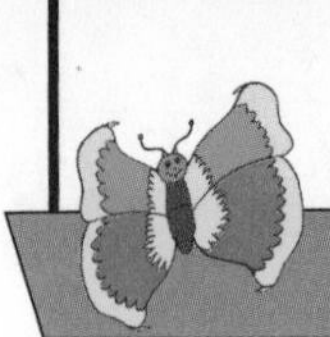

# Colors, Shapes and Numbers

Trace the rectangles at the top of the page.
Draw your own rectangles at the bottom. Then color the shapes.

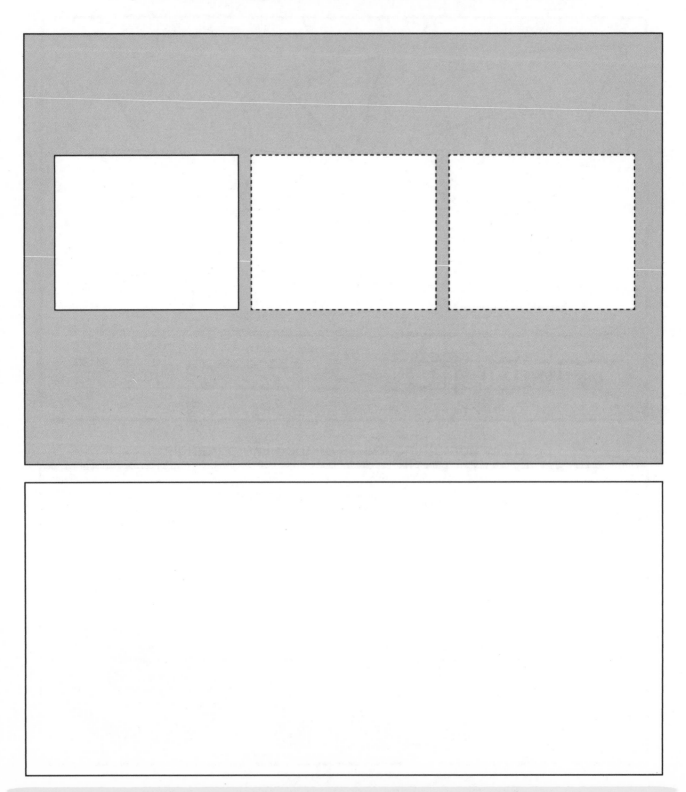

**Skills:** Recognizing shapes; Forming geometric shapes

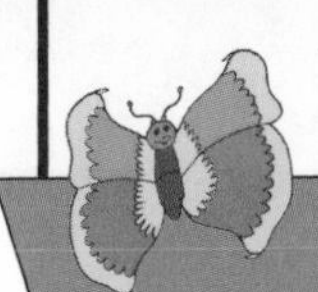

# Colors, Shapes and Numbers

Look at the circles at the top of the page.
Circle the objects below that are shaped like circles.

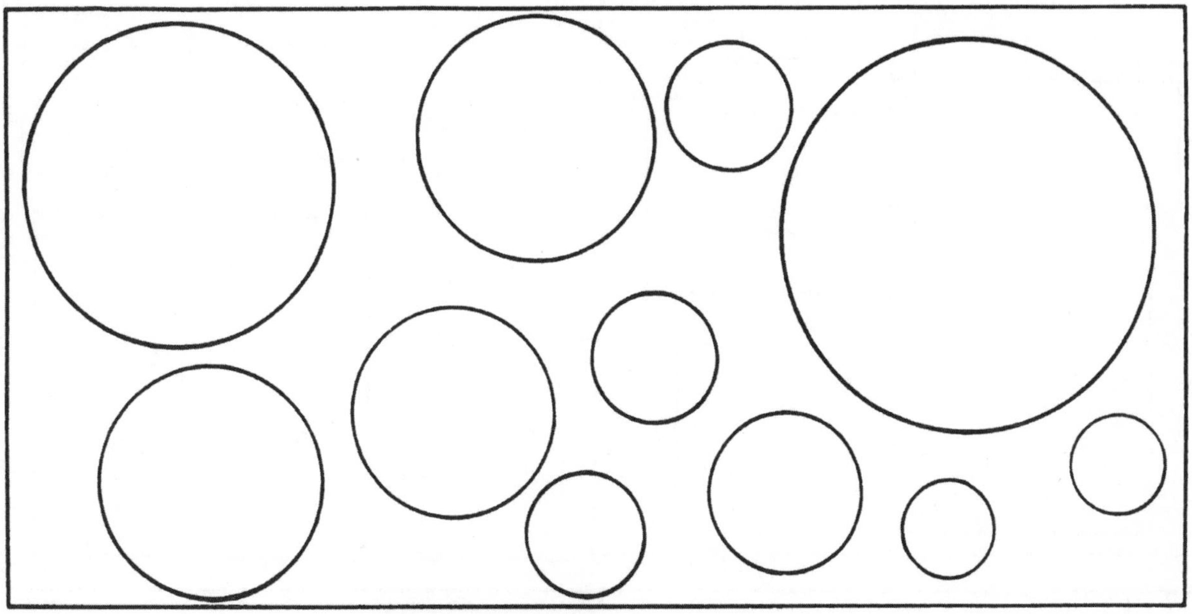

Skills: Recognizing shapes in objects

Look at the squares at the top of the page.
Circle the objects below that are shaped like squares.

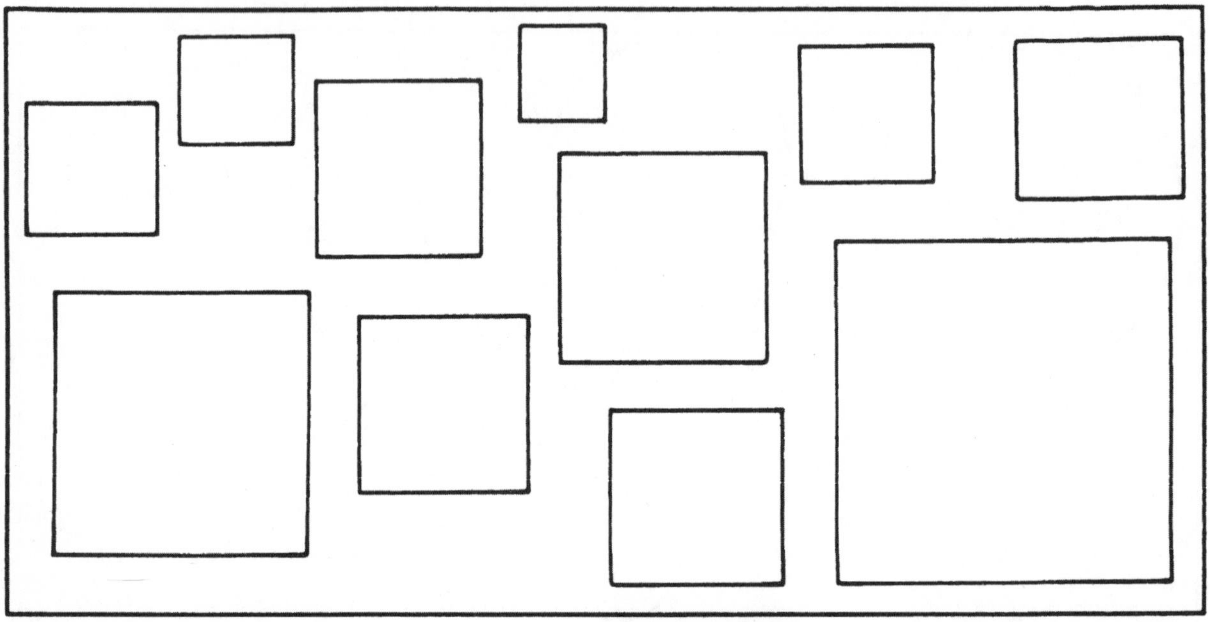

**Skills:** Recognizing shapes in objects

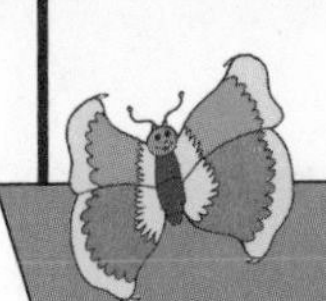



Look at the triangles at the top of the page.
Circle the objects below that are shaped like triangles.

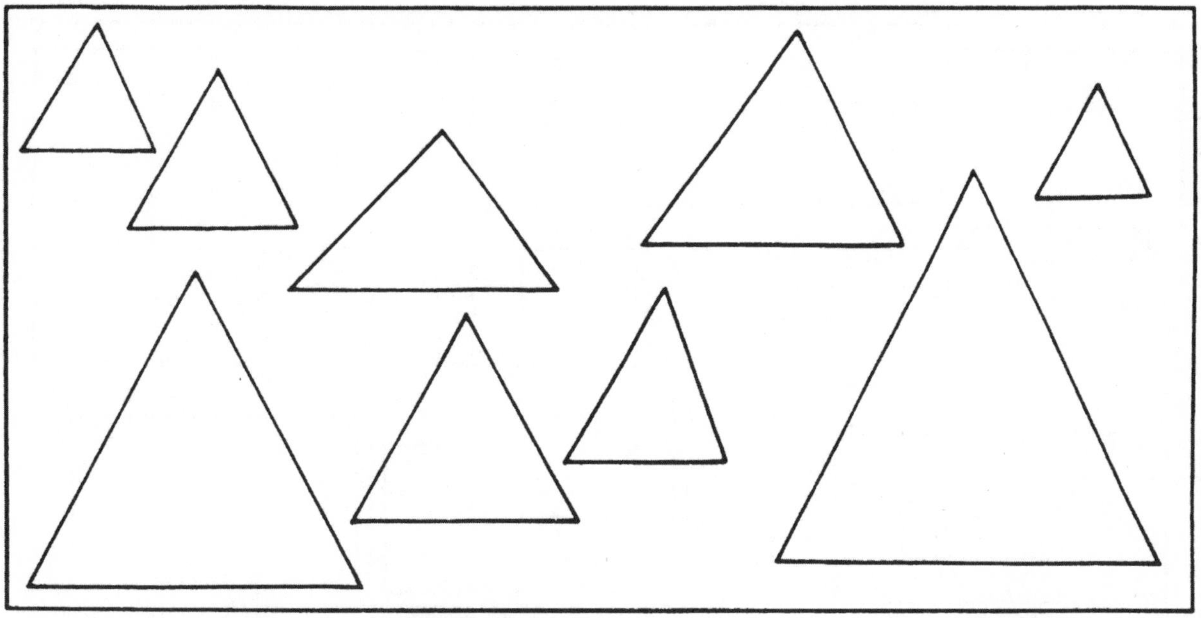

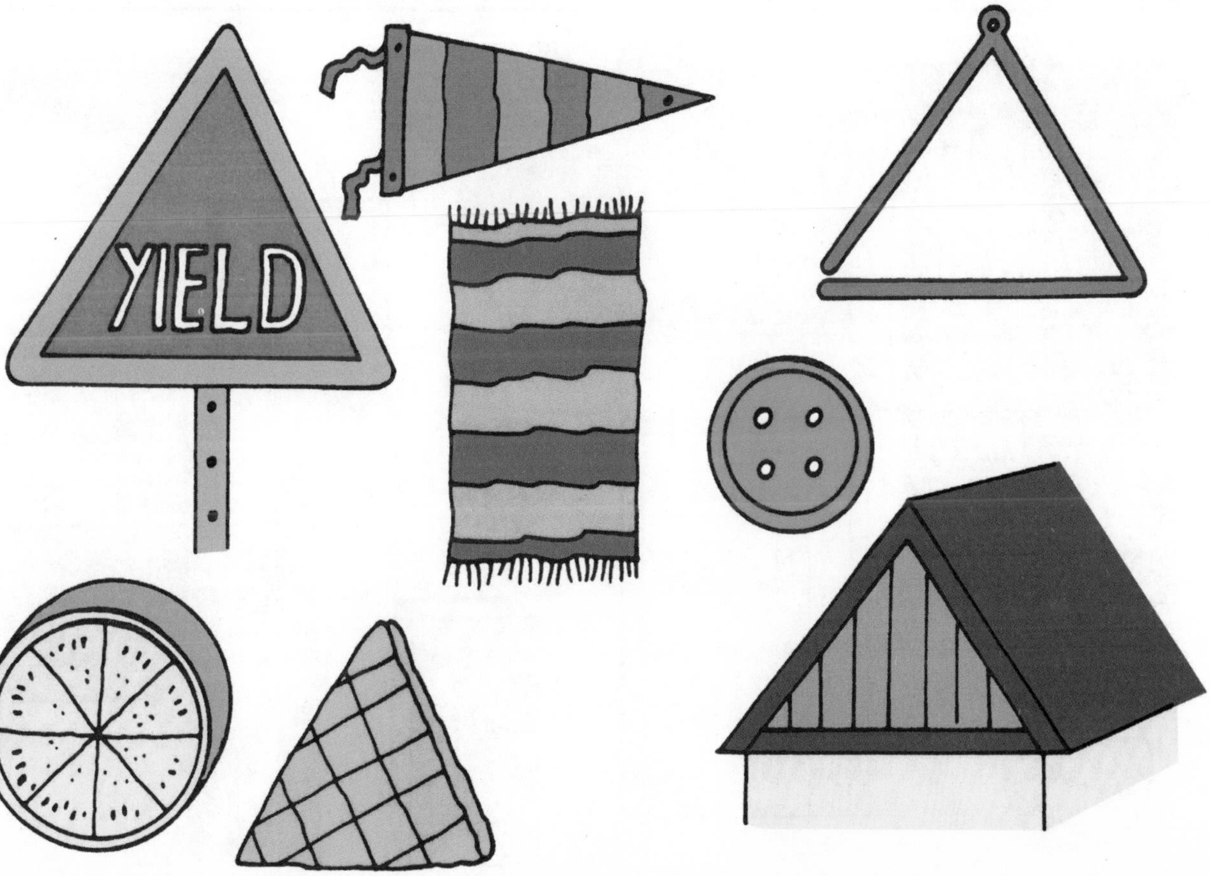

**Skills:** Recognizing shapes in objects

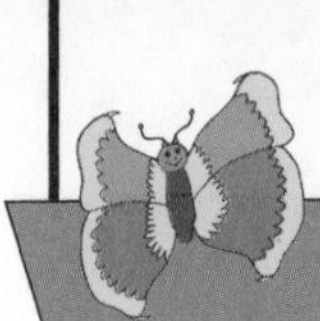

# Colors, Shapes and Numbers

Look at the rectangles at the top of the page.
Circle the objects below that are shaped like rectangles.

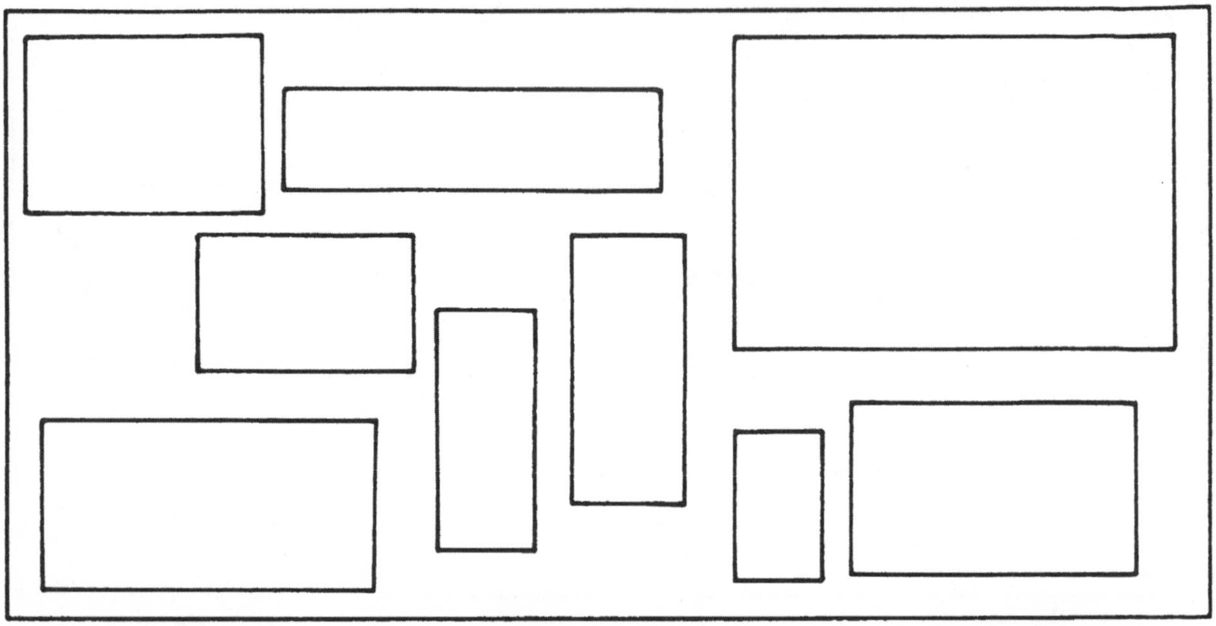

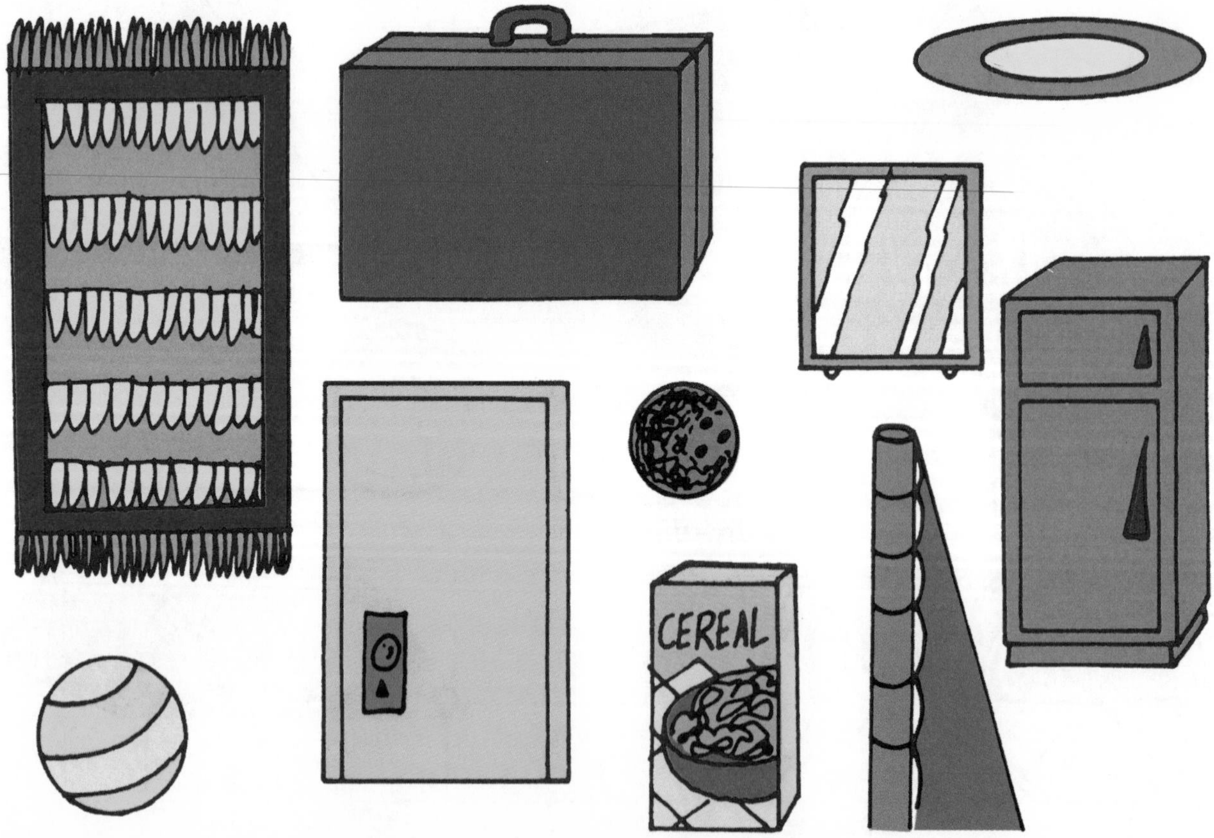

CEREAL

**Skills:** Recognizing shapes in objects

Color the shape that matches the word.

| | |
|---|---|
| **Triangle** | |
| **Square** | |
| **Circle** | |
| **Rectangle** | |

**Skills:** Following directions; Association between sight vocabulary and shapes; Sight vocabulary recognition

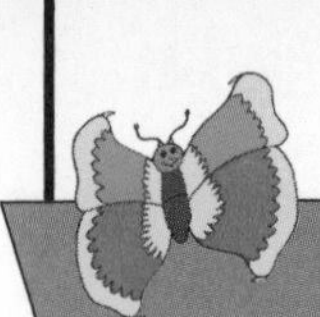

# Colors, Shapes and Numbers

Color the squares red. Color the circles blue.
Color the triangles yellow. Color the rectangles green.

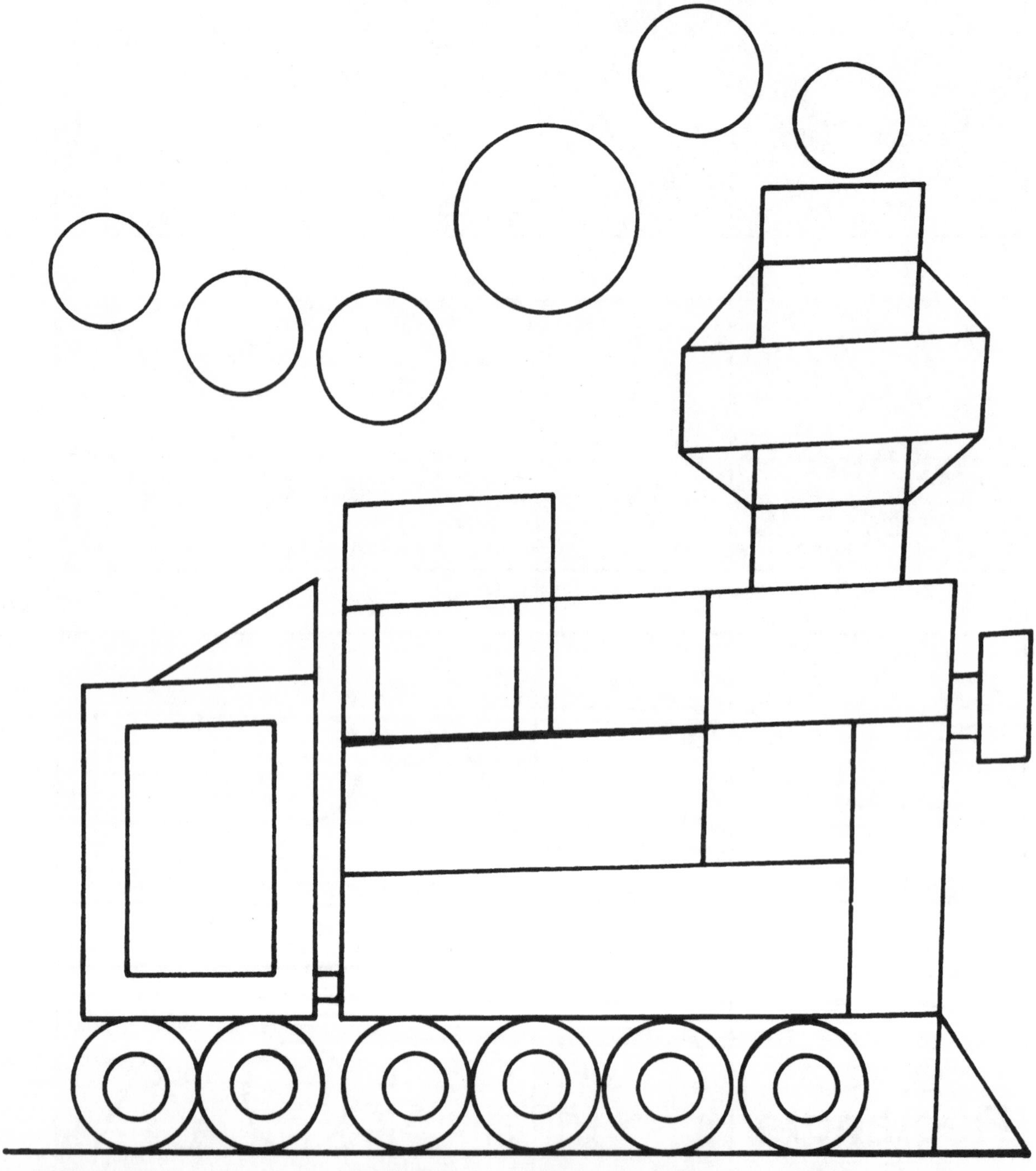

**Skills:** Following directions; Association between sight vocabulary and shapes

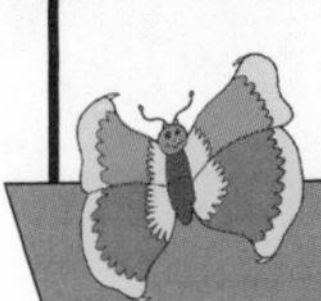

# Colors, Shapes and Numbers

Look at each shape.
Find and circle the shapes that have two sides that match.
Then color all of the shapes.

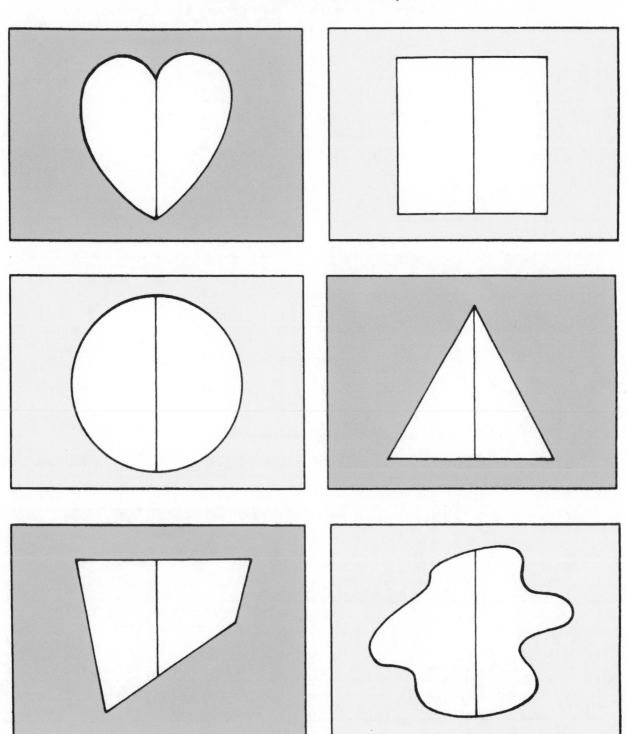

Skills: Recognizing symmetrical shapes

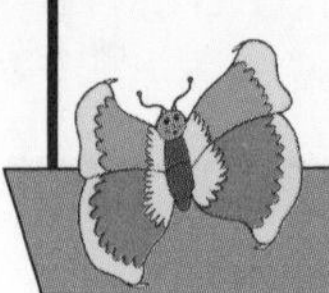



Look at each picture.
Find and circle the pictures that have two sides that match.
Then color all of the pictures.

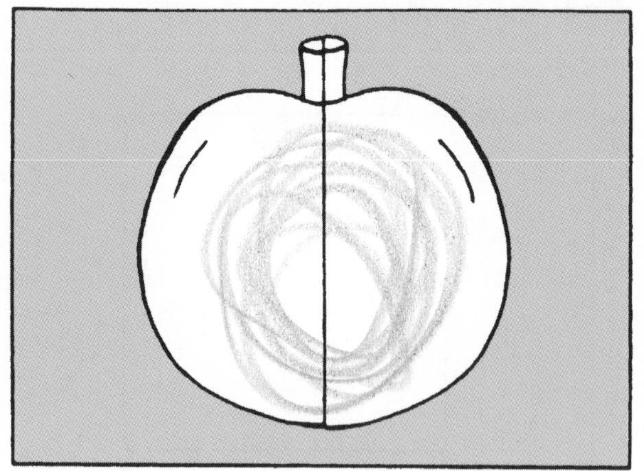

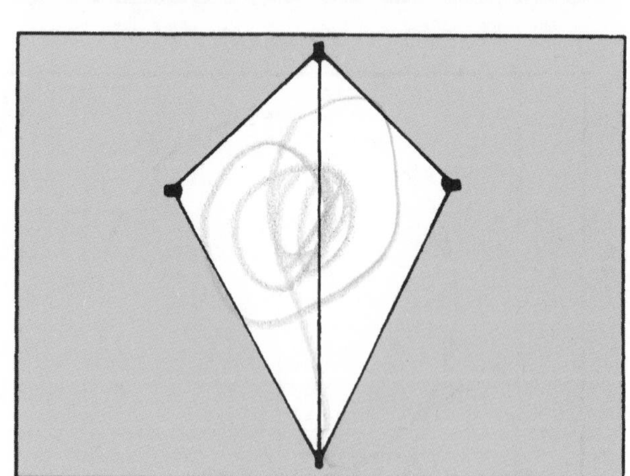

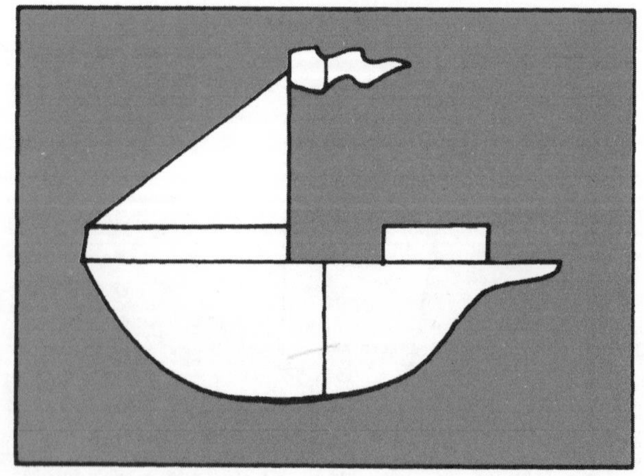

**Skills:** Recognizing symmetry in objects

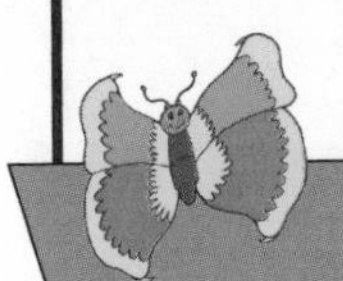

# Colors, Shapes and Numbers

Circle the correct number.

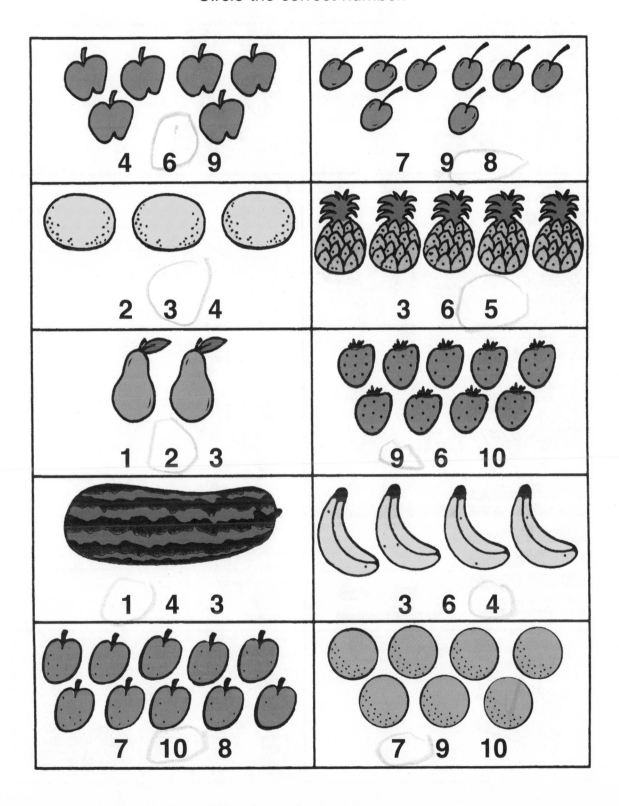

| | |
|---|---|
| 4 6 9 | 7 9 8 |
| 2 3 4 | 3 6 5 |
| 1 2 3 | 9 6 10 |
| 1 4 3 | 3 6 4 |
| 7 10 8 | 7 9 10 |

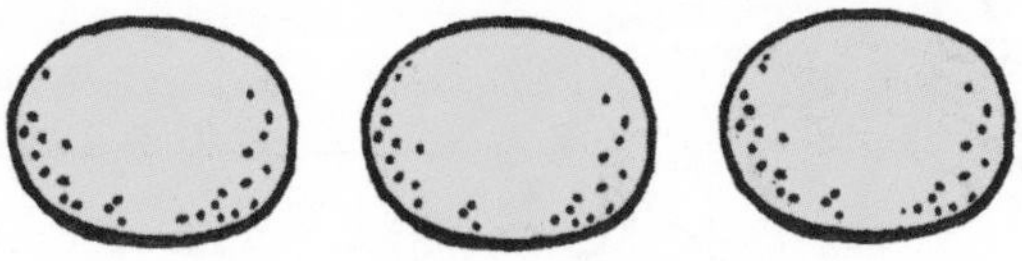

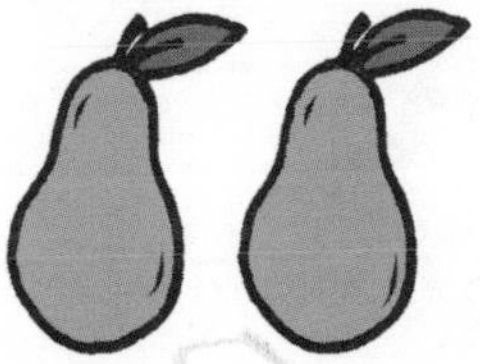

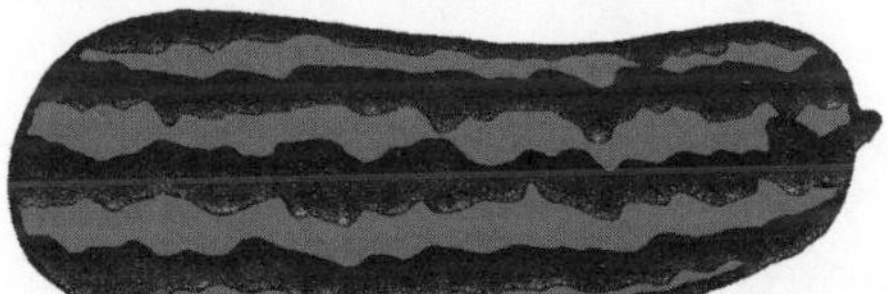

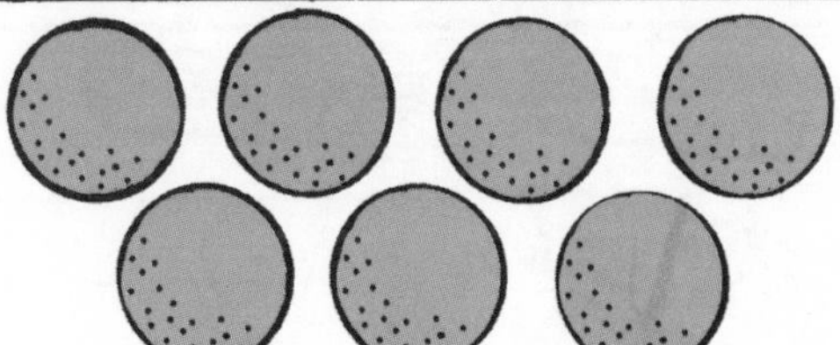

**Skills:** Recognizing sets of objects and the corresponding numeral; Following directions

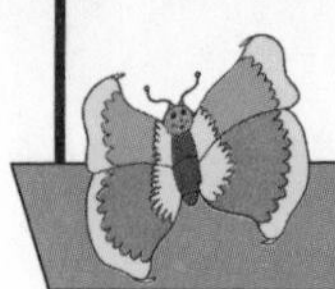

# Colors, Shapes and Numbers

Print the correct number.

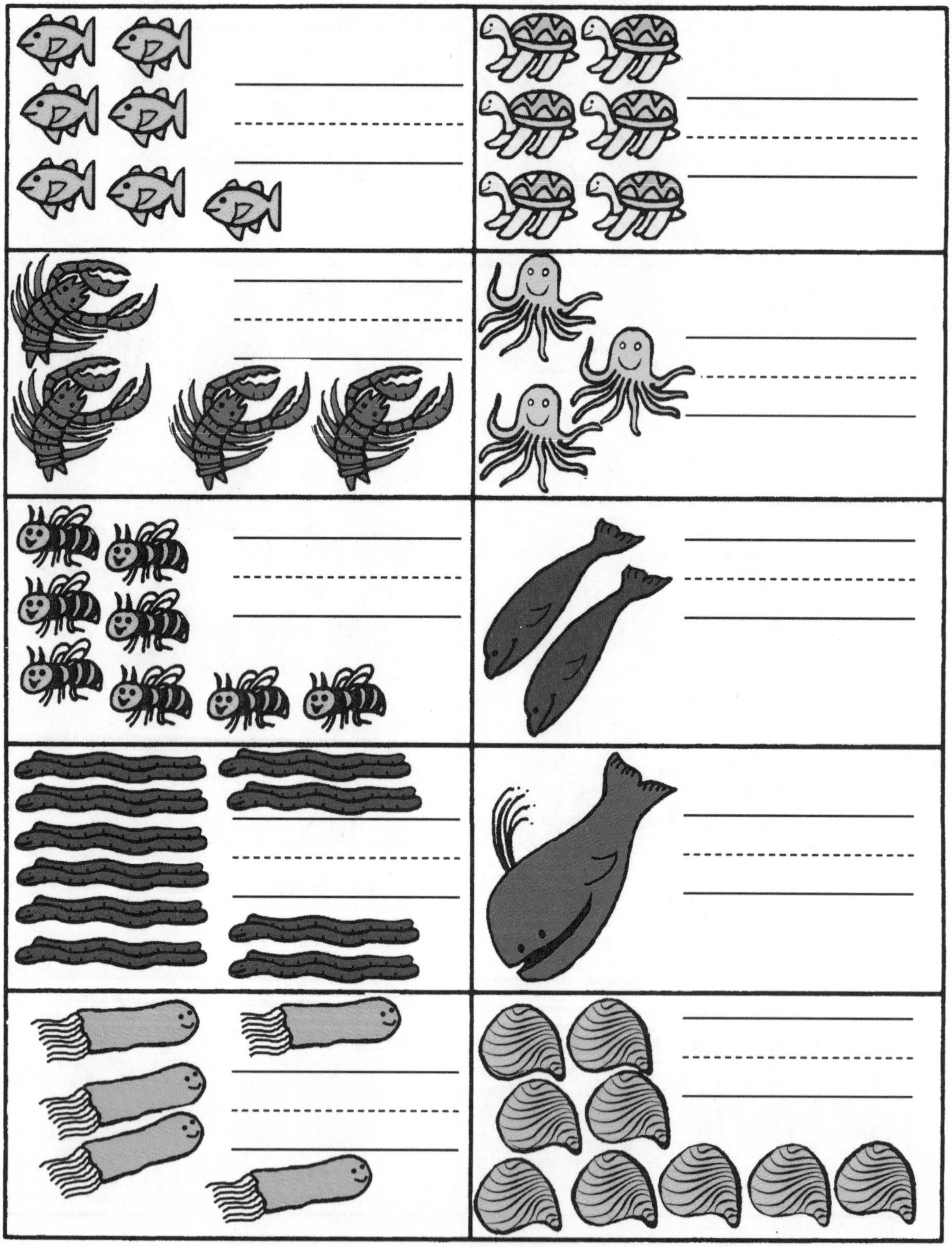

Skills: Recognizing sets of objects; Forming numerals

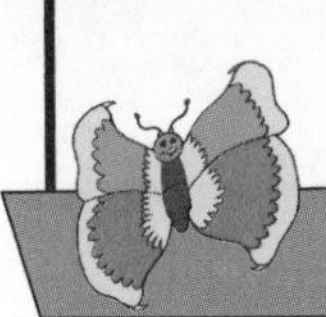



Trace and print the numbers and the number words.

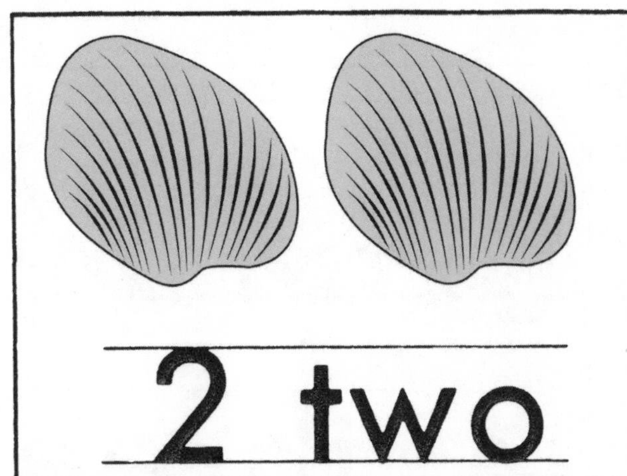


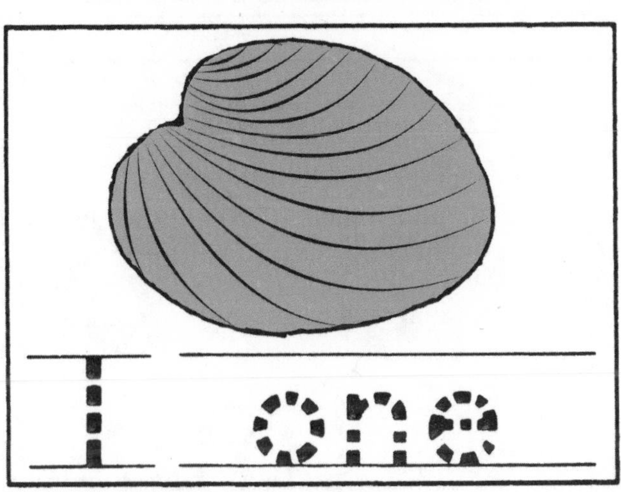


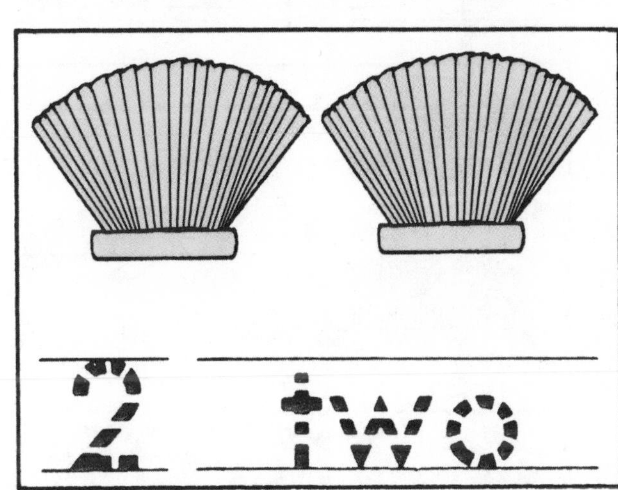


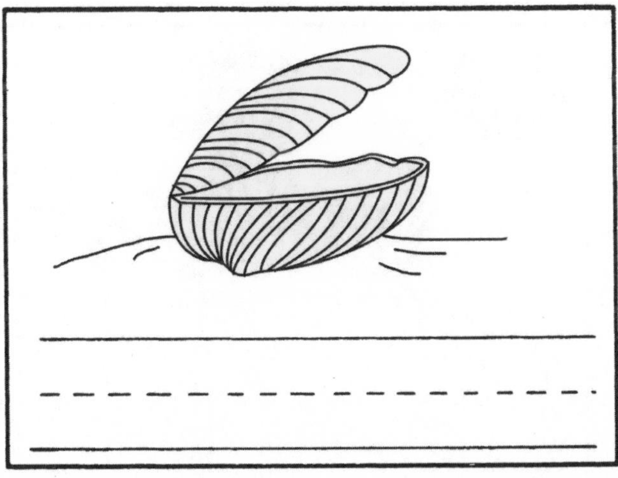

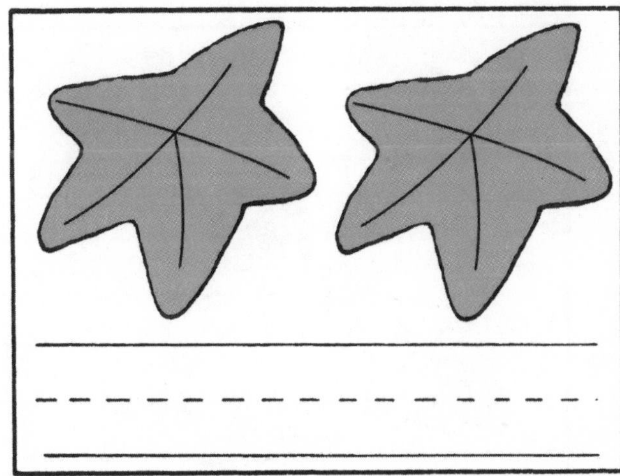

**Skills:** Recognizing sets of one and two;
Association between sight vocabulary, numerals and sets

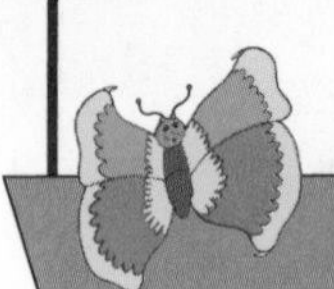

# Colors, Shapes and Numbers

Trace and print the numbers and the number words.

3 three

4 four

3 three

4 four

**Skills:** Recognizing sets of three and four;
Association between sight vocabulary, numerals and sets

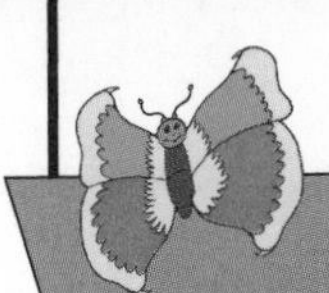

# Colors, Shapes and Numbers

Trace and print the numbers and the number words.

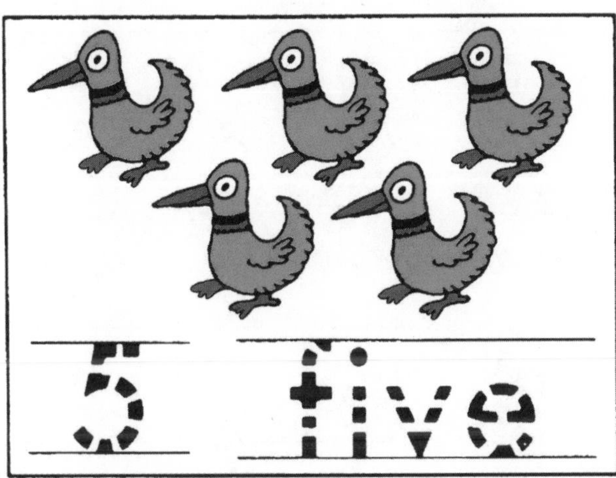

**Skills:** Recognizing sets of five and six;
Association between sight vocabulary, numerals and sets

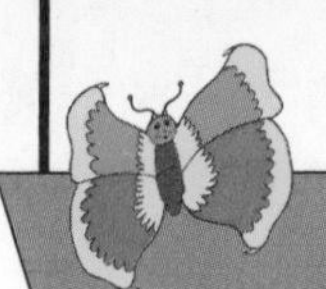

# Colors, Shapes and Numbers

Trace and print the numbers and the number words.

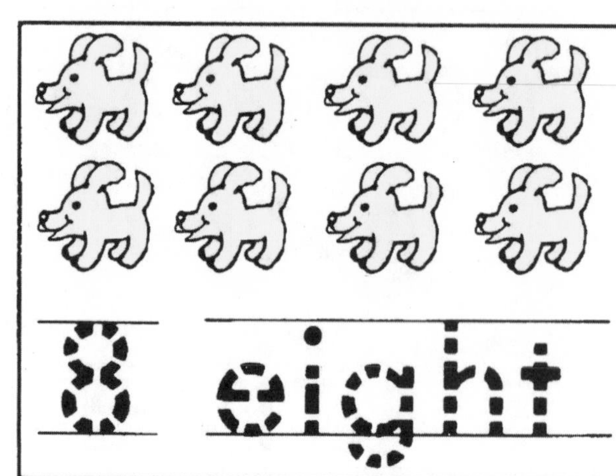

**Skills:** Recognizing sets of seven and eight;
Association between sight vocabulary, numerals and sets

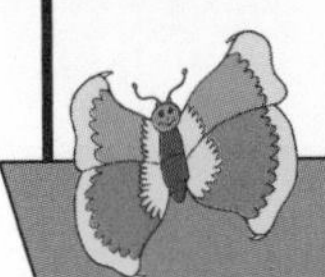

# Colors, Shapes and Numbers

Trace and print the numbers and the number words.

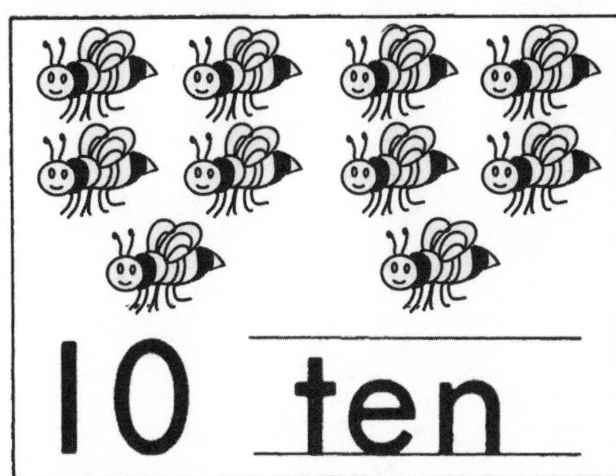

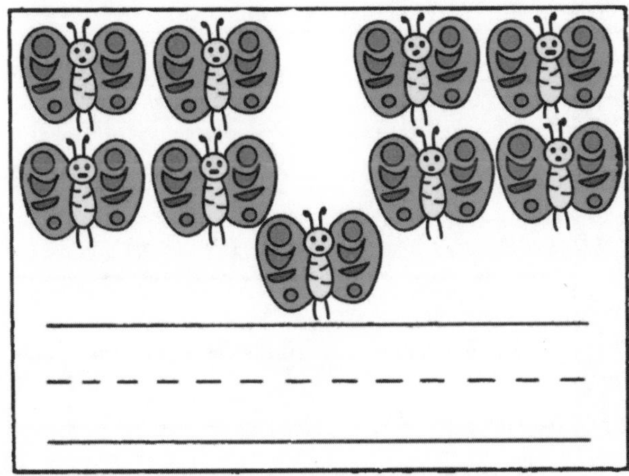

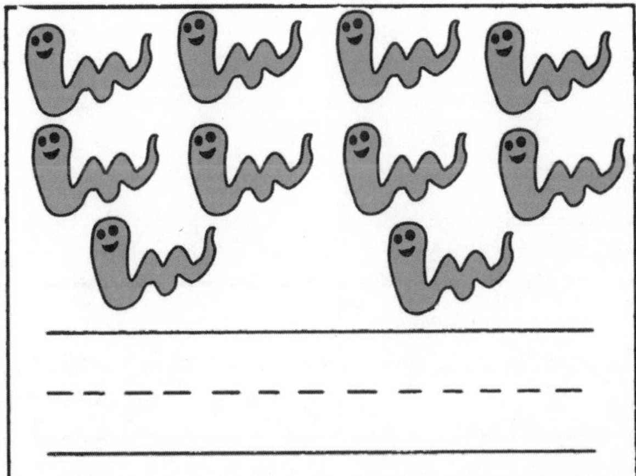

**Skills:** Recognizing sets of nine and ten;
Association between sight vocabulary, numerals and sets

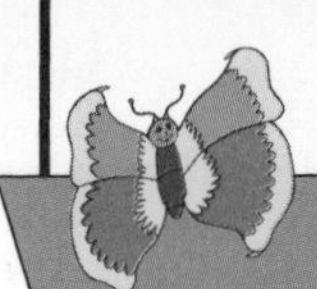

# Colors, Shapes and Numbers

Trace the numbers and the number words.
Then draw that many objects.

1 one

2 two

3 three

4 four

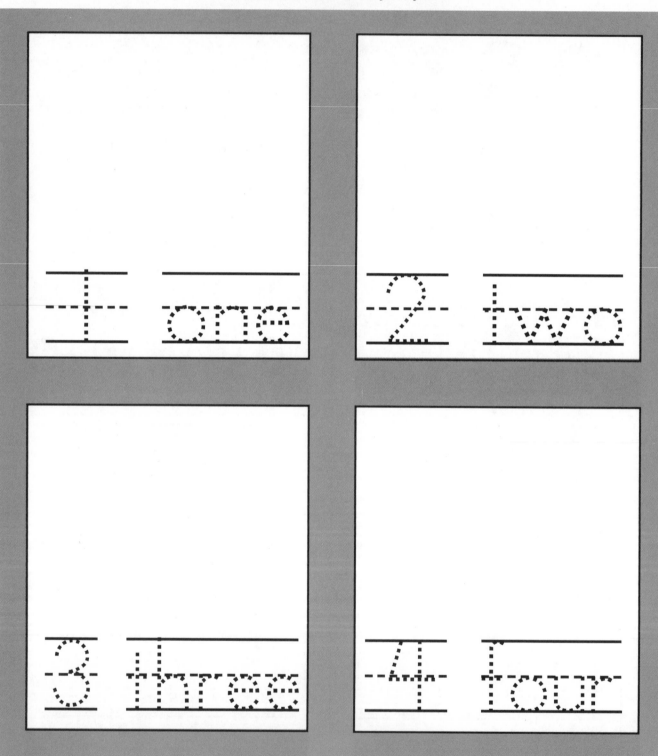

**Skills:** Recognizing numerals; Writing number words; Forming corresponding sets of objects

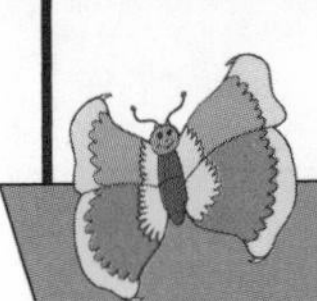

## Colors, Shapes and Numbers

Trace the numbers and the number words.
Then draw that many objects.

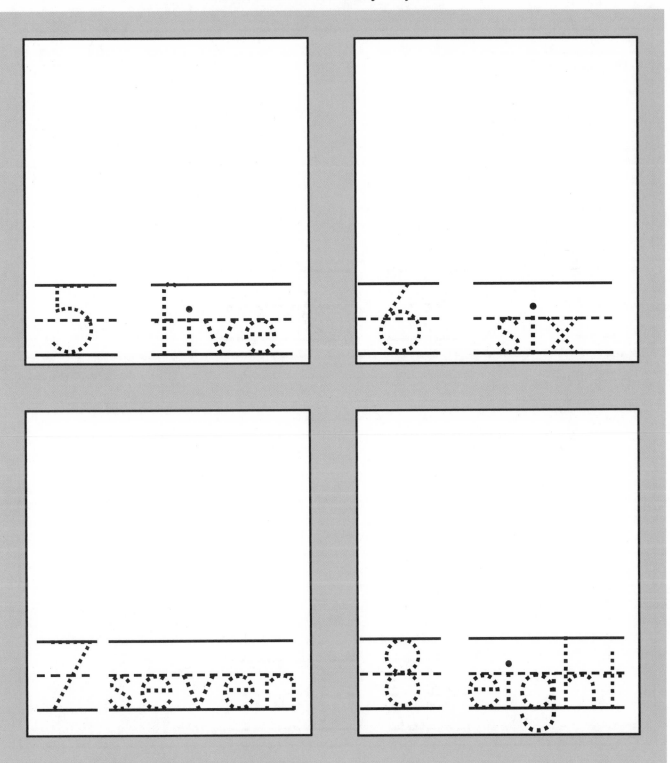

5 five

6 six

7 seven

8 eight

**Skills:** Recognizing numerals; Writing number words; Forming corresponding sets of objects

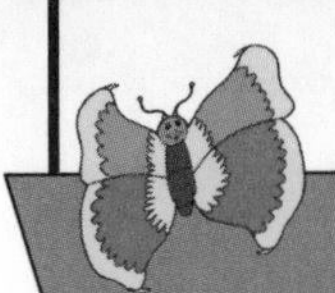

# Colors, Shapes and Numbers

Trace the numbers and the number words.
Then draw that many objects.

9 nine

10 ten

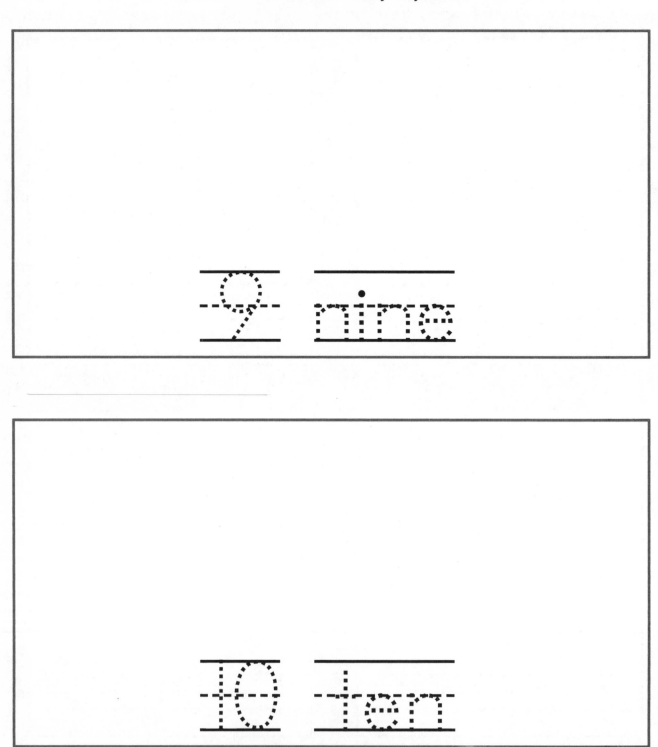

**Skills:** Recognizing numerals; Writing number words; Forming corresponding sets of objects

# Excellent!

## Give yourself a star!

# Counting and Math Skills

# Counting and Math Skills

Trace the numbers from 1 to 100.

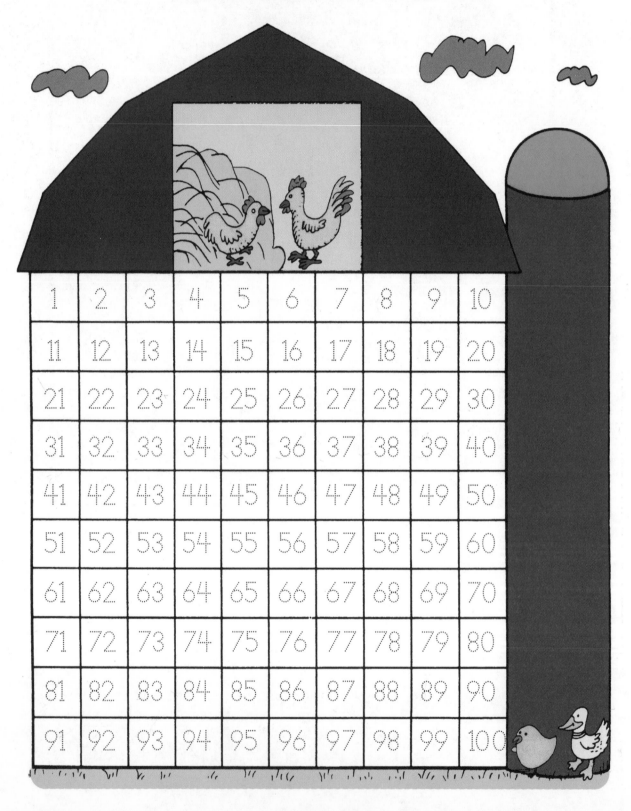

| 1 | 2 | 3 | 4 | 5 | 6 | 7 | 8 | 9 | 10 |
|---|---|---|---|---|---|---|---|---|---|
| 11 | 12 | 13 | 14 | 15 | 16 | 17 | 18 | 19 | 20 |
| 21 | 22 | 23 | 24 | 25 | 26 | 27 | 28 | 29 | 30 |
| 31 | 32 | 33 | 34 | 35 | 36 | 37 | 38 | 39 | 40 |
| 41 | 42 | 43 | 44 | 45 | 46 | 47 | 48 | 49 | 50 |
| 51 | 52 | 53 | 54 | 55 | 56 | 57 | 58 | 59 | 60 |
| 61 | 62 | 63 | 64 | 65 | 66 | 67 | 68 | 69 | 70 |
| 71 | 72 | 73 | 74 | 75 | 76 | 77 | 78 | 79 | 80 |
| 81 | 82 | 83 | 84 | 85 | 86 | 87 | 88 | 89 | 90 |
| 91 | 92 | 93 | 94 | 95 | 96 | 97 | 98 | 99 | 100 |

**Skills:** Counting to 100; Forming numerals

# Counting and Math Skills

Look at the balloons. Which number comes next?

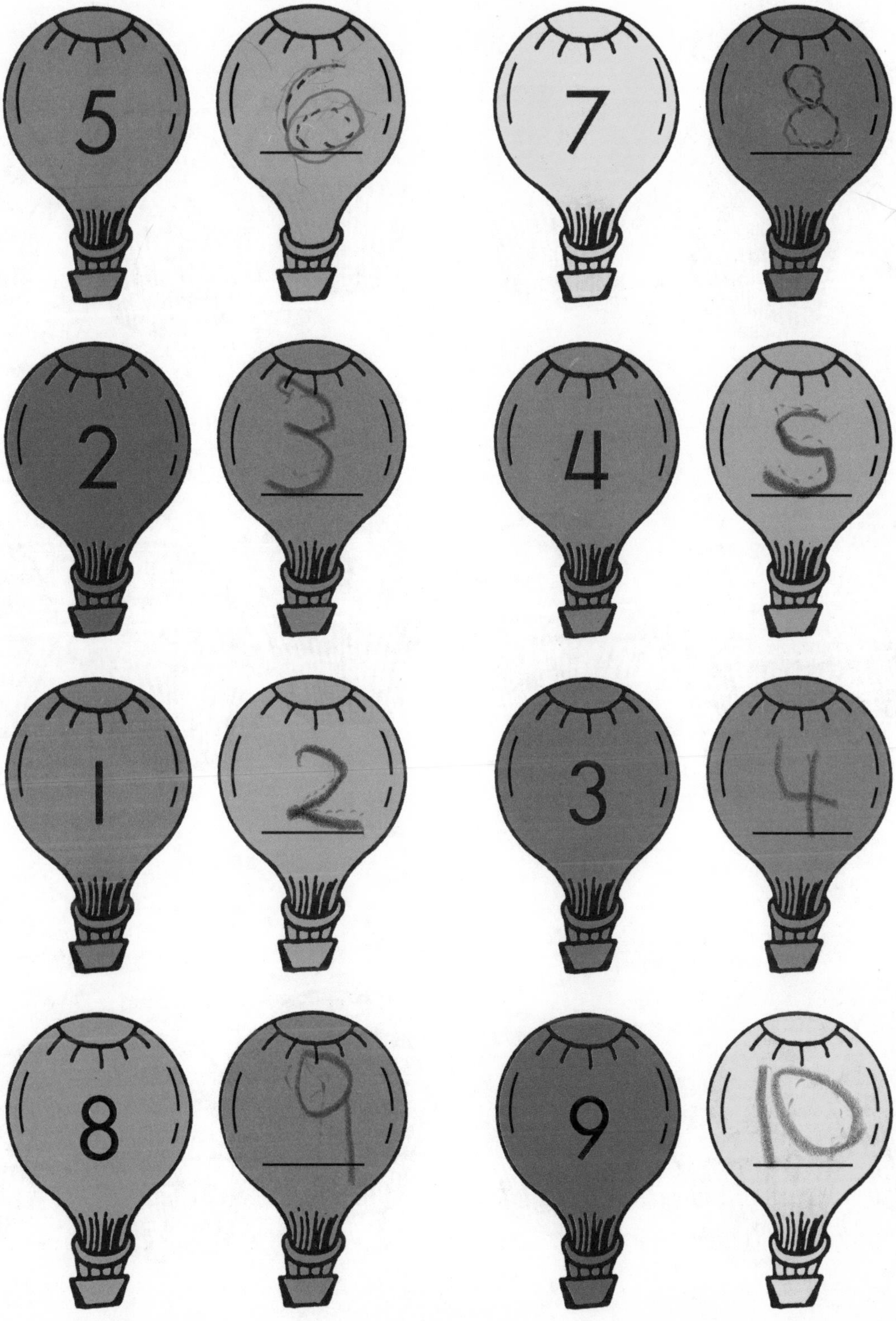

5 ___ 7 ___

2 ___ 4 ___

1 ___ 3 ___

8 ___ 9 ___

**Skills:** Ordering numbers to 10; Writing numerals

# Counting and Math Skills

Look at each group of cupcakes.
Which number comes between?

4 5 6    7 ___ 9

3 ___ 5    6 ___ 8

2 ___ 4    5 ___ 7

**Skills:** Ordering numbers to 10; Writing numerals

# Counting and Math Skills

Look at the set in each box.
Circle the number that tells how many.

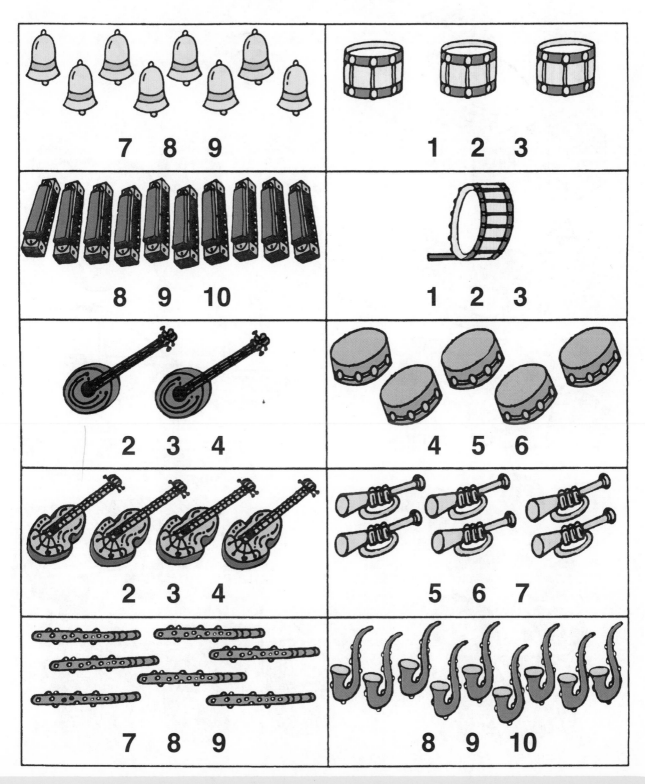

| | |
|---|---|
| 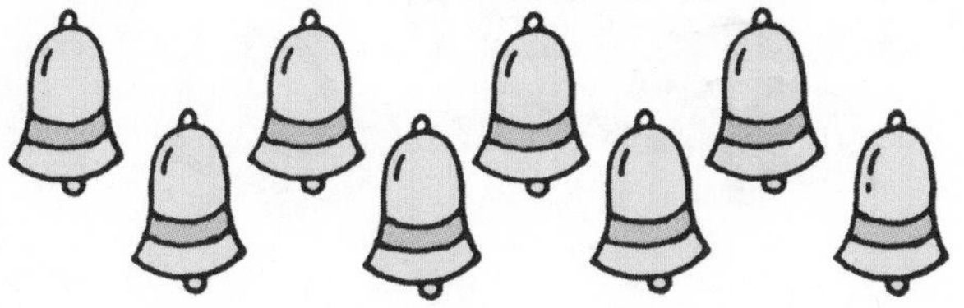 7 8 9 |  1 2 3 |
|  8 9 10 | 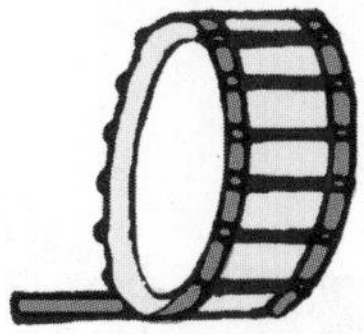 1 2 3 |
|  2 3 4 |  4 5 6 |
|  2 3 4 |  5 6 7 |
| 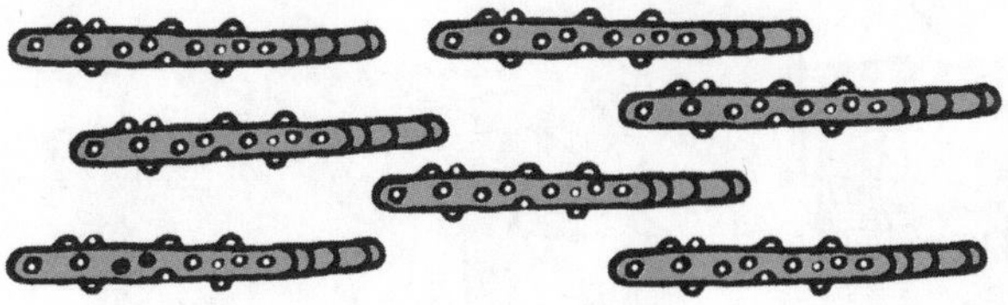 7 8 9 | 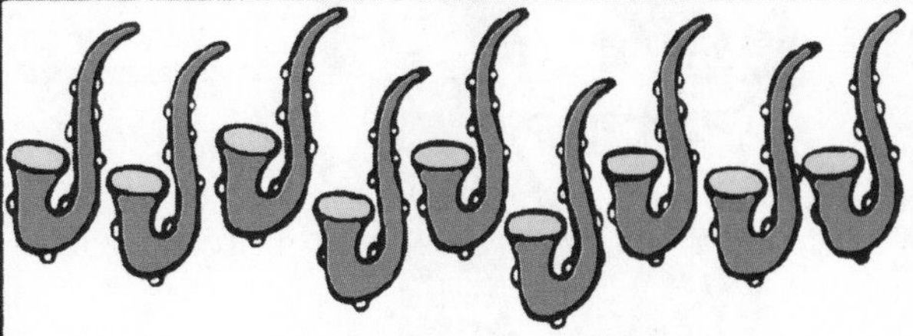 8 9 10 |

**Skills:** Recognizing sets of objects and the corresponding numeral

# Counting and Math Skills

How many objects are in each set?
Draw a line to match the sets with the same number of objects.

**Skills:** Identifying and matching sets

## Counting and Math Skills

Look at the number on each necklace.
Draw that many beads on each necklace.

7

10

9

6

8

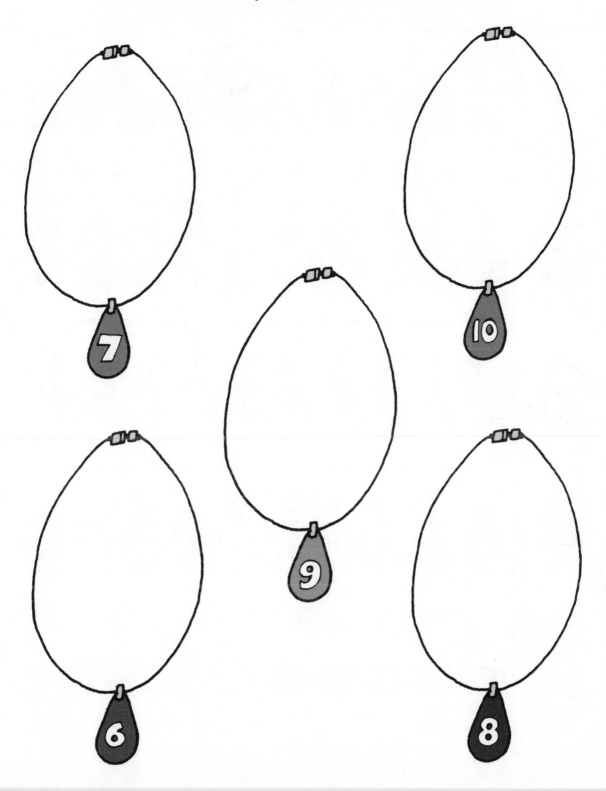

**Skills:** Recognizing numerals; Creating sets to show an amount

# Counting and Math Skills

Look at the number at the beginning of each row.
Circle that number of fruits.

| | |
|---|---|
| 1 | |
| 2 | |
| 3 | |
| 4 | |
| 5 | |

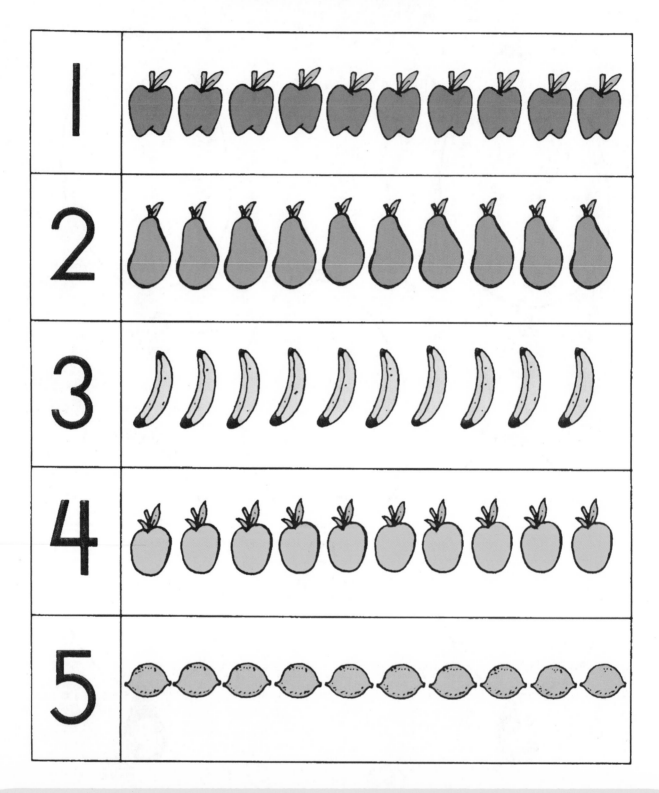

**Skills:** Creating sets of objects; Recognizing numerals

# Counting and Math Skills

Look at the number at the beginning of each row.
Circle that number of objects.

| | |
|---|---|
| 6 | |
| 7 | |
| 8 | |
| 9 | |
| 10 | |

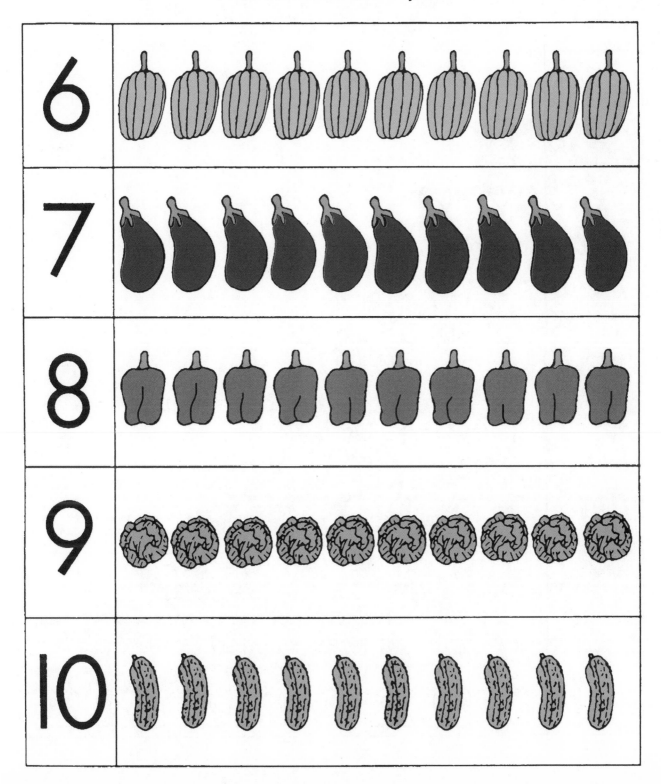

**Skills:** Creating sets of objects; Recognizing numerals

# Counting and Math Skills

Look at the objects in each row. Count the objects in each row. Write the number in each box. Then color the page.

1

2

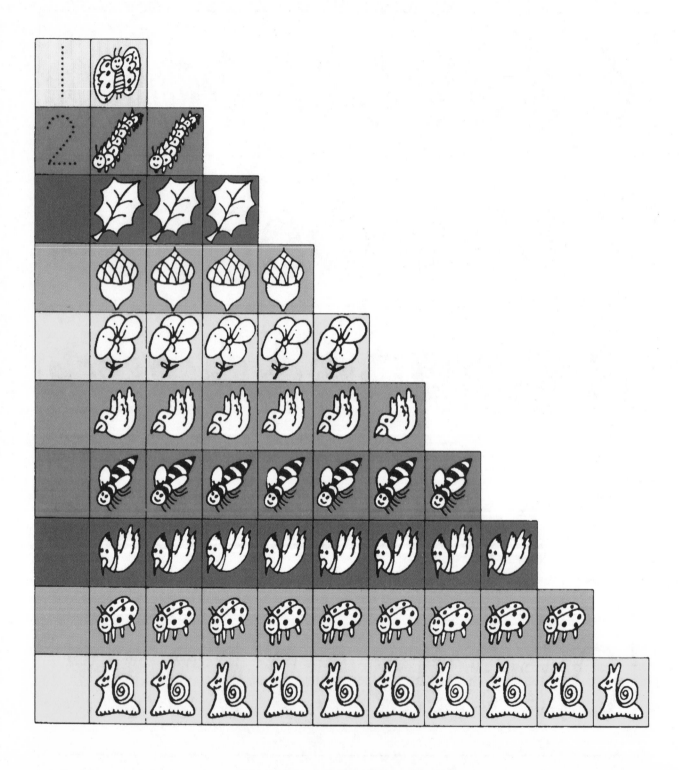

Skills: Recognizing sets of objects; Forming numerals

# Counting and Math Skills

Color the balloons with numbers that are greater than 20.

50 30
18 3 21 11
49 33 27 36 46
12 19
43 47 16 38 45 31
13 9
32 42 24 17 37 48
23

**Skills:** Comparing numbers

# Counting and Math Skills

Look at the seesaws.
Circle the number that is larger.

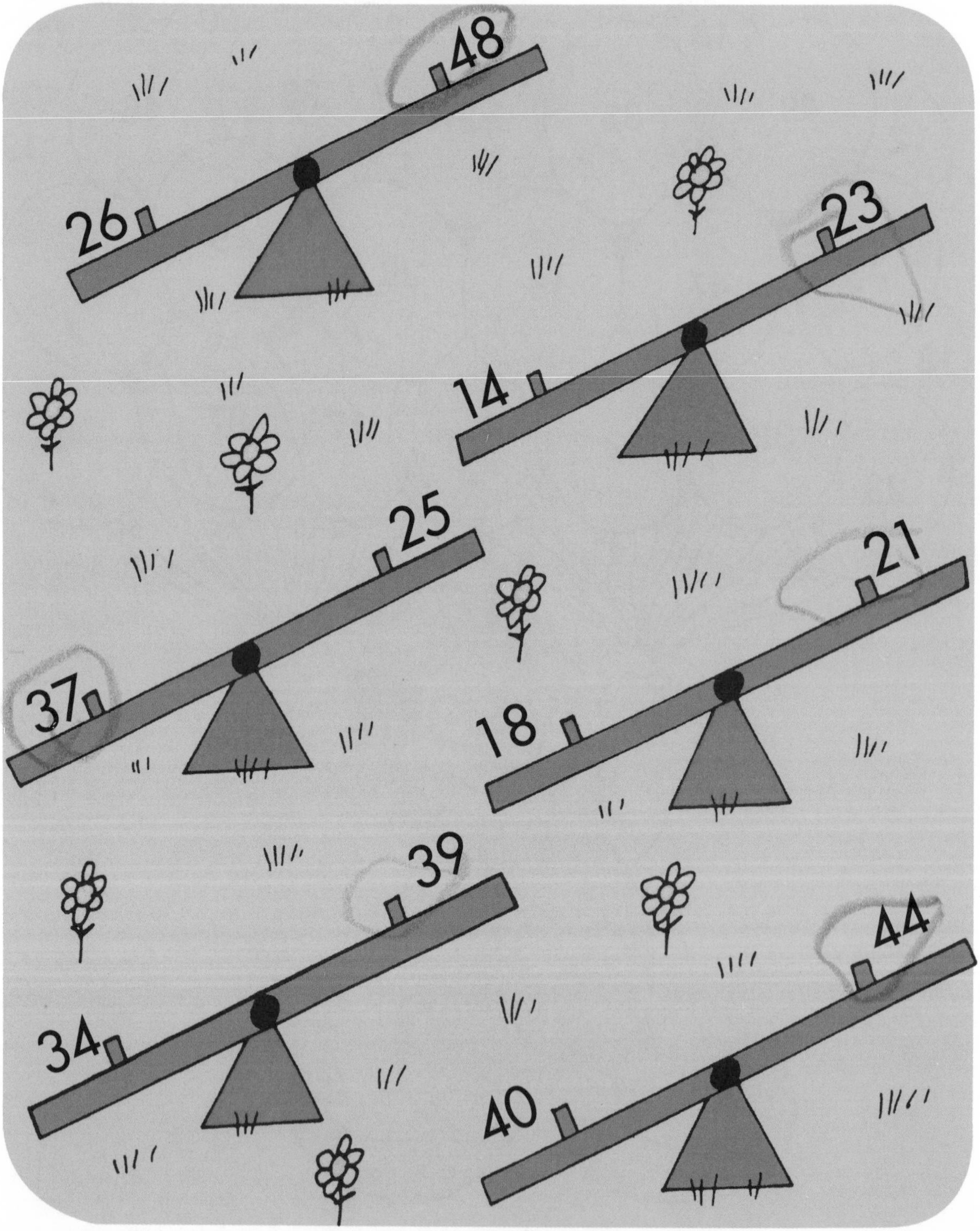

26 48

14 23

37 25

18 21

34 39

40 44

Skills: Comparing numbers

# Counting and Math Skills

Look at the bicycles. Circle the number that is smaller.

15 42

25 18

33 41

27 35

46 22

20 39

Skills: Comparing numbers

# Counting and Math Skills

Can you count to 100?
Write the missing numbers.

| 1 | 2 |  |  | 5 |  | 7 | 8 |  | 10 |
|---|---|---|---|---|---|---|---|---|---|
| 11 |  | 13 | 14 |  | 16 |  |  | 19 | 20 |
|  | 22 | 23 | 24 |  |  | 27 |  |  |  |
| 31 |  |  | 34 | 35 |  |  | 38 |  | 40 |
|  |  | 43 |  |  | 46 | 47 |  | 49 |  |
| 51 | 52 |  |  |  |  |  | 58 |  | 60 |
|  |  |  | 64 | 65 | 66 |  |  |  |  |
|  | 72 |  |  |  | 76 |  | 78 |  |  |
| 81 |  |  |  | 85 | 86 |  | 88 | 89 |  |
|  |  |  |  |  |  |  |  | 99 |  |

**Skills:** Counting to 100; Forming numerals

# Counting and Math Skills

Connect the dots from 1 to 100 to find out who lives near the castle.

**Skills:** Ordering numerals from 1 to 100

# Counting and Math Skills

Look at the even numbers. Look at the odd numbers.
Fill in the missing numbers.

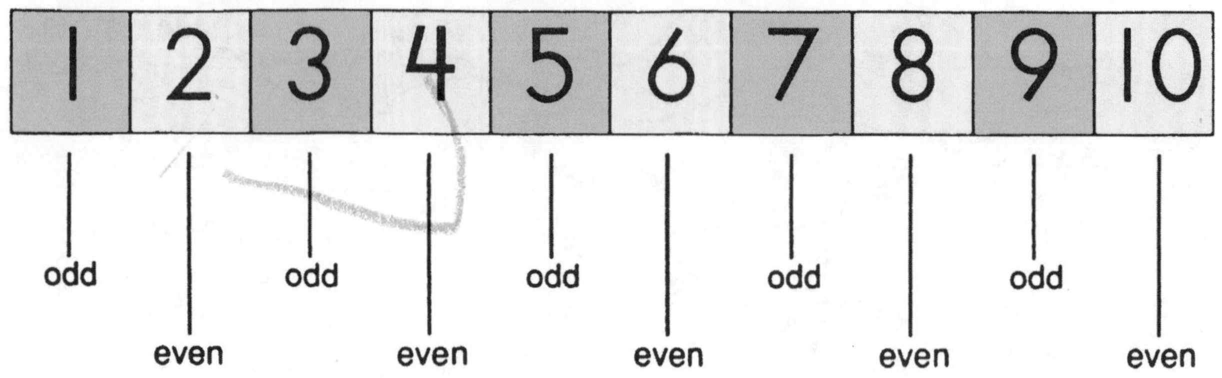



| | | | | |
|---|---|---|---|---|
| 1 | 3 | 5 | | |
| 2 | 4 | 6 | | |
| 9 | 7 | 5 | | |

**Skills:** Recognizing and using odd and even numbers

Connect the dots.
Start with 2 and count by 2's.

44 46 40 42 38 48 36 34 50 20 32 22 28 24 18 30 26 6 16 8 10 12 4 14 2

**Skills:** Counting by 2's to 50

Color the odd numbers to see which animal is swimming in the pond.

**Skills:** Identifying odd numbers

# Counting and Math Skills

Color the even numbers to see which animal is hiding in the jungle.

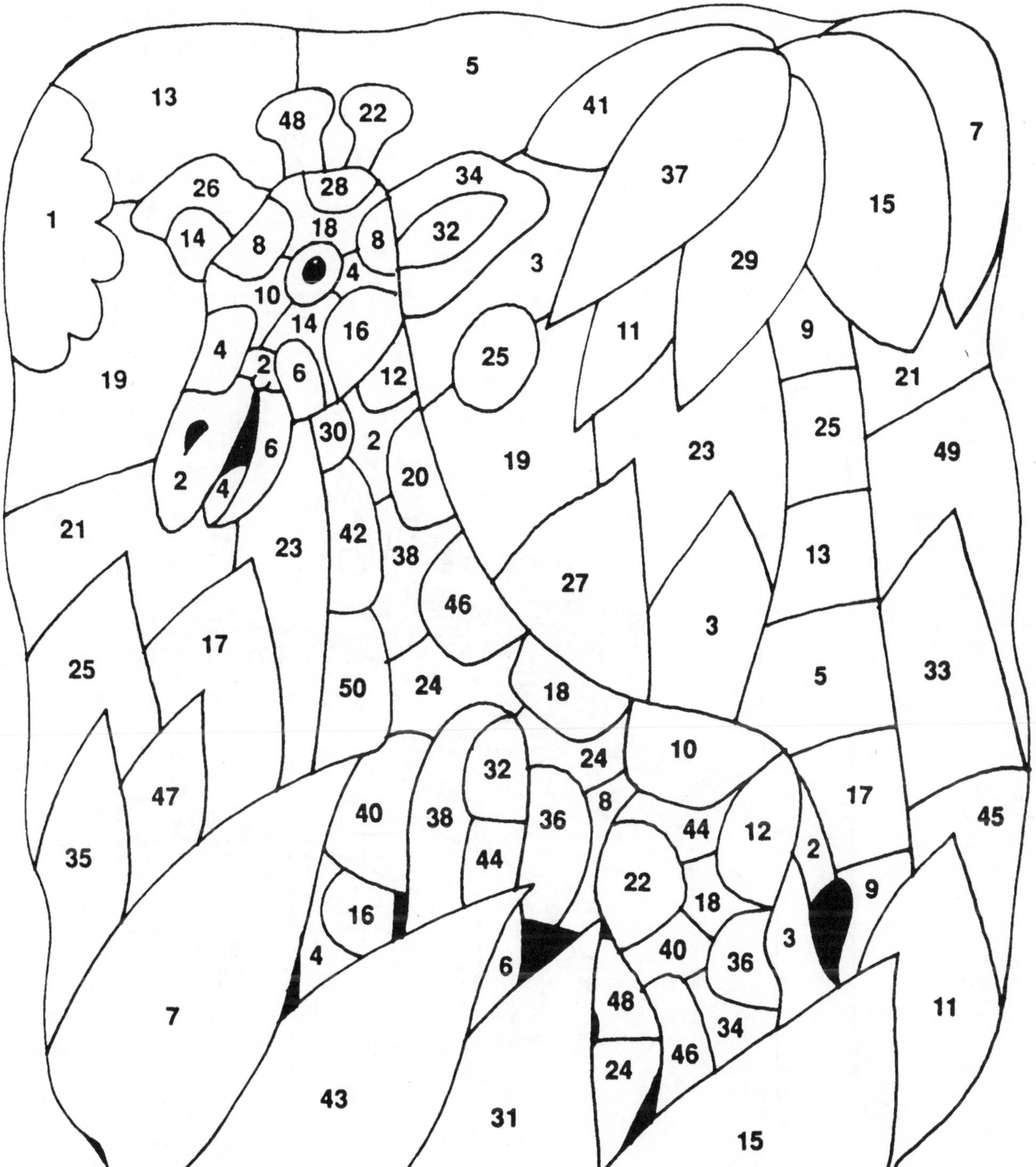

**Skills:** Identifying even numbers

Connect the dots.
Start with 5 and count by 5's.

**Skills:** Counting by 5's to 100

# Counting and Math Skills

Look at these marbles. Put them into groups of 10.

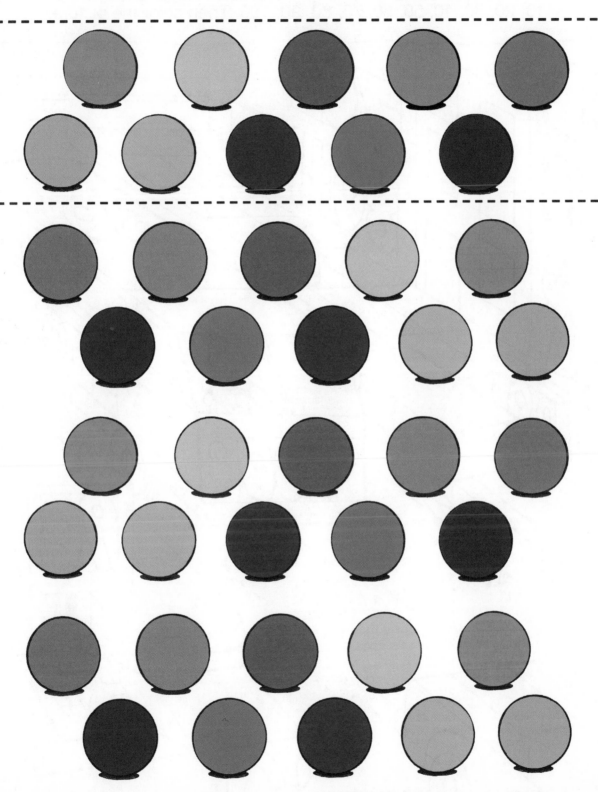

Skills: Forming groups of 10; Counting objects to form groups

Look closely at this picture. Find and circle these numbers hidden in the picture: 10, 20, 30, 40, 50, 60, 70, 80, 90, 100. Then color the picture.

**Skills:** Recognizing decade numbers

# Counting and Math Skills

Look at each picture. How many are in the first group?
How many are in the second group? How many are there in all?

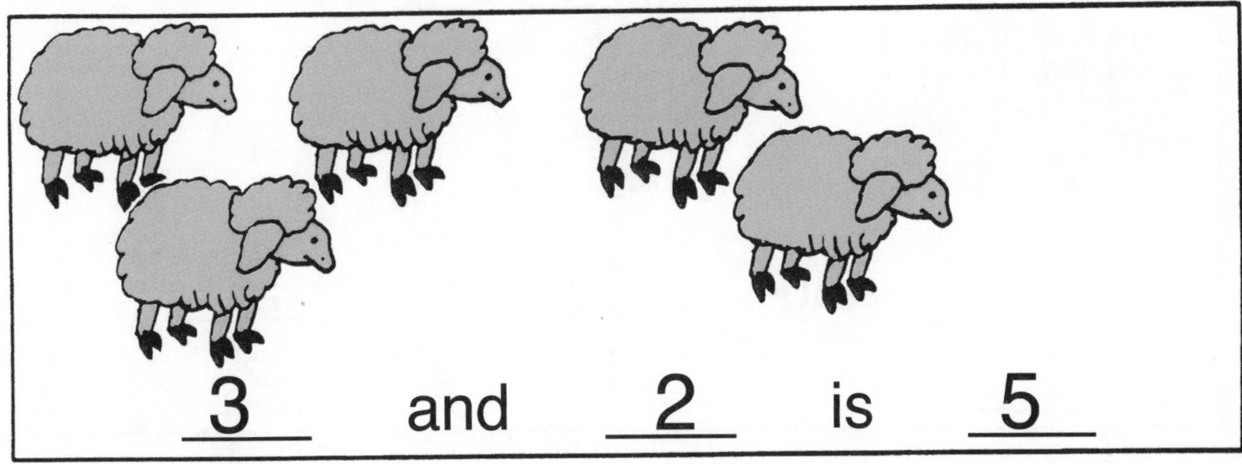

3 and 2 is 5

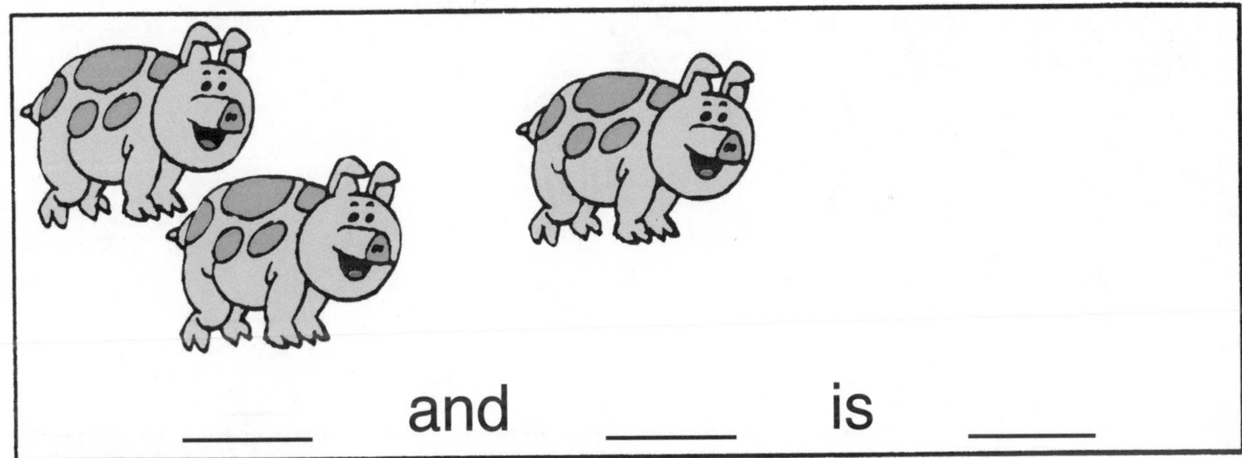

____ and ____ is ____

____ and ____ is ____

**Skills:** Recognizing sets of objects and writing corresponding numerals; Adding groups of objects; Understanding addition sentences

# Counting and Math Skills

Look at each picture. How many are in the first group?
How many are in the second group? How many are there in all?

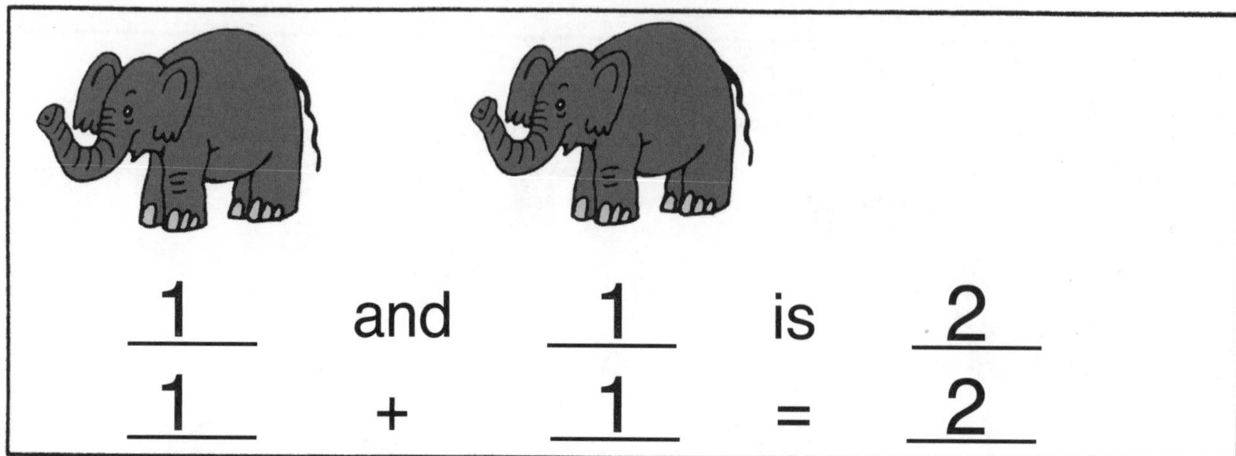

1 and 1 is 2

1 + 1 = 2

___ and ___ is ___

___ + ___ = ___

___ and ___ is ___

___ + ___ = ___

**Skills:** Recognizing sets of objects and writing corresponding numerals; Adding groups of objects; Understanding addition sentences

# Counting and Math Skills

Look at each picture. How many are in the first group?
How many are in the second group?
How many are there in all?

____ and ____ is ____

____ + ____ = ____

____ and ____ is ____

____ + ____ = ____

____ and ____ is ____

____ + ____ = ____

**Skills:** Recognizing sets of objects and writing corresponding numerals; Adding groups of objects; Understanding addition sentences

# Counting and Math Skills

Look at each picture. How many are in the first group?
How many are in the second group?
How many are there in all?

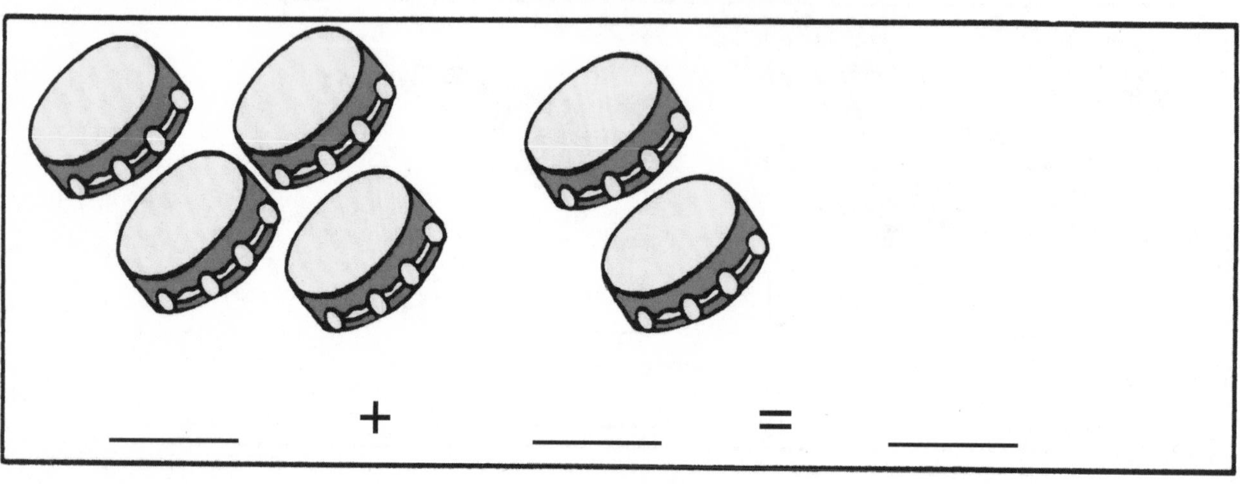

____ + ____ = ____

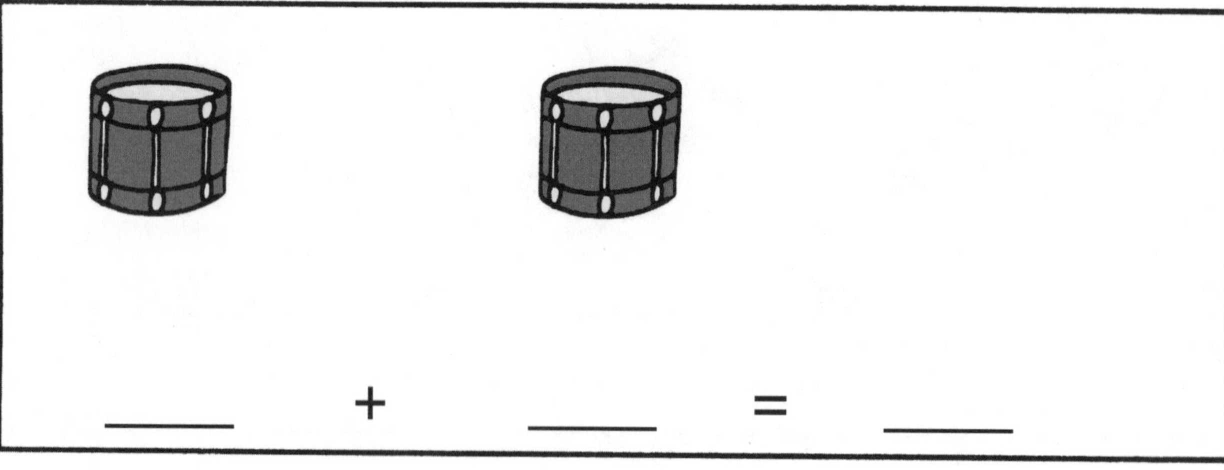

____ + ____ = ____

____ + ____ = ____

**Skills:** Recognizing sets of objects and writing corresponding numerals; Adding groups of objects; Practicing addition problem

## Counting and Math Skills

How many vegetables are there in each box?
Add them to find out.

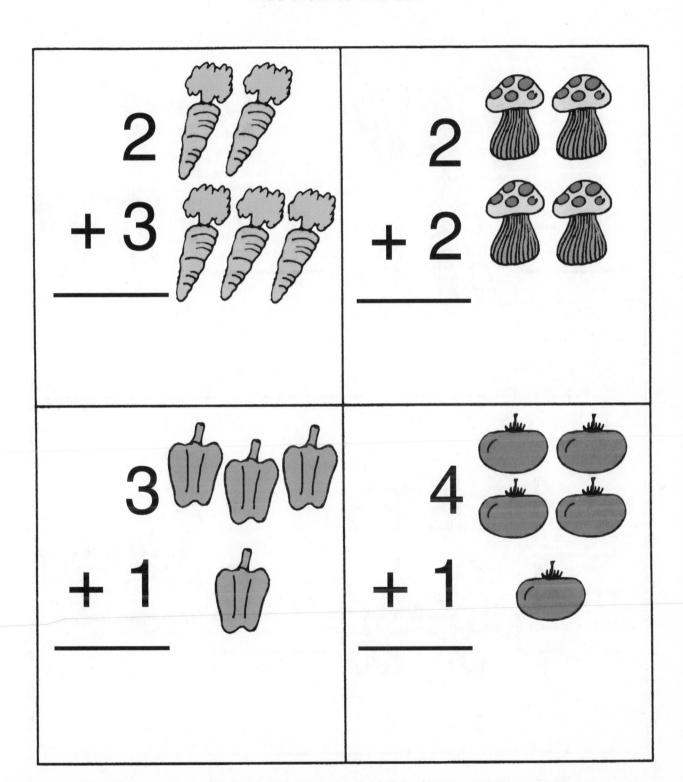

| | |
|---|---|
| 2<br>+ 3<br>____ | 2<br>+ 2<br>____ |
| 3<br>+ 1<br>____ | 4<br>+ 1<br>____ |

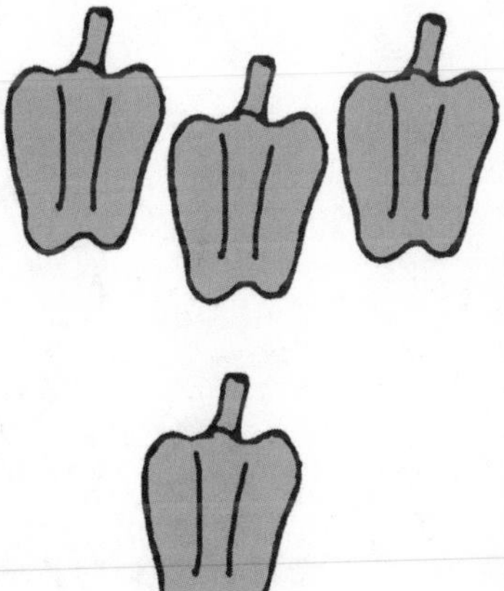

**Skills:** Solving vertical addition problems; Writing numeral problems

How many objects are in each box?
Add them to find out.

| | |
|---|---|
| 6<br>+ 2<br>____ | 3<br>+ 7<br>____ |
| 4<br>+ 4<br>____ | 1<br>+ 6<br>____ |

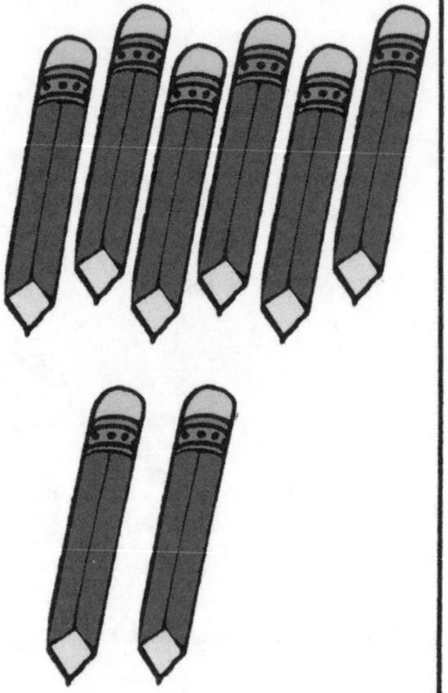

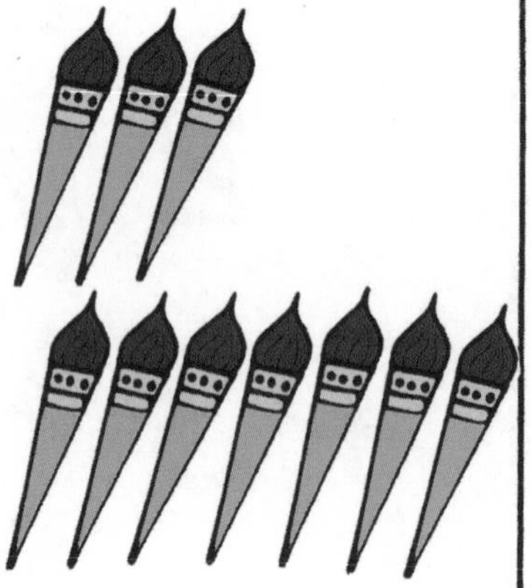

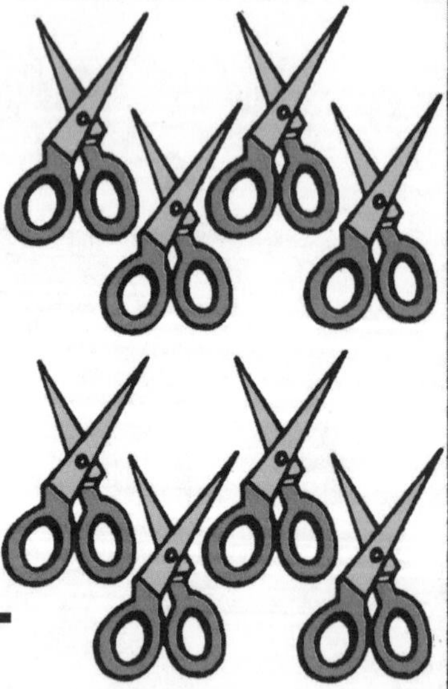

**Skills:** Solving vertical addition problems to ten; Writing numeral problems

# Counting and Math Skills

Add the numbers in each flower. If the answer is six, color it yellow. If the answer is seven, color it red. If the answer is eight, color it orange.

$$\begin{array}{r} 3 \\ +\,3 \\ \hline \end{array}$$

$$\begin{array}{r} 4 \\ +\,3 \\ \hline \end{array}$$

$$\begin{array}{r} 2 \\ +\,4 \\ \hline \end{array}$$

$$\begin{array}{r} 5 \\ +\,3 \\ \hline \end{array}$$

$$\begin{array}{r} 2 \\ +\,6 \\ \hline \end{array}$$

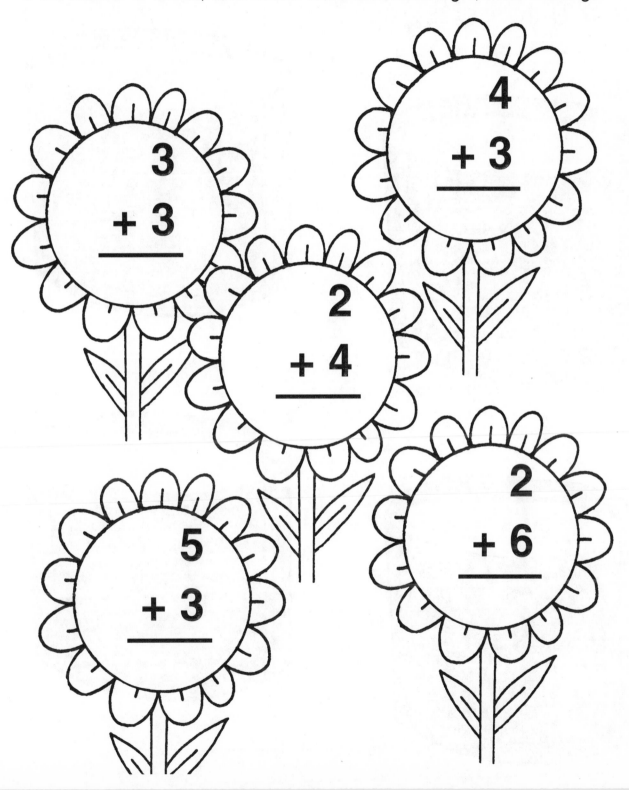

**Skills:** Solving vertical addition problems; Writing numerals

How many in all?
Add the numbers on the drums.

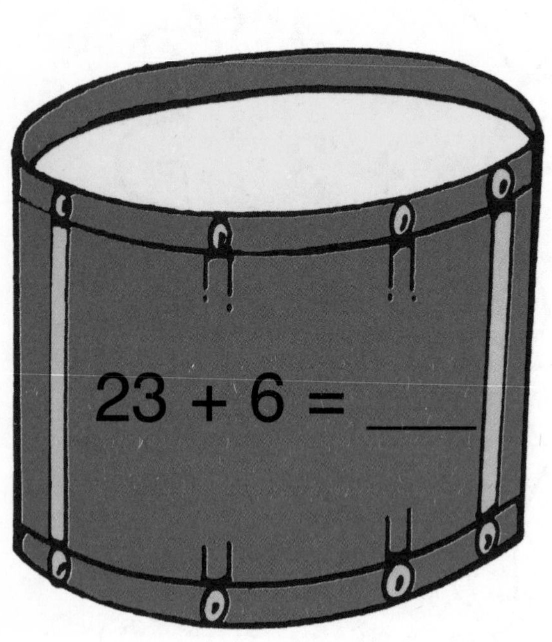


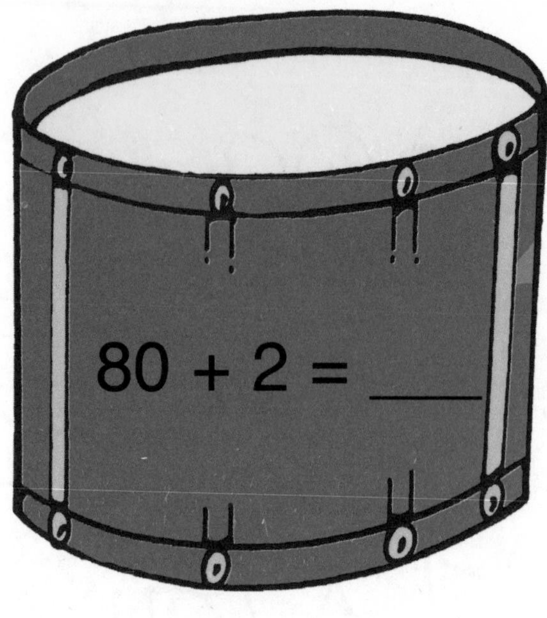

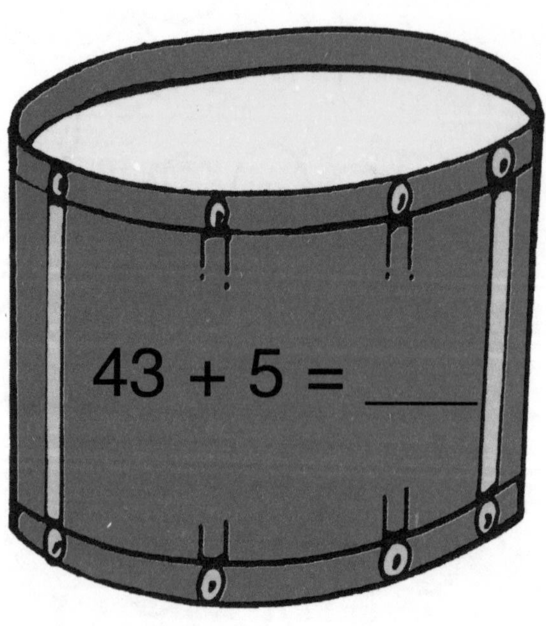


**Skills:** Solving 2-digit addition problems; Writing numerals

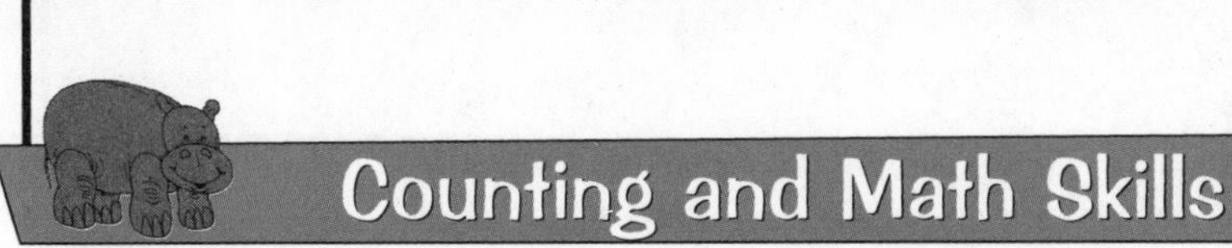


Add the numbers in each section. If the answer is 18, color it orange. If the answer is 27, color it black. If the answer is 15, color it brown.

15 + 12

20 + 7

14 + 4

10 + 5

9 + 6

16 + 2

11 + 4

21 + 6

12 + 3

12 + 6

13 + 14

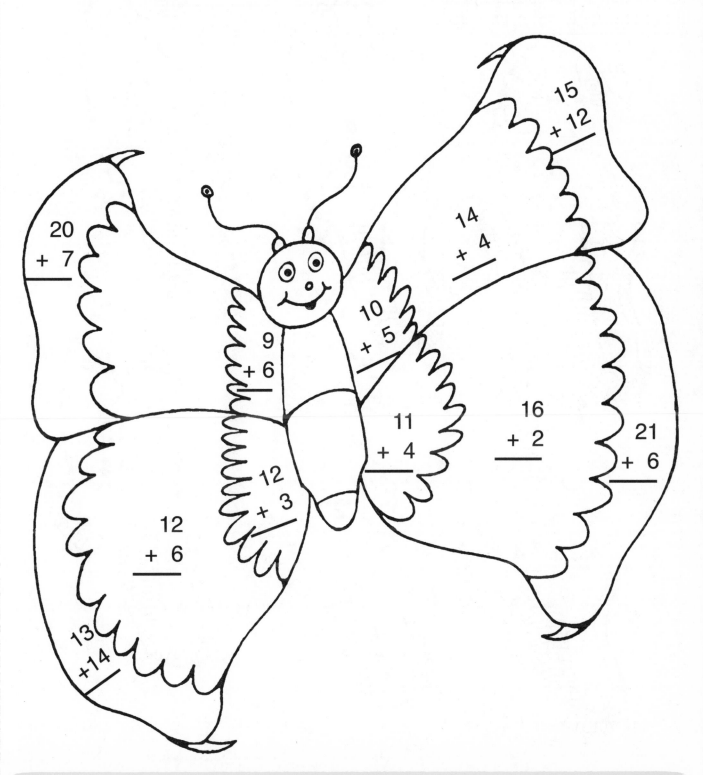

**Skills:** Solving 2-digit addition problems; Writing numerals

Add the numbers on each sea horse.
If the answer is 24, color it red.
If the answer is 36, color it blue.
If the answer is 45, color it yellow.

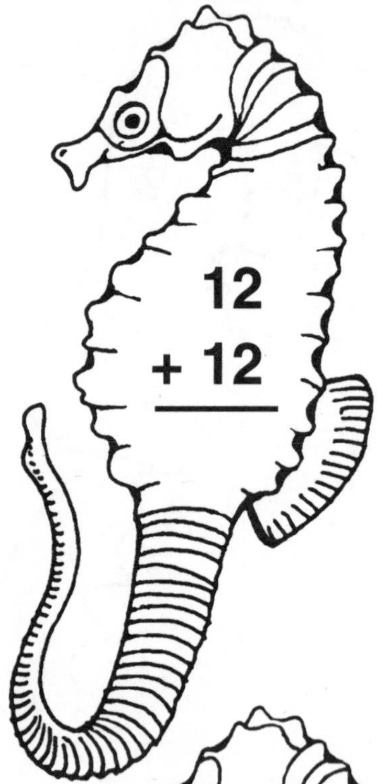

  12
+ 12

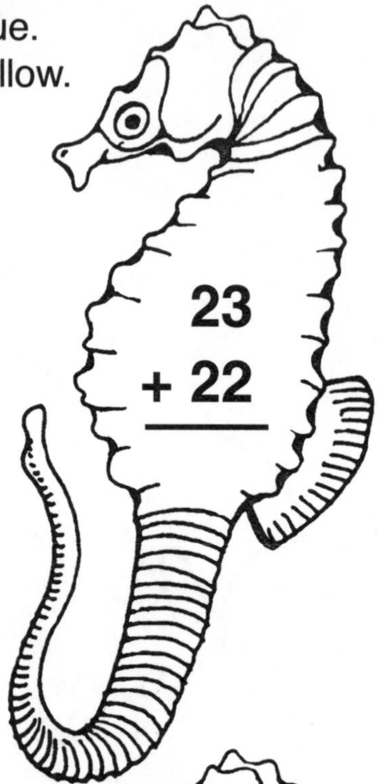

  23
+ 22

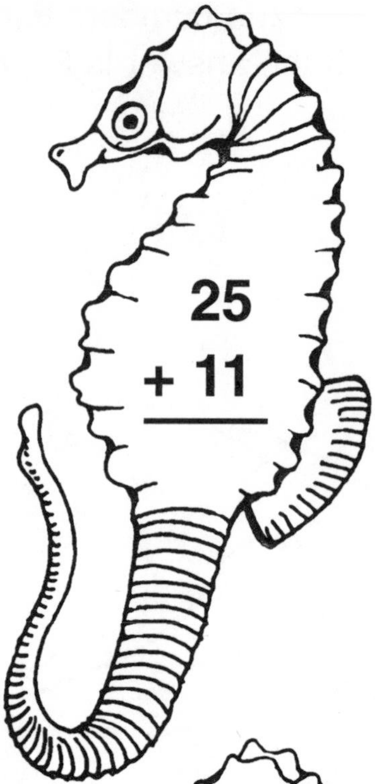

  25
+ 11

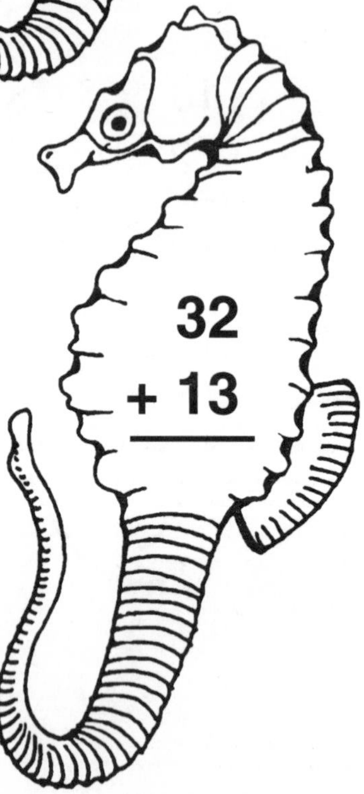

  32
+ 13

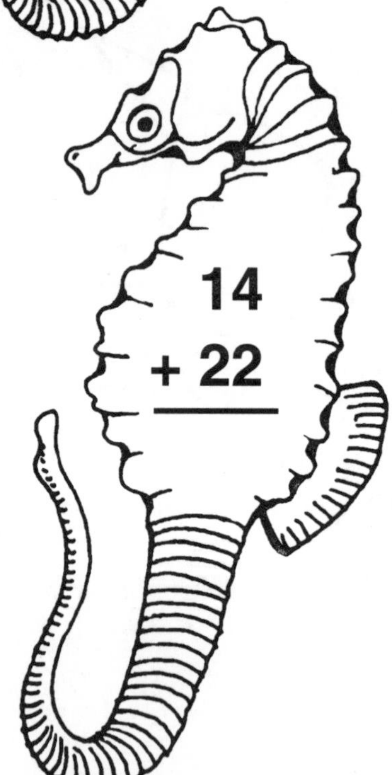

  14
+ 22

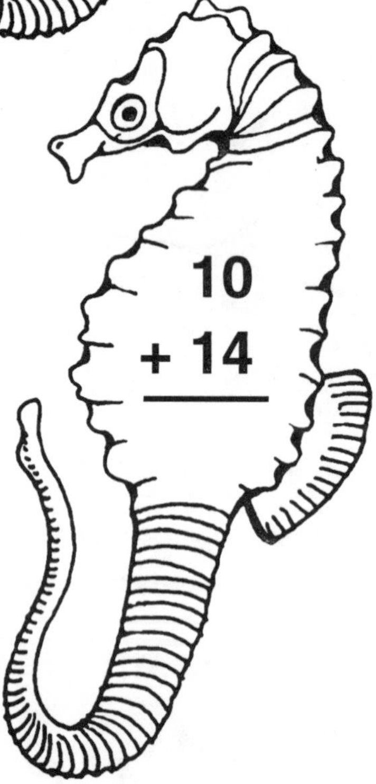

  10
+ 14

**Skills:** Solving 2-digit addition problems; Writing numerals

# Counting and Math Skills

Look at each picture.
How many animals are left?

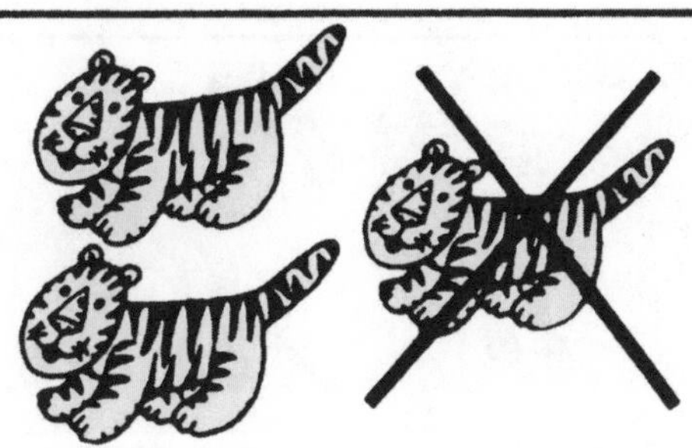

3 take away 1 is 2

4 take away 2 is ____

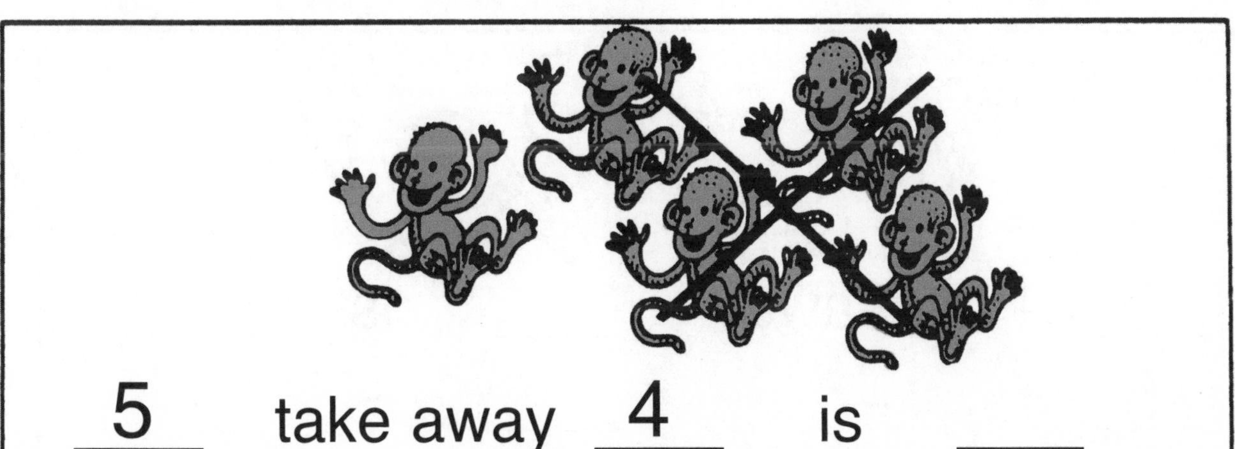

5 take away 4 is ____

**Skills:** Recognizing sets of objects and writing corresponding numerals; Subtracting groups of objects; Practicing subtraction problems

Look at each picture.
How many animals are left?

2 take away ____ is ____

2 – ____ = ____

4 take away ____ is ____

4 – ____ = ____

5 take away ____ is ____

5 – ____ = ____

**Skills:** Recognizing sets of objects and writing corresponding numerals; Subtracting groups of objects; Understanding subtraction sentences

# Counting and Math Skills

Look at each picture.
How many animals are left?

5 take away ____ is ____

5 – ____ = ____

3 take away ____ is ____

3 – ____ = ____

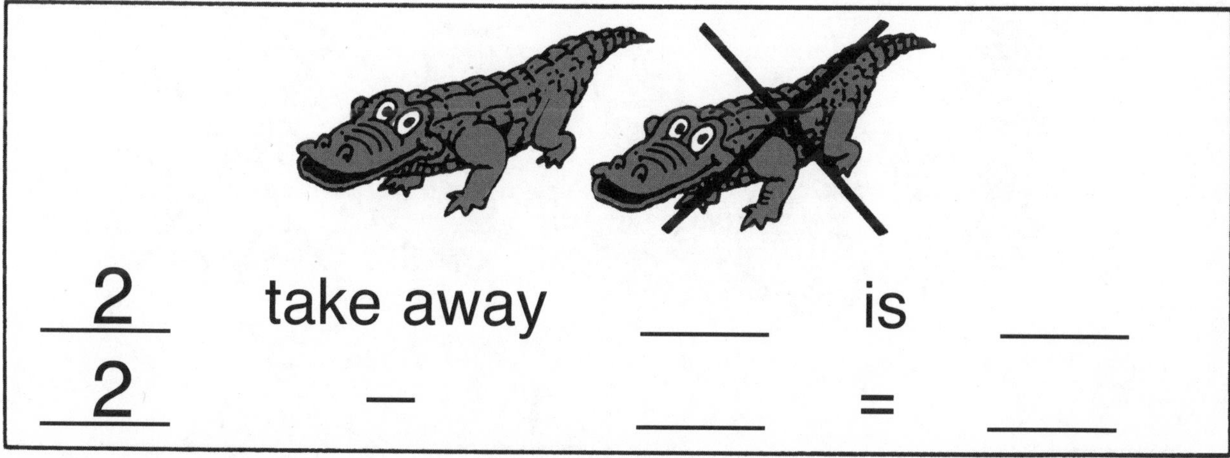

2 take away ____ is ____

2 – ____ = ____

**Skills:** Recognizing sets of objects and writing corresponding numerals; Subtracting groups of objects; Understanding subtraction sentences

# Counting and Math Skills

Look at each picture.
How many animals are left?

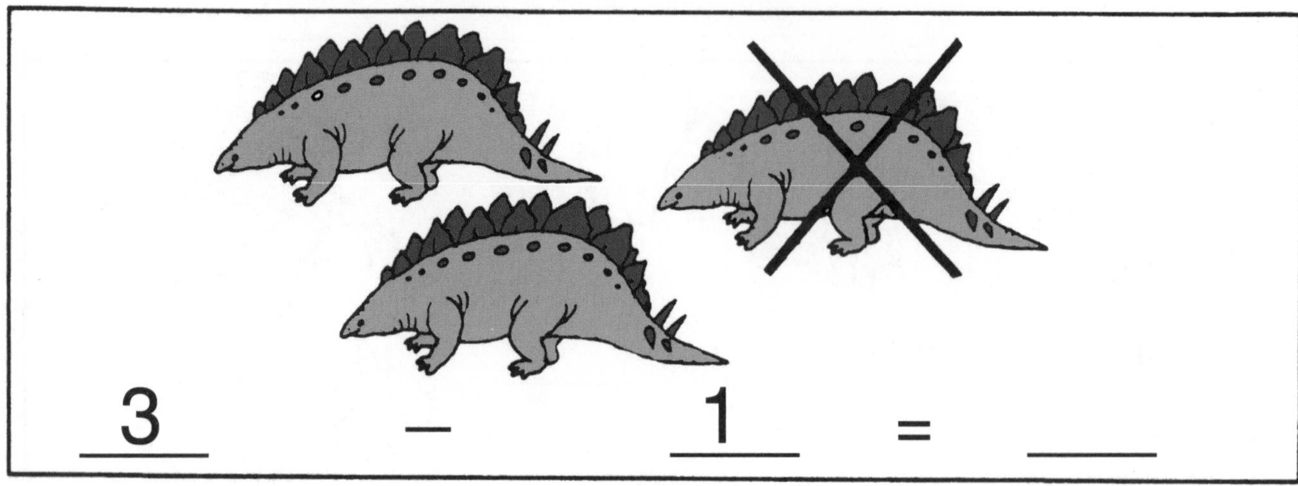

3 – 1 = ___

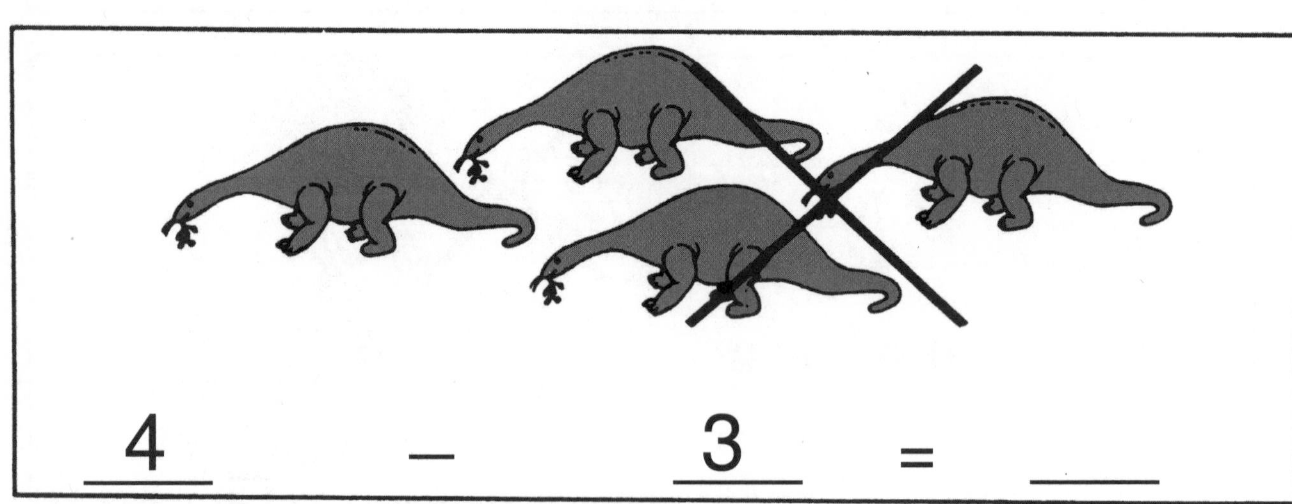

4 – 3 = ___

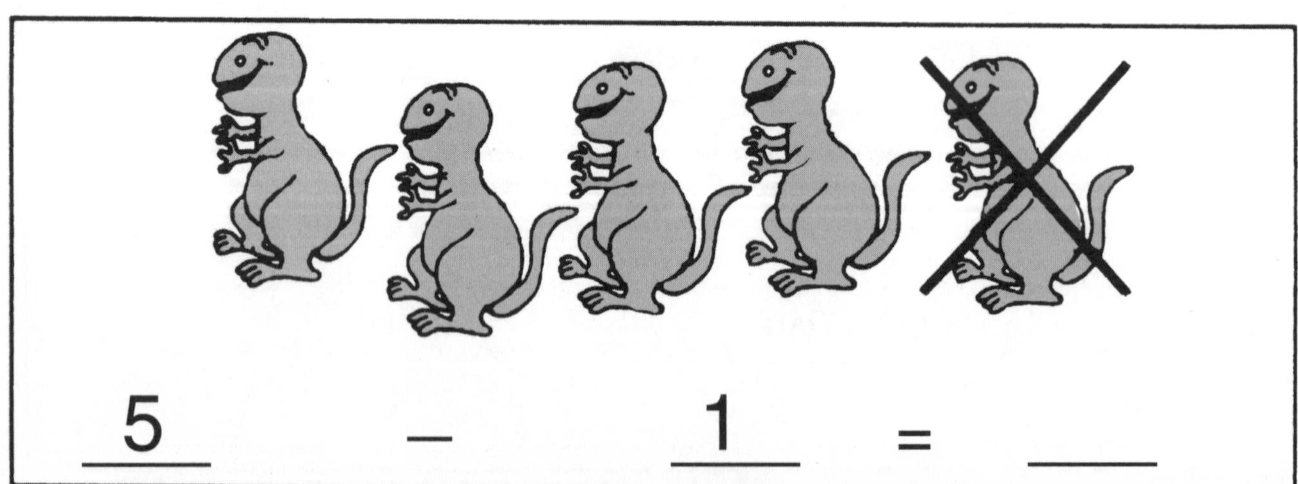

5 – 1 = ___

**Skills:** Recognizing sets of objects and writing corresponding numerals; Subtracting groups of objects; Practicing subtraction problems

# Counting and Math Skills

How many animals are left?
Subtract to find out.

| | |
|---|---|
| 4<br>− 2<br>______ | 5<br>− 1<br>______ |
| 3<br>− 2<br>______ | 5<br>− 3<br>______ |

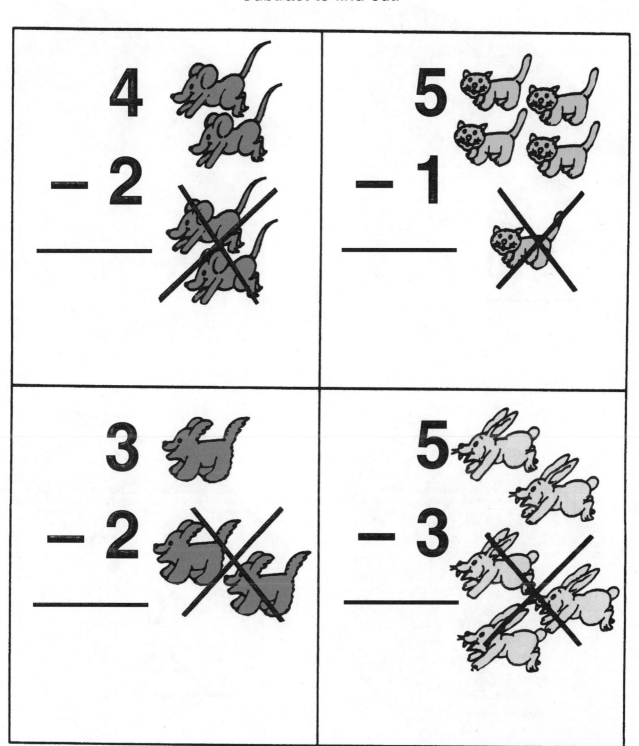

**Skills:** Solving vertical subtraction problems; Writing numerals

# Counting and Math Skills

Subtract the numbers on the birdhouses.

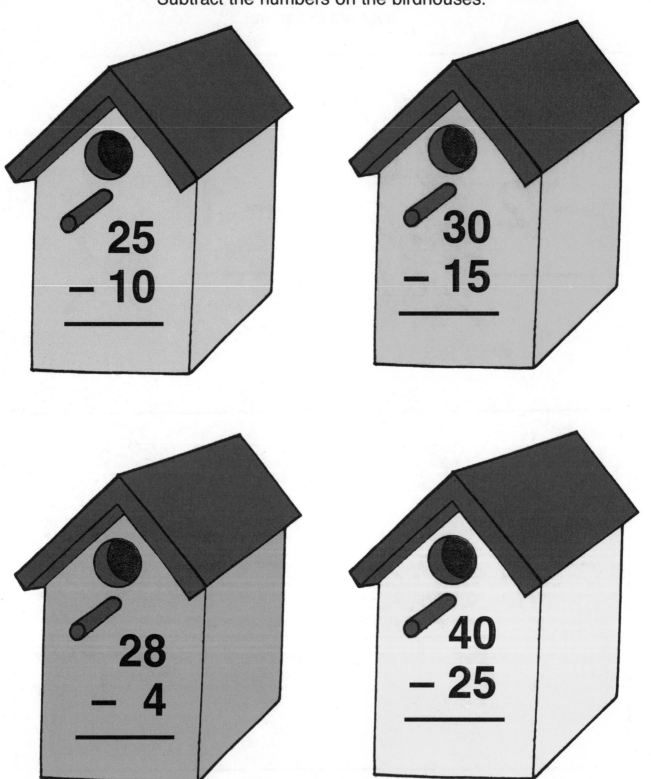

$$\begin{array}{r} 25 \\ -\ 10 \\ \hline \end{array}$$

$$\begin{array}{r} 30 \\ -\ 15 \\ \hline \end{array}$$

$$\begin{array}{r} 28 \\ -\ 4 \\ \hline \end{array}$$

$$\begin{array}{r} 40 \\ -\ 25 \\ \hline \end{array}$$

**Skills:** Solving 2-digit subtraction problems; Writing numerals

# Excellent!

## Give yourself a star!

# Measuring

# Measuring

Look at the pictures in each box.
Circle the ones that are the same length.
Then color the pictures.

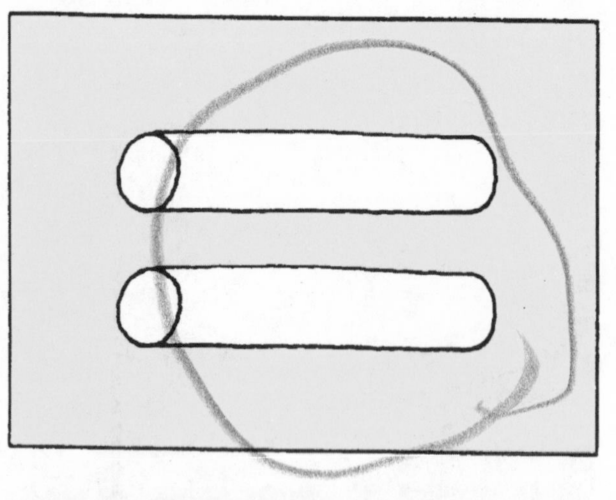

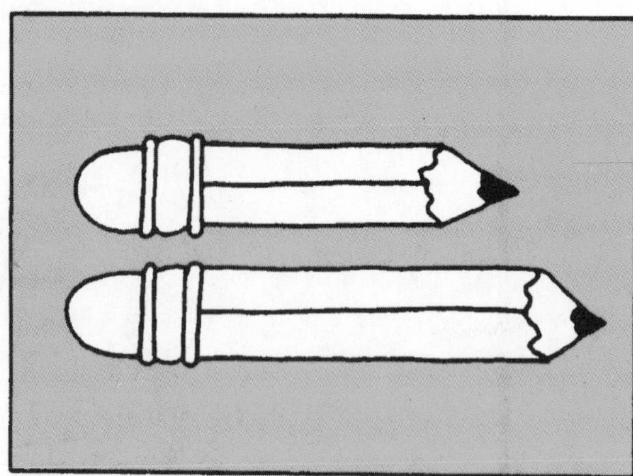

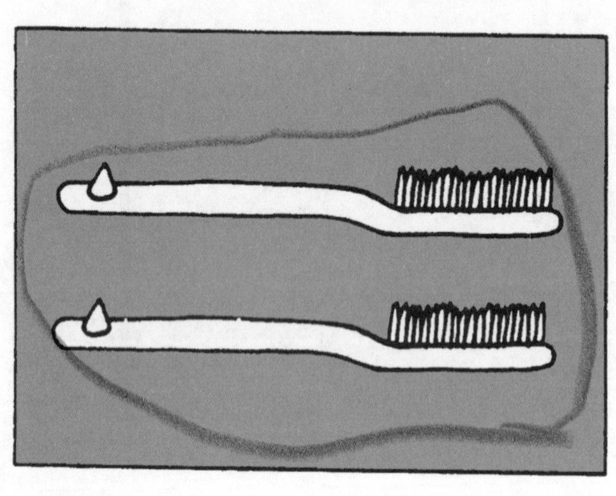

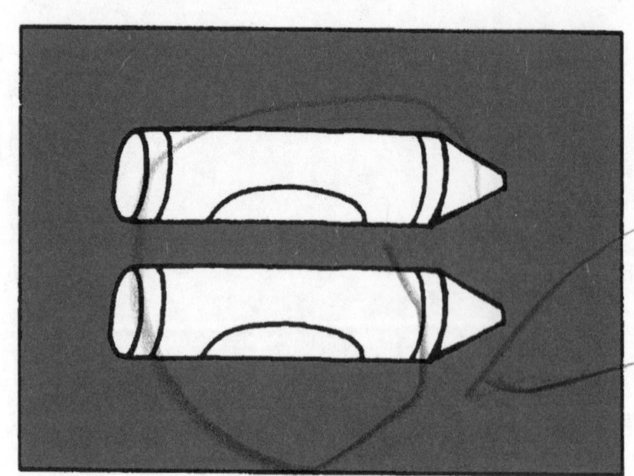

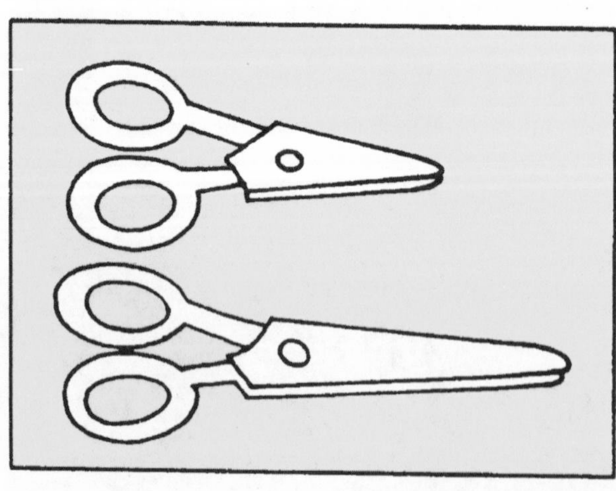

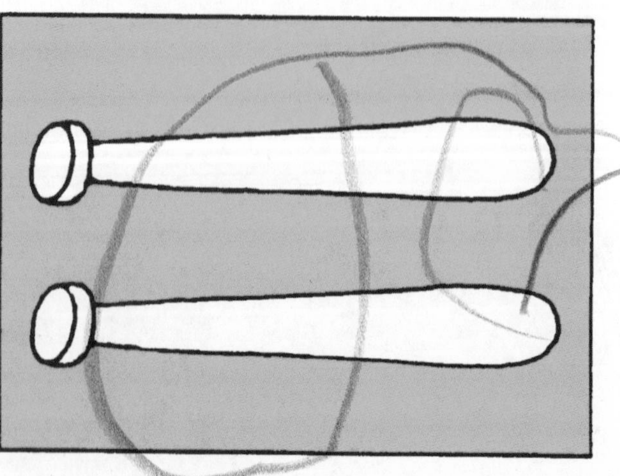

Skills: Recognizing objects that are the same length

# Measuring

Look at the pictures in each box.
Circle the one that is shorter.
Then color the pictures.

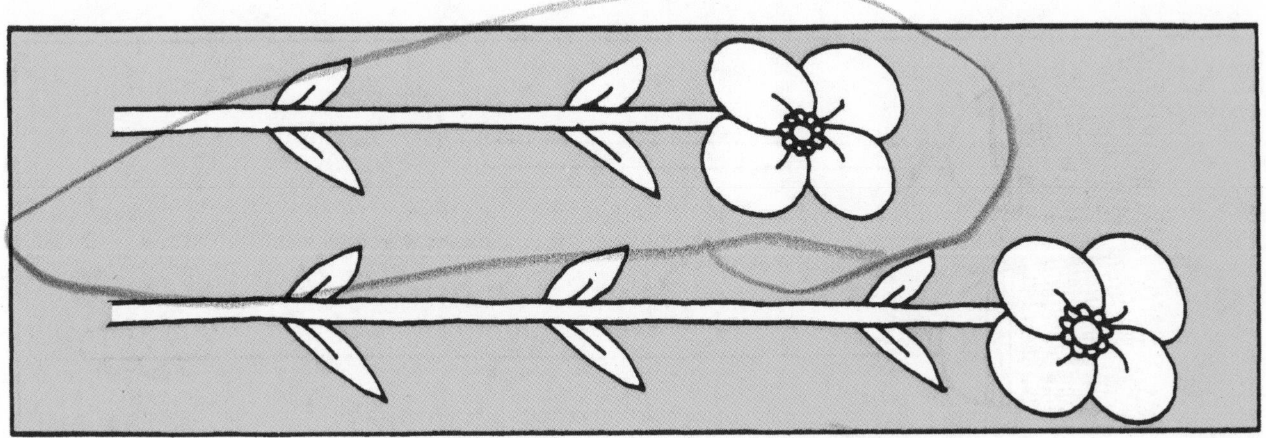

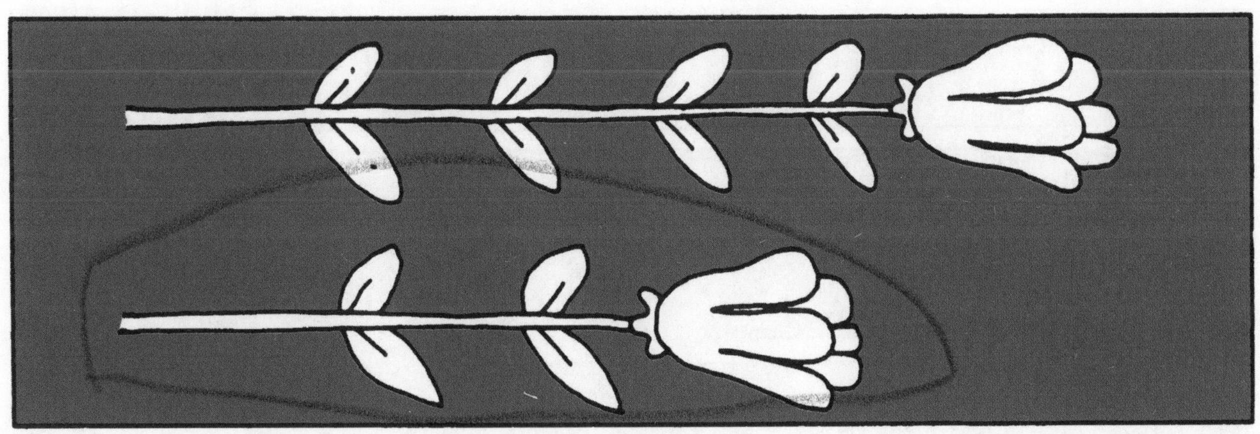

**Skills:** Comparing length

# Measuring

Look at the pictures in each box.
Circle the one that is longer.
Then color the pictures.

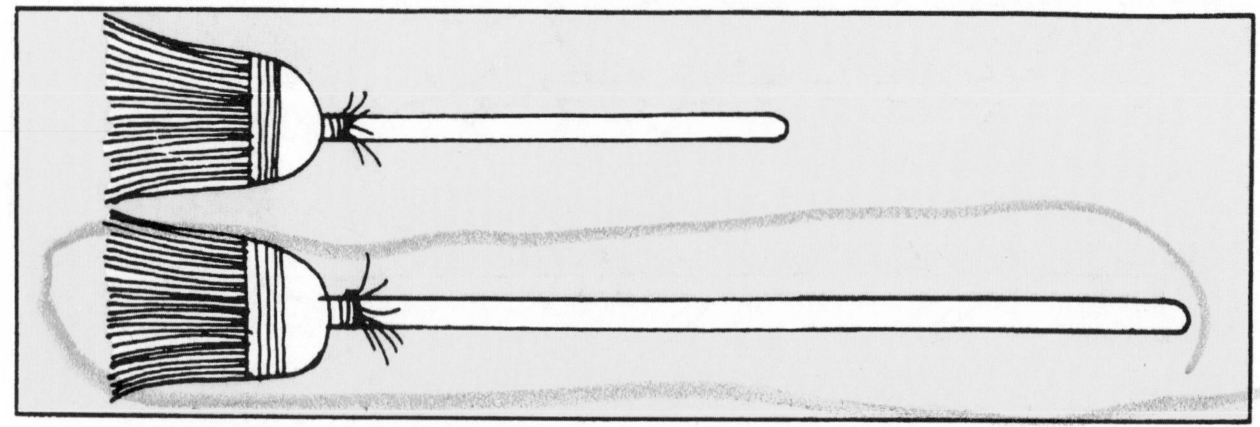

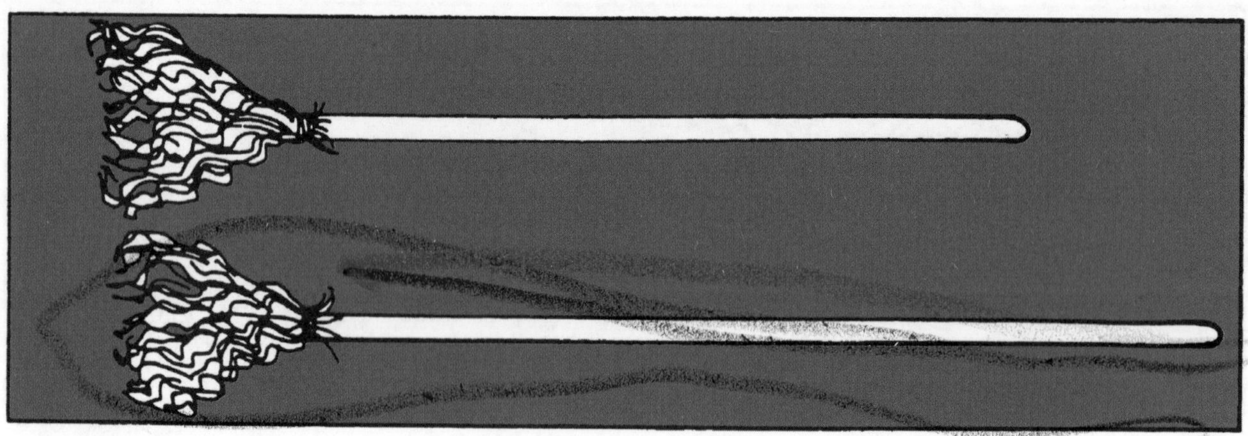

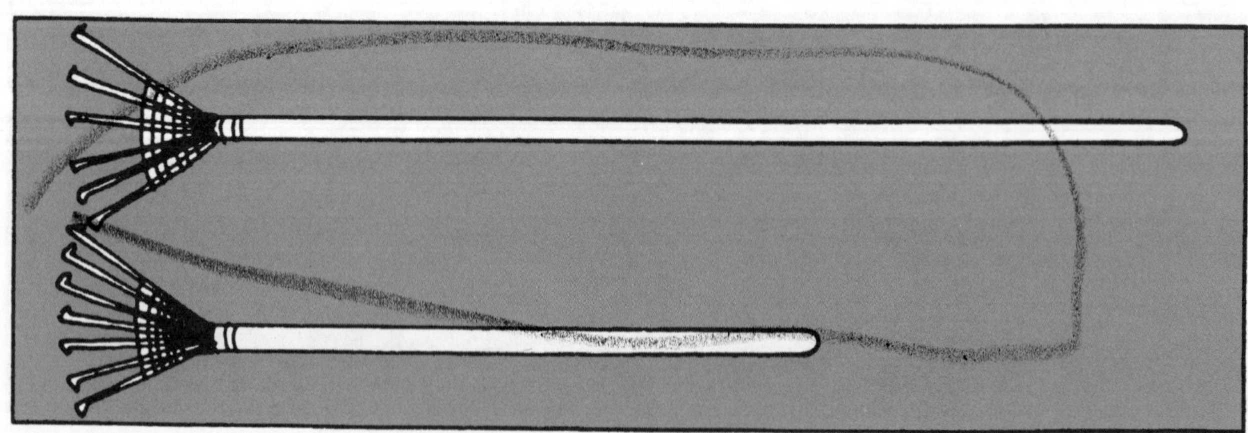

Skills: Comparing length

# Measuring

Look at the pictures in each box.
Circle the one that is longer.
Then color the pictures.

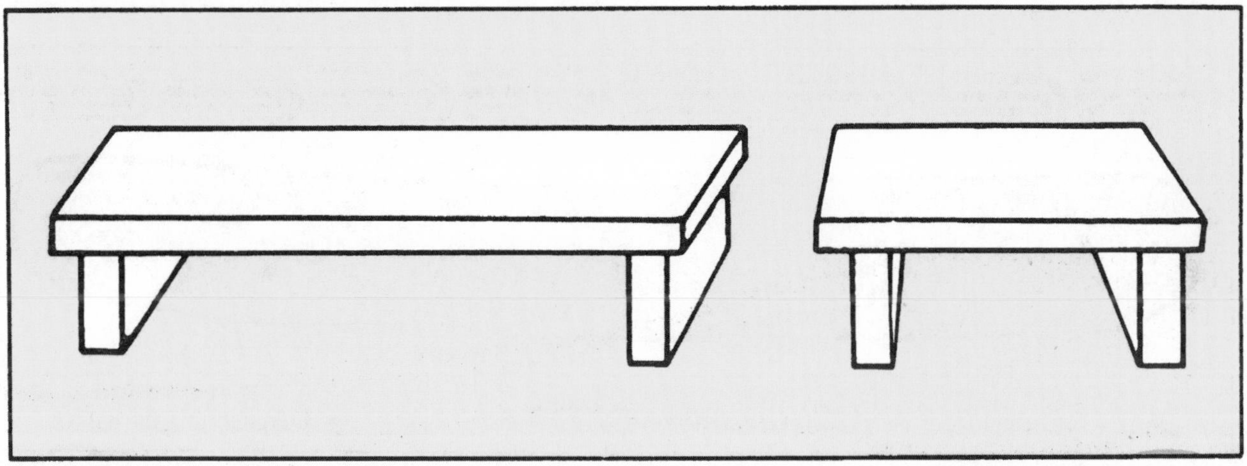

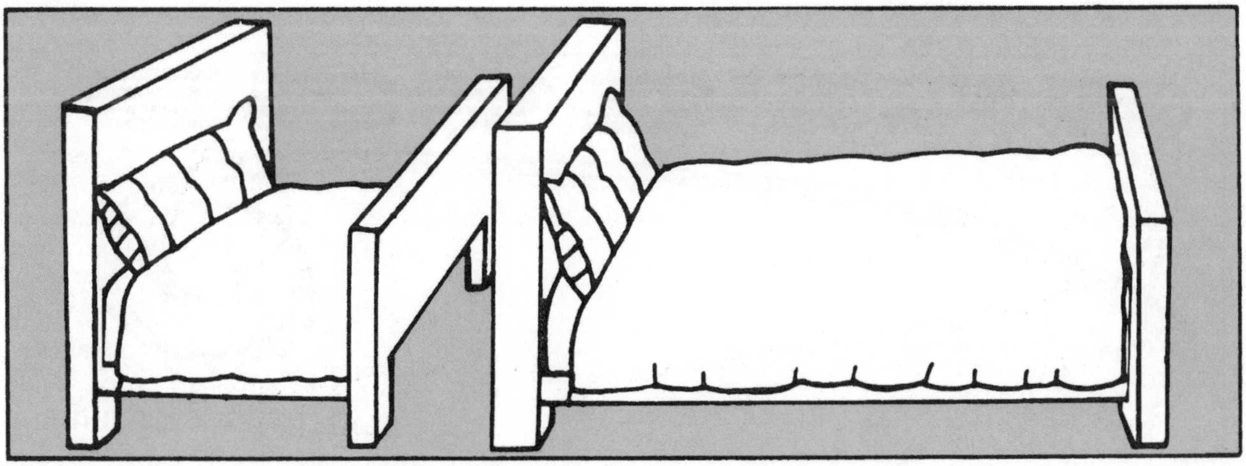

Skills: Making comparisons; Visual discrimination; Vocabulary

# Measuring

Look at the picture in each box.
Count how many paper clips long it is.
Then write that number on the line.

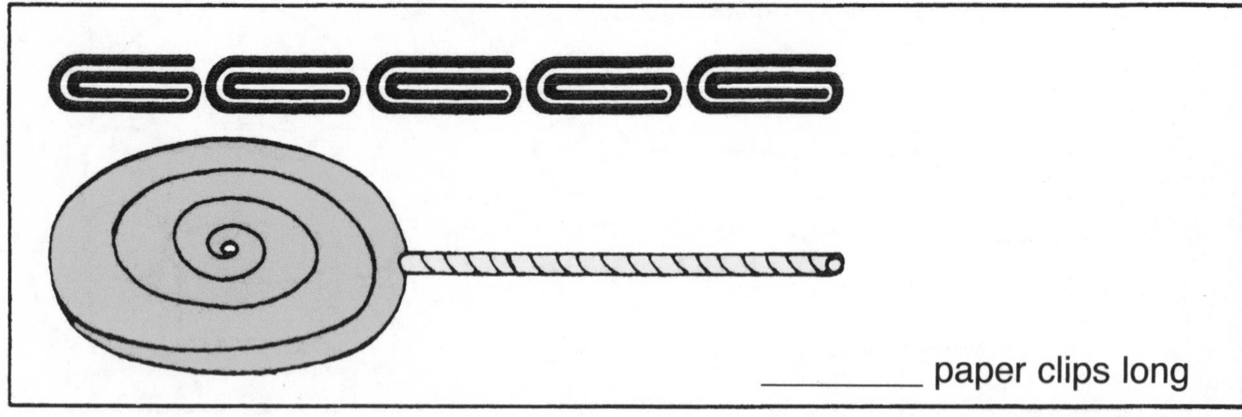

_______ paper clips long

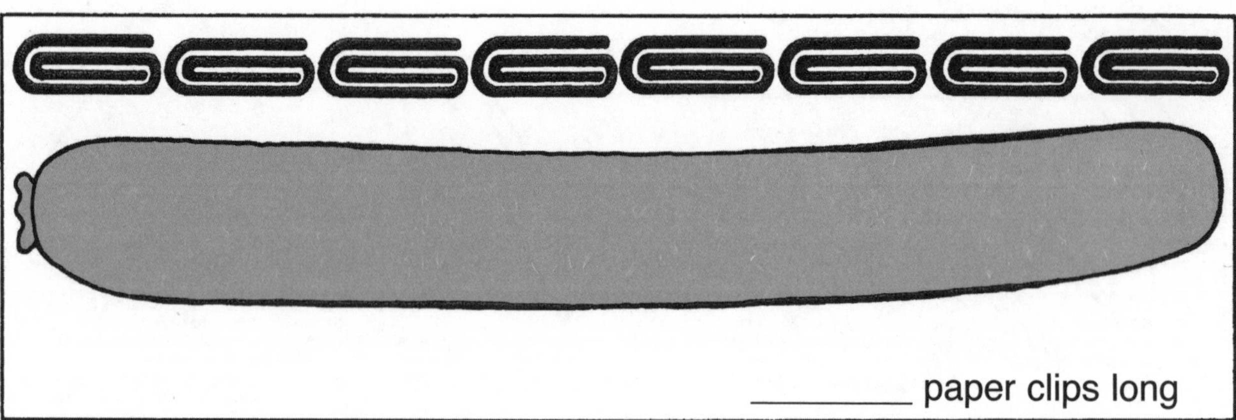

_______ paper clips long

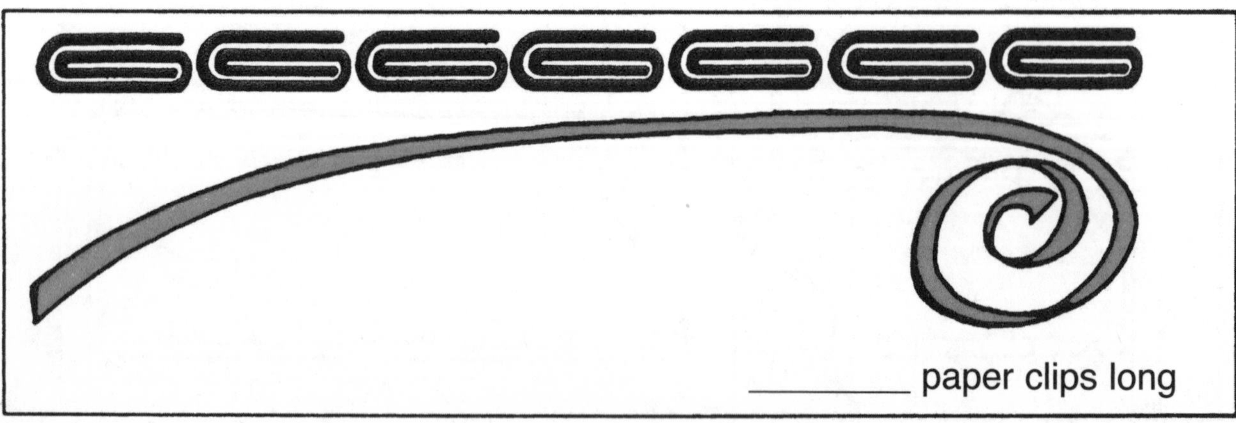

_______ paper clips long

**Skills:** Measuring lengths; Using non-standard units

# Measuring

Look at the pictures in each box.
Circle the picture of the person who is taller.
Then color the pictures.

Skills: Comparing height

# Measuring

Look at the pictures in each box.
Circle the picture of the person who is shorter.
Then color the pictures.

**Skills:** Comparing height

# Measuring

Look at the pictures in each box.
Circle the one that holds more.
Then color the pictures.

Skills: Comparing capacity

# Measuring

Look at the pictures in each box.
Circle the one that holds less.
Then color the pictures.

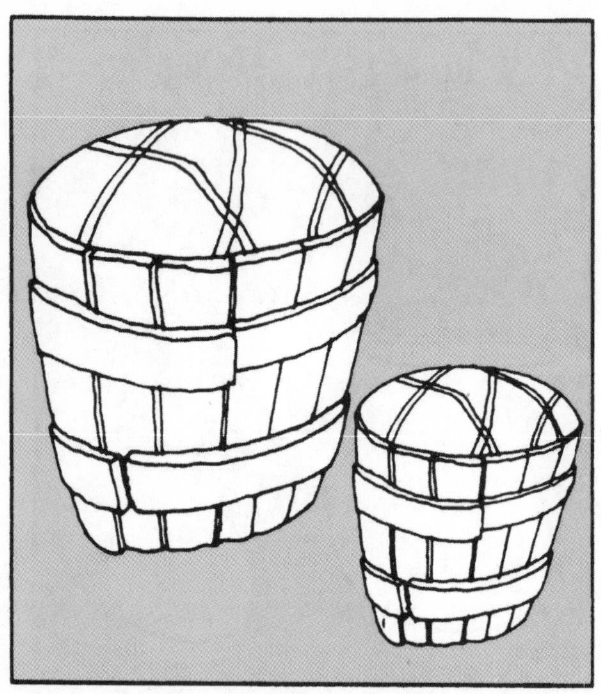

**Skills:** Comparing capacity

# Measuring

Look at the pictures in each box.
Circle the one that is heavier.
Then color the pictures.

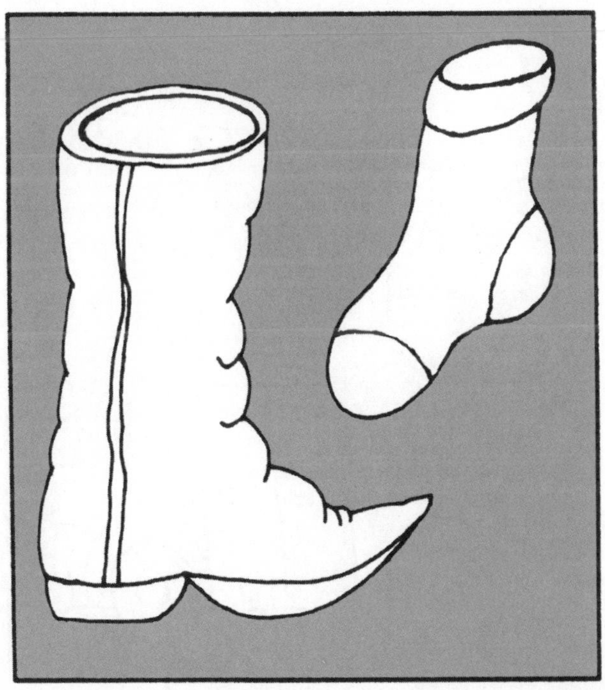

Skills: Comparing weight

# Measuring

Look at the pictures in each box.
Circle the one that is lighter.
Then color the pictures.

Skills: Comparing weight

# Measuring

Look at the pictures in each row.
Circle the one that is small.
Then color the pictures.

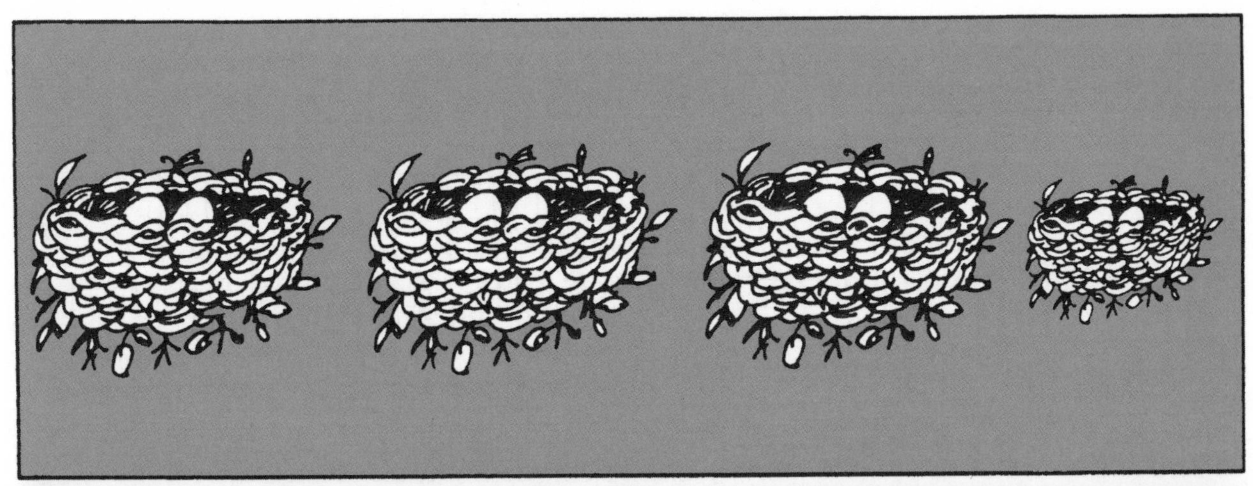

Skills: Comparing size

# Measuring

Look at the pictures in each row.
Circle the one that is large.
Then color the pictures.

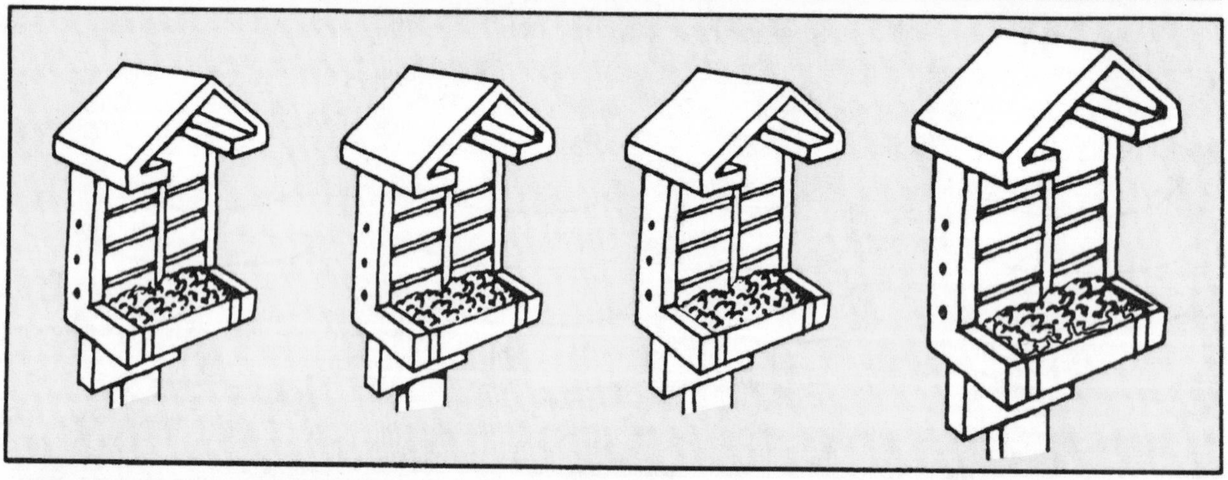

**Skills:** Comparing size

# Excellent!

## Give yourself a star!

# Time and Money

# Time and Money

Look at the pictures in each row.
Which activity takes longer to do?
Color that picture.

**Skills:** Determining time duration

# Time and Money

Look at the clock.
Trace the numbers.
Then color the picture.

**Skills:** Identifying and tracing the numbers on the clock

Look at the clock in each box.
Write the time in the space below each clock.

2 o'clock

_______ o'clock

_______ o'clock

_______ o'clock

_______ o'clock

_______ o'clock

**Skills:** Identifying time to the hour

# Time and Money

Look at the clock in each box.
Write the time in the space below each clock.

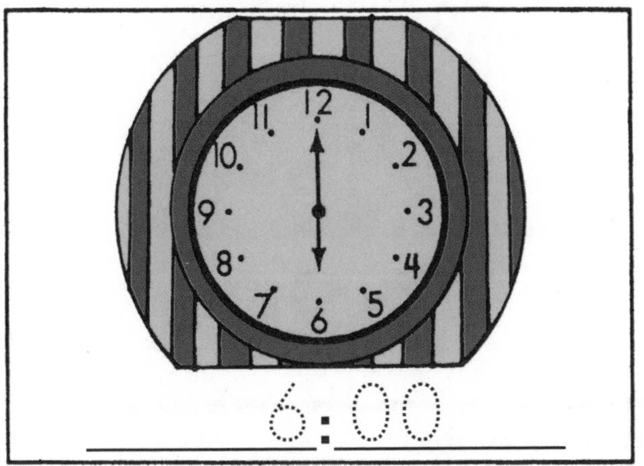


6:00

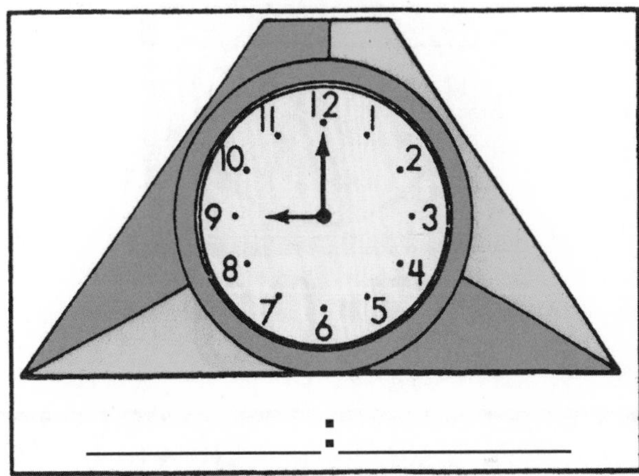


_____:_____

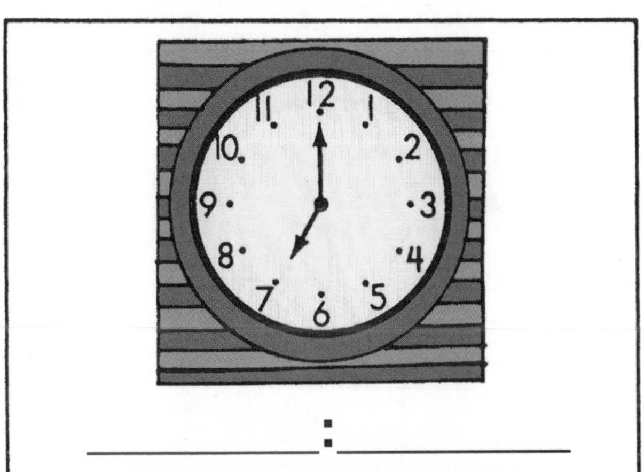


_____:_____

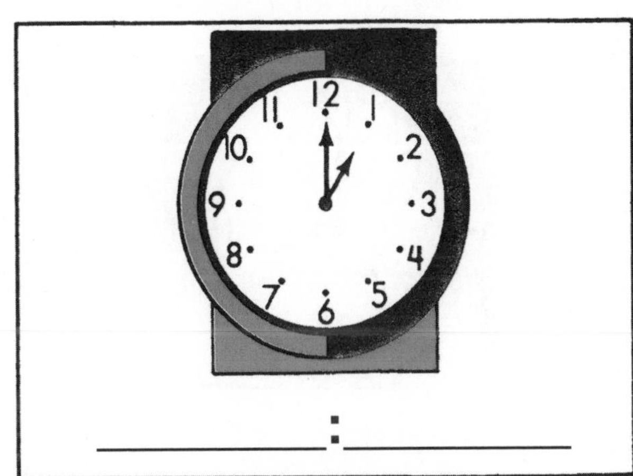


_____:_____

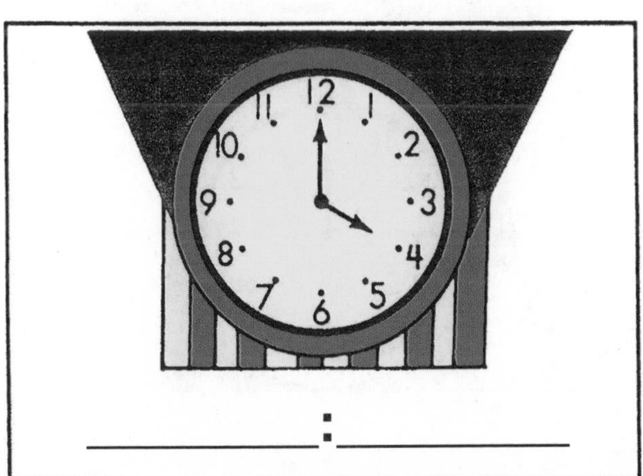


_____:_____

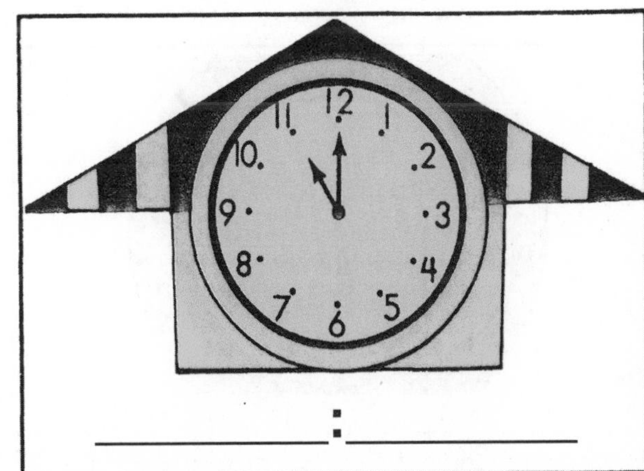


_____:_____

**Skills:** Identifying time to the hour

60 minutes is one hour.

# 7:00

30 minutes is one half hour.

# 7:30

Look at the clock in each box.
Write the time in the space below each clock.

8:00

_____:_____

_____:_____

_____:_____

**Skills:** Identifying time to the hour and the half hour

# Time and Money

Look at the clock in each box.
Write the time in the space below each clock.

3 : 30

______ : ______

______ : ______

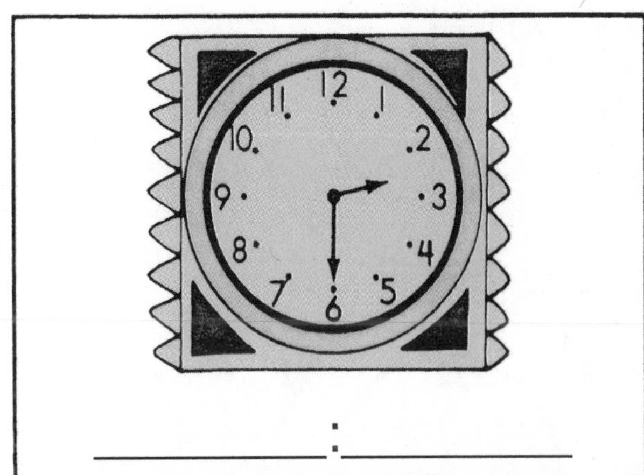

______ : ______

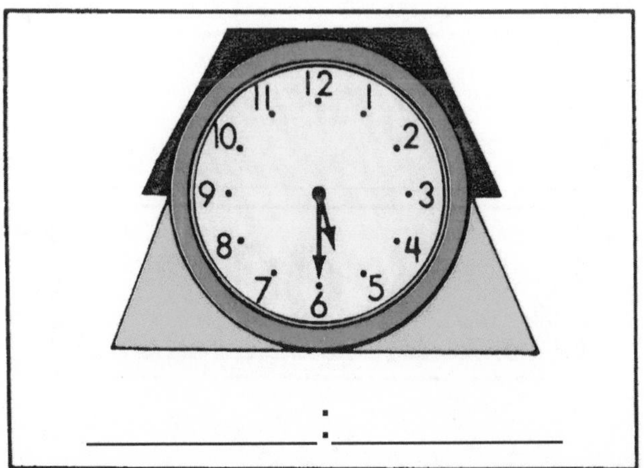

______ : ______

______ : ______

**Skills:** Identifying time to the half hour

# Time and Money

Look at the clocks on each side of the page.
Match the clocks that show the same time.
Then color the pictures.

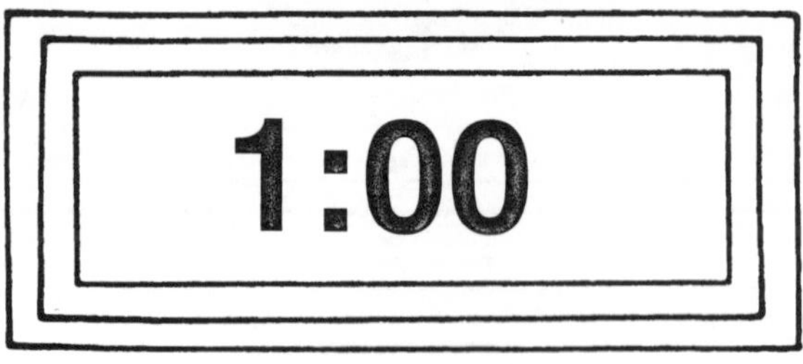


3:00

**Skills:** Using number skills to determine the same time

Look at the first clock in each row.
Find and circle a clock that shows the same time.

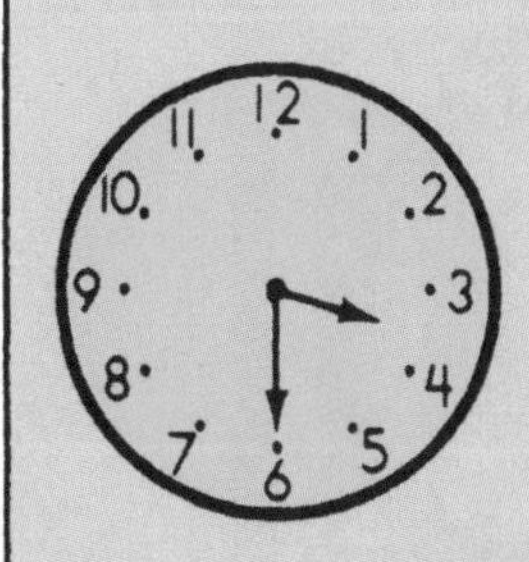

12:30

7:30

2:30

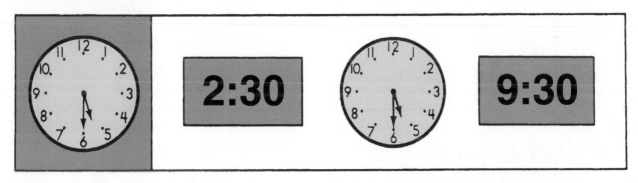

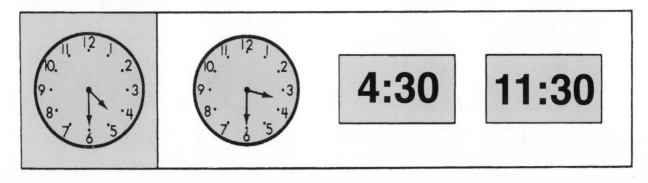

9:30

4:30

11:30

**Skills:** Using number skills to determine the same time

Look at the minute hand on each clock.
Draw the hour hand to show the correct time.

9:00

2:00

4:00

10:00

5:00

1:00

**Skills:** Showing time to the hour on the clock

# Time and Money

Look at the minute hand on each clock.
Draw the hour hand to show the correct time.

3:30

5:30

7:30

12:30

9:30

1:30

**Skills:** Showing time to the half hour on the clock

# Time and Money

Look at the coins. Draw a circle around each penny.
Draw a square around each nickel. Draw a line under each dime.

1¢ 5¢ 10¢

1¢ 10¢ 5¢ 1¢ 10¢ 5¢ 10¢ 1¢ 5¢ 5¢ 10¢ 1¢ 10¢ 1¢ 5¢ 1¢ 10¢ 5¢ 10¢

**Skills:** Identifying pennies, nickels and dimes

# Time and Money

Circle how many cents are in each box.

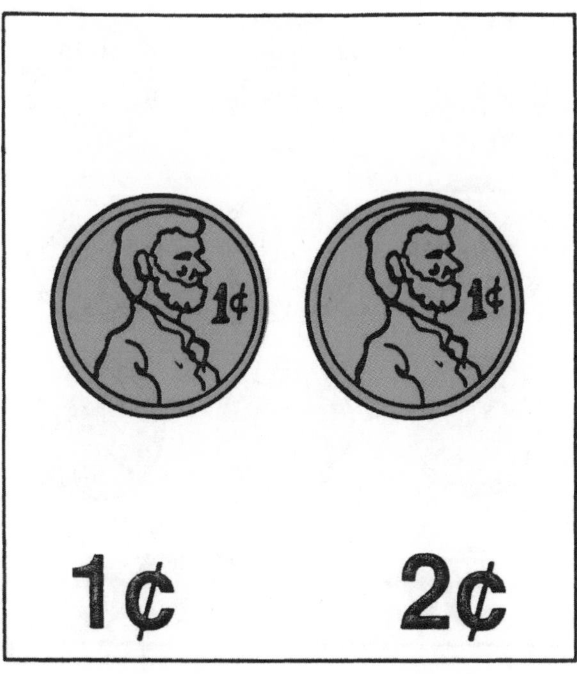


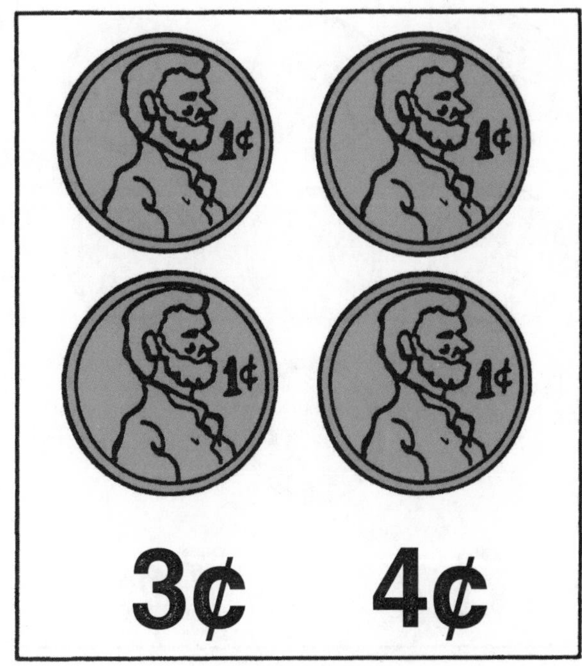


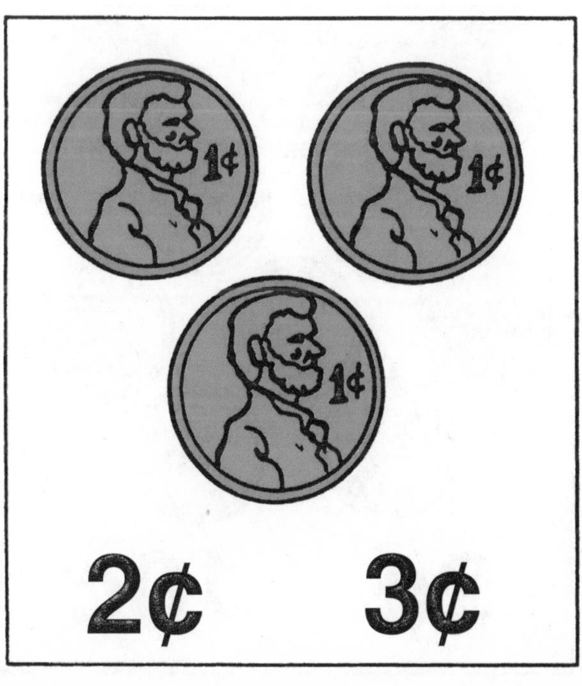

**Skills:** Identifying amounts of money

# Time and Money

Circle how many cents are in each box.

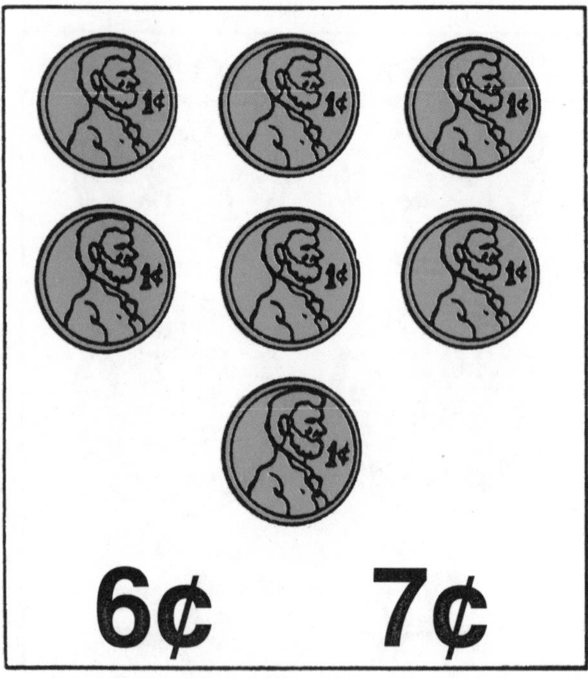


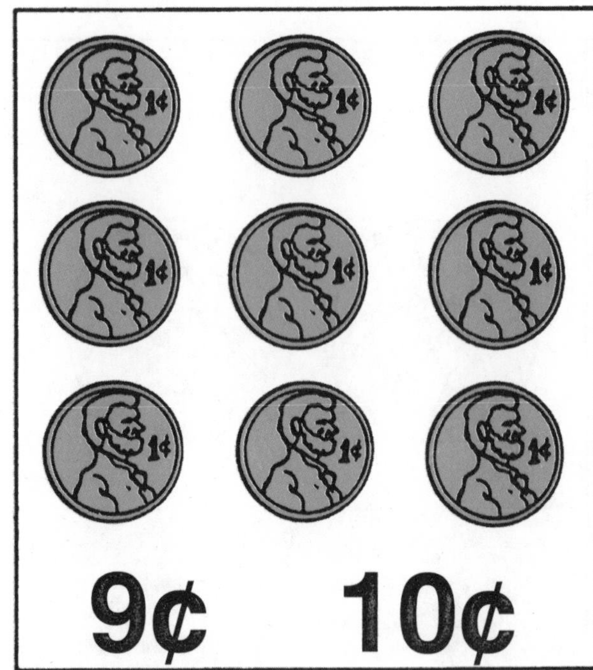


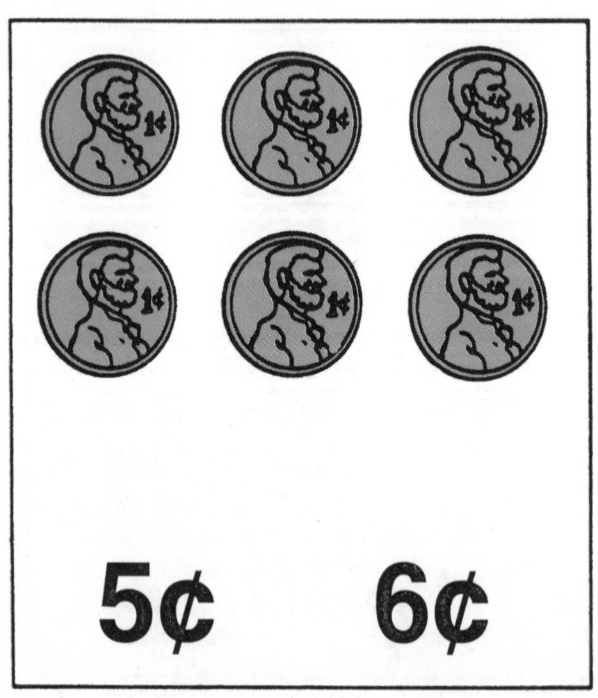

**Skills:** Identifying amounts of money

# Time and Money

5 pennies are the same as 1 nickel. Look at the amounts of money on this page. Circle the amounts that show 5¢.

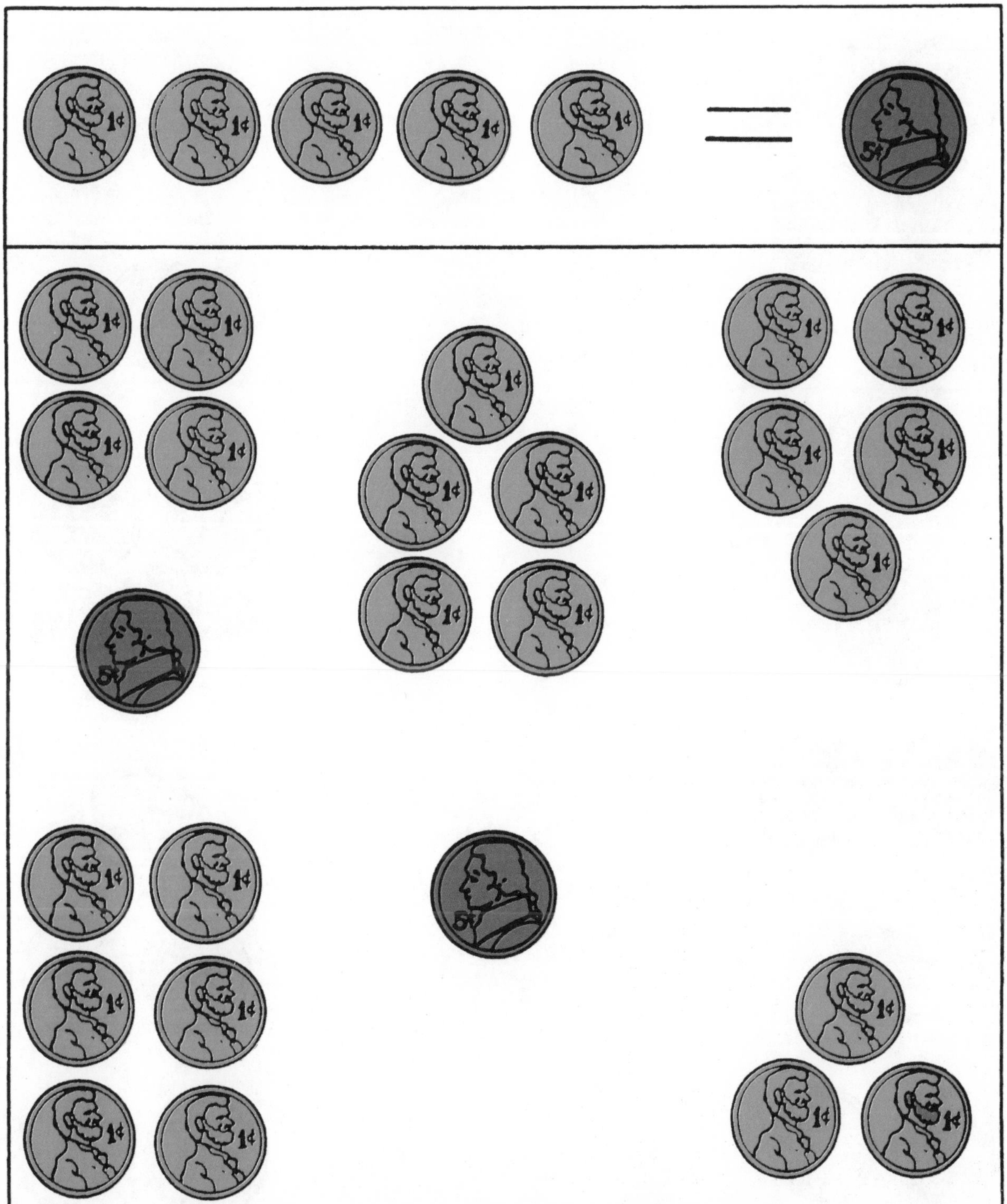

**Skills:** Identifying amounts of money

# Time and Money

Look at the money on each side of the page.
Match the groups of coins that show the same amount of money.

| | |
|---|---|
| 1¢ 1¢ 1¢ 1¢ | 5¢ |
| 5¢ | 1¢ |
| 1¢ | 1¢ 1¢ 1¢ 1¢ |
| 5¢ 5¢ | 10¢ |
| 10¢ | 1¢ 1¢ |
| 1¢ 1¢ | 5¢ 5¢ |

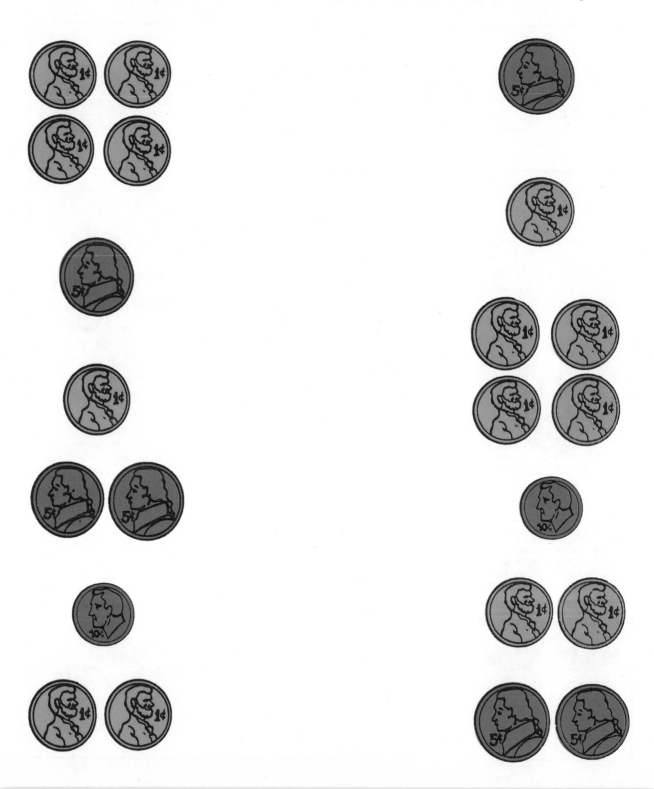

**Skills:** Identifying amounts of money; Matching same amounts of money

# Time and Money

10 pennies are the same as 1 dime.
2 nickels are the same as 1 dime.

Look at the amounts of money on this page.
Circle the amounts that show 10¢.

**Skills:** Identifying amounts of money

# Time and Money

Look at the coins in each purse.
Write the amount of money that is in each purse.

______ ¢

______ ¢

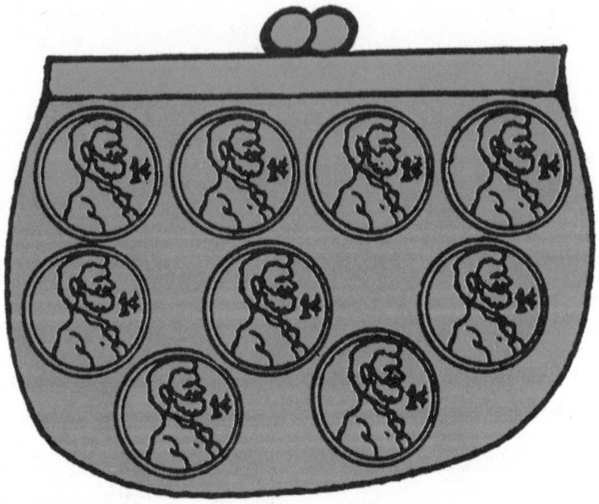

______ ¢

______ ¢

Skills: Identifying amounts of money

# Time and Money

Look at the coins in each piggy bank.
Write the amount of money that is in each piggy bank.

_______¢

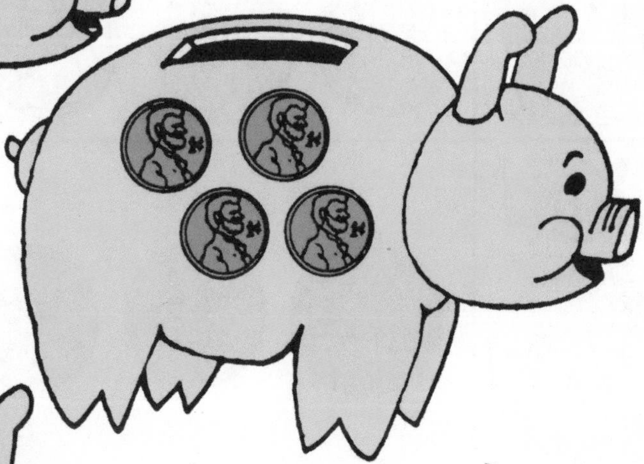

_______¢

_______¢

_______¢

**Skills:** Identifying amounts of money

# Time and Money

Look at the price tag in each box.
Circle the amount of money that each fruit costs.

| | |
|---|---|
| 4¢ | 1¢ 1¢ 1¢ 1¢ 1¢ 1¢ 1¢ |
| 6¢ | 5¢ 1¢ 1¢ 1¢ |
| 10¢ | 10¢ 1¢ 1¢ |
| 5¢ | 1¢ 1¢ 1¢ 1¢ 1¢ 1¢ 1¢ 1¢ |

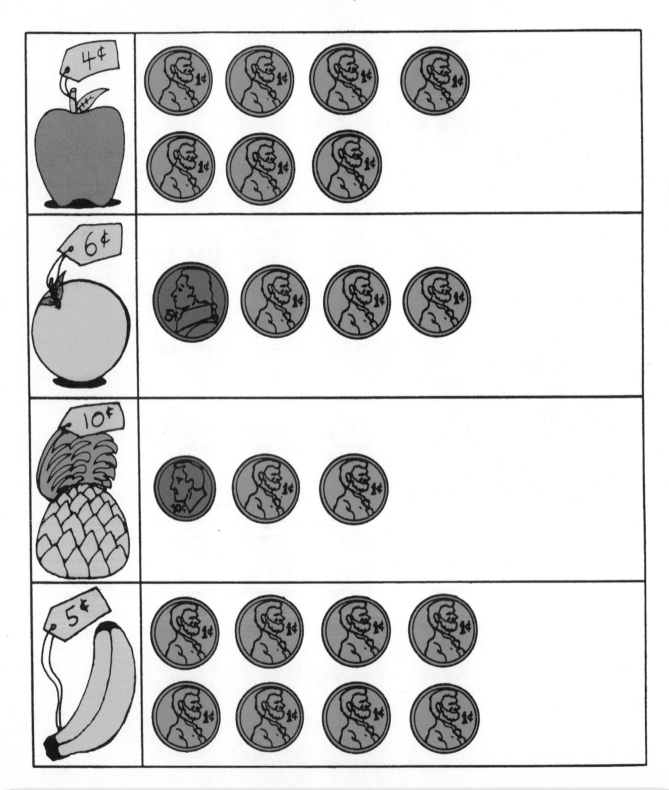

**Skills:** Understanding the use of money

# Excellent!

## Give yourself a star!

# Reading Readiness

# Reading Readiness

Look at the pictures on this page.
Draw lines to match the pictures that are the same.
Then color the pictures.

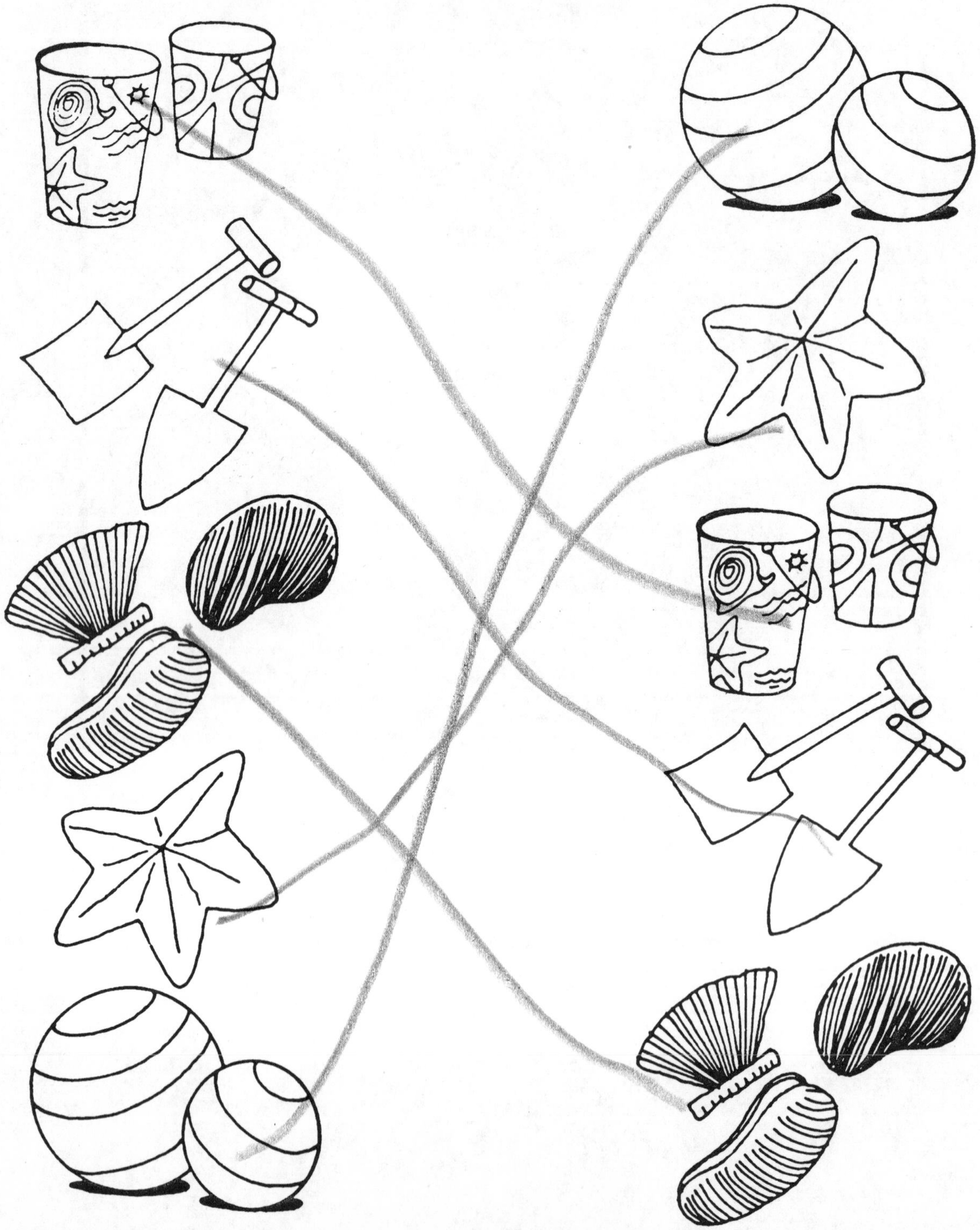

**Skills:** Association; Visual discrimination

## Reading Readiness

Look at the pictures in each row.
Cross out the one that doesn't belong.
Color the others.

**Skills:** Association; Classification

# Reading Readiness

Color the pictures in each row that belong together.

**Skills:** Association; Classification; Logical reasoning

## Reading Readiness

Look at the pictures in each box. Draw lines to match the number of objects on top to the number of objects on the bottom. Then color the pictures.

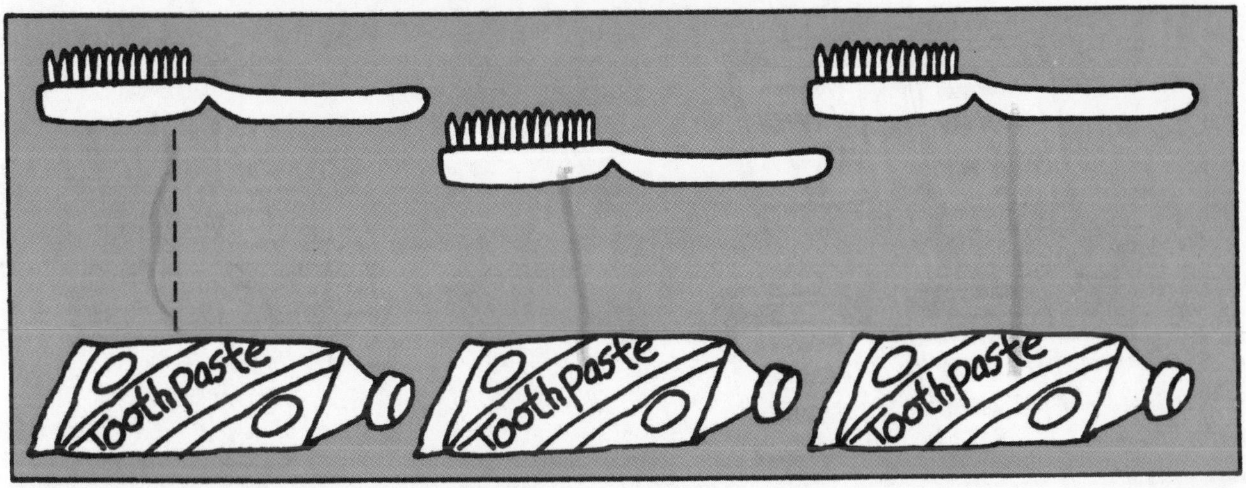

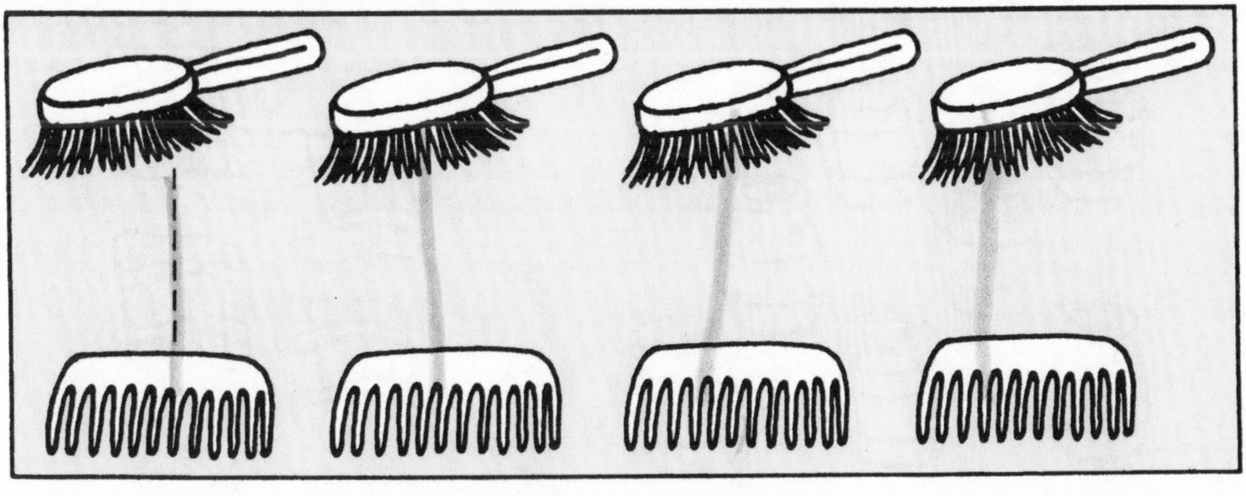

Toothpaste Toothpaste Toothpaste

**Skills:** One-to-one correspondence

## Reading Readiness

Look at the pictures in each box. Circle the group that shows more.
Then color the pictures.

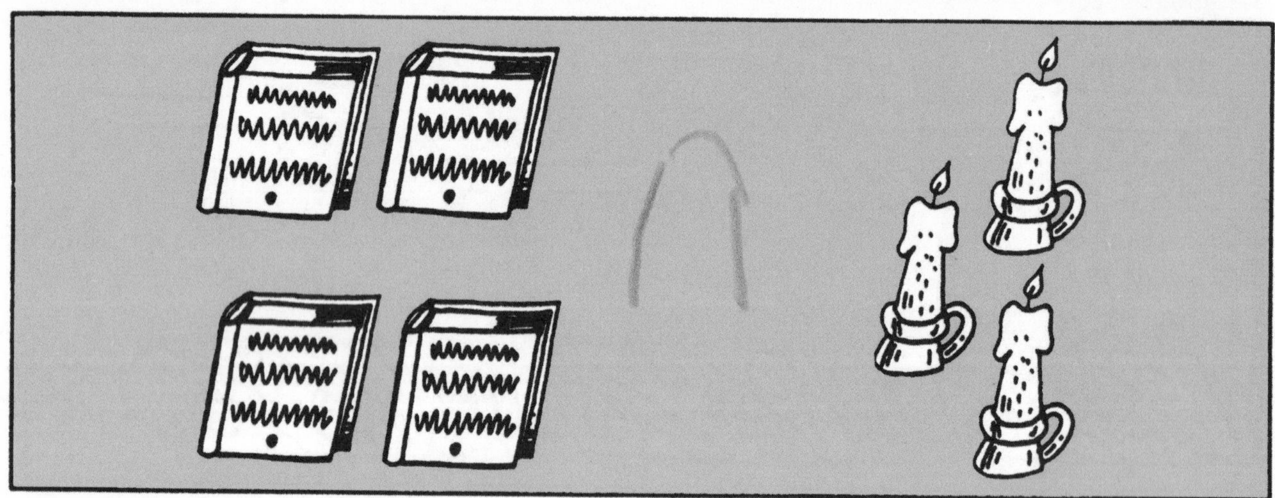

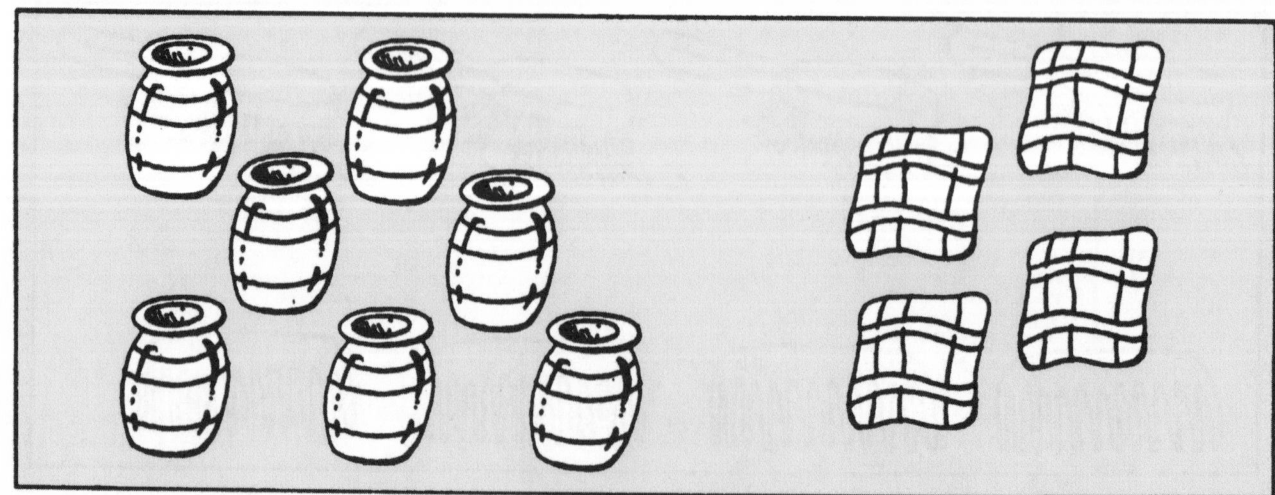

**Skills:** One-to-one correspondence; Understanding more and less

# Reading Readiness

Look at the pictures in each box.
Circle the group that shows less.
Then color the pictures.

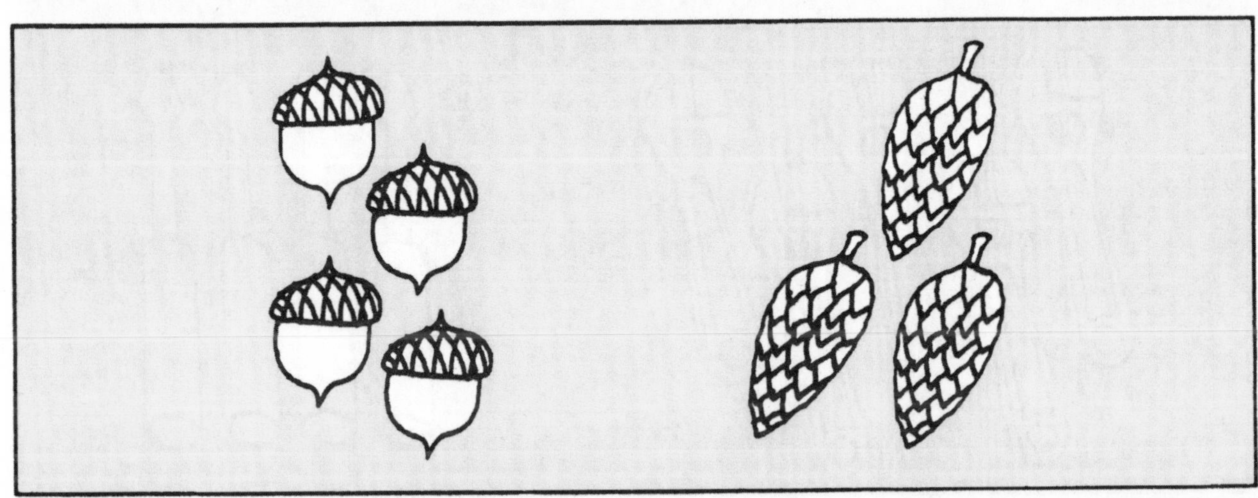

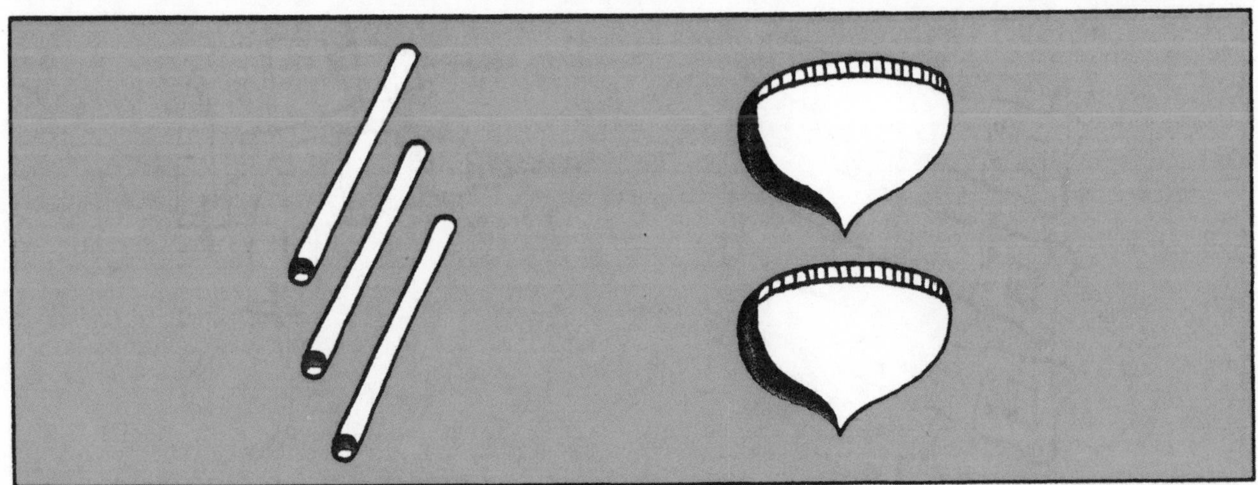

**Skills:** One-to-one correspondence; Understanding more and less

# Reading Readiness

Look at the pictures in each box.
Circle the group that shows less.
Then color the pictures.

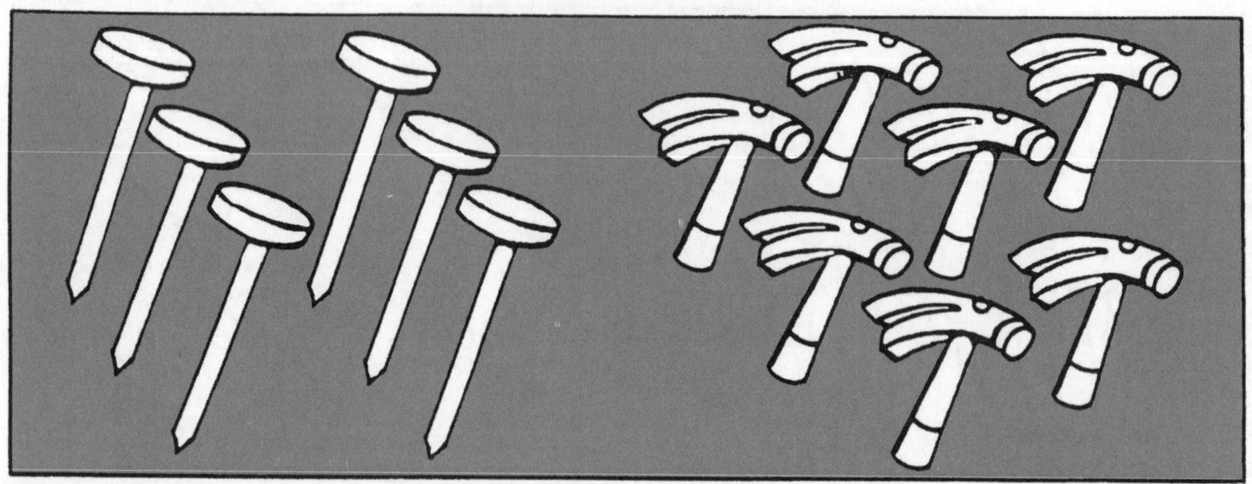

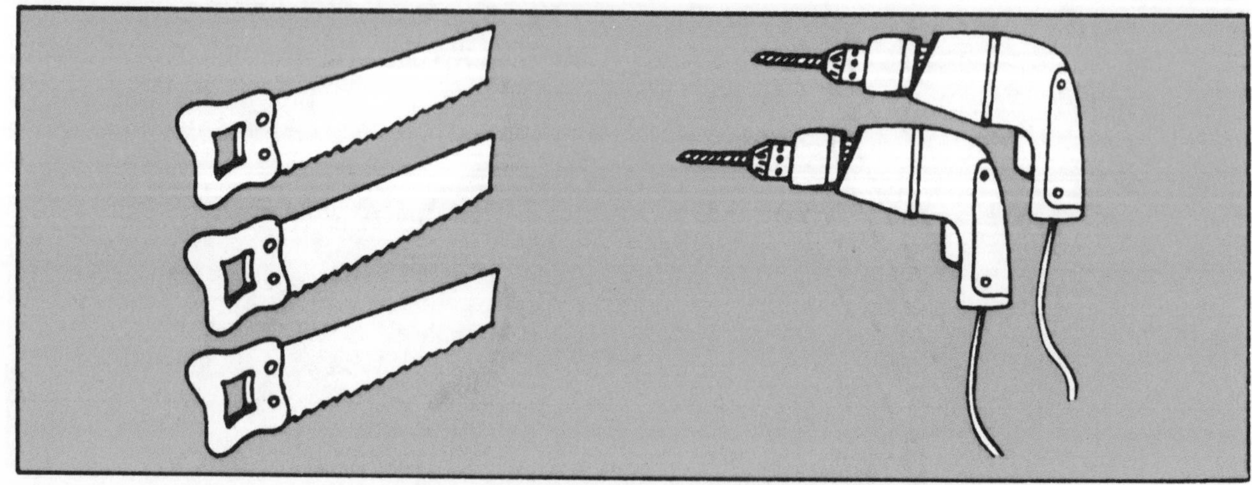

**Skills:** One-to-one correspondence; Understanding more and less

# Reading Readiness

Color the pictures in each box that belong together.

**Skills:** Association; Classification; Logical reasoning

# Reading Readiness

Look at this picture. Circle five things that do not belong.
Then color the picture.

**Skills:** Visual discrimination; Logical reasoning; Counting

# Reading Readiness

Look at the pictures in each box.
Cross out the one that is different.
Color the others.

**Skills:** Visual discrimination; Noticing details; Following directions

# Reading Readiness

Look closely at the pictures in each row.
One of the objects is in a different position.
Cross it out. Then color the other pictures.

**Skills:** Visual discrimination; Noticing details; Following directions

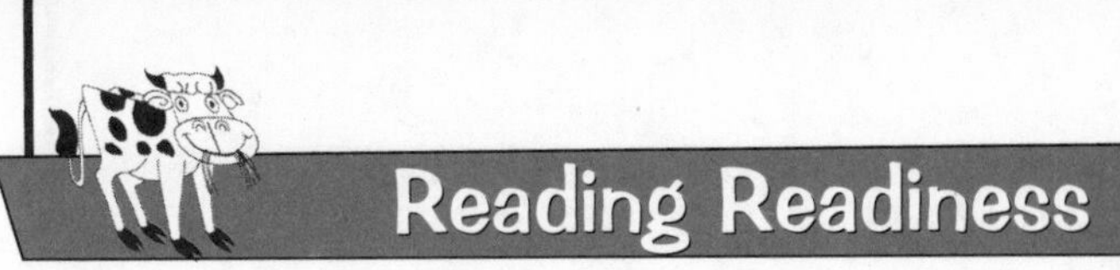


The car at the top of the page is heading right. Look at the rest of the pictures. Circle the pictures that show cars heading right.

**right**

**Skills:** Recognizing directionality; Word recognition

# Reading Readiness

The bicycle at the top of the page is heading left. Look at the rest of the pictures. Circle the pictures that show bicycles heading left.

**left**

**Skills:** Recognizing directionality; Word recognition

# Reading Readiness

Look at the pictures at the top of this page. One child is facing right. One child is facing left. Then look at the rest of the pictures.
Circle the pictures that show children facing right.
Draw a line under the pictures that show children facing left.

left

right

**Skills:** Recognizing right and left; Word recognition

# Reading Readiness

Look at the uniform each person is wearing.
Draw a line to match the type of vehicle each person uses at work.

**Skills:** Association; Classification

# Reading Readiness

Look at the person at the beginning of each row.
Circle the picture that shows what each person uses at work.

Skills: Association; Classification

# Reading Readiness

Look at the pictures.
Draw a line between the pictures that are opposites.

**Skills:** Vocabulary; Opposites

## Reading Readiness

The shoes in the shoe store got mixed up.
Draw lines between the shoes that belong together.

**Skills:** Understanding pairs; Vocabulary; Visual matching

# Reading Readiness

Look at the pictures at the top of the page.
Find and circle them in the larger picture below.

**Skills:** Association; Classification

# Reading Readiness

Look at the pattern in each row.
Draw pictures that continue each pattern.

**Skills:** Observing and reproducing patterns; Visual memory; Fine motor skill development

# Reading Readiness

Look at the pictures. Think about the story they tell.
Write the numbers 1, 2, 3, and 4 in the boxes to put the story in order.
Then color the pictures.

**Skills:** Sequencing; Identifying parts of a story; Writing numerals

# Excellent!

## Give yourself a star!

# Vocabulary and Math Skill Builder

## Vocabulary and Math Skill Builder

First, read the story with the child and discuss the plot. In the yellow boxes, you will find the math in the story simply illustrated. You will also find questions designed to encourage children to notice words and use related vocabulary. Read the story again and discuss the math concepts as outlined below. Discuss the vocabulary concepts as part of another separate reading.

**About the Math in this Book**

Show the child each type of coin and discuss the value of each coin. Talk about how coins can be combined to make equal amounts. Let the child notice details on the coins such as words, dates and what each coin feels like. Notice the different sizes of each coin.

Point out words in the story such as cost, equals, plus, minus, not enough, count and bought. Discuss when these words are used.

Review each money equation with the child. Use real coins to show how each addition or subtraction problem works. Ask the child to try to make 25¢ in as many ways as possible. Then ask the child to try this with 50¢.

**About the Vocabulary and Language in this Book**

First, read the story, pointing out what happens in the pictures. Then read the story a second time and encourage the child to retell the story using the pictures.

The element of repetition in this story encourages beginning readers to follow the story and predict words. Help the child notice how some sentences have similar words in them.

As you read the story a second time, pause and let the child fill in a predictable word. Learning to finish a sentence and predict words can be very beneficial to a beginning reader.

Make a list of big words or words that are unfamiliar to the child. Encourage the child to say the words and even use the words in a sentence. Children often enjoy saying or spelling long complicated words such as lemonade or carnival.

Vocabulary and Math Skill Builder

# LEMONADE LIL

Lil woke up one morning.
She wanted something fun to do.

# Vocabulary and Math Skill Builder

Lil ate breakfast.
Lil played with toys.
Lil played with Bill.
Lil ate lunch.
But still she wanted something fun to do.

**Skills:** What do you like to eat for breakfast?
What is your favorite toy?

# Vocabulary and Math Skill Builder

Then Lil had an idea.
"I can go to the carnival!
I can go on the rides!
I can eat cotton candy!
I will need $2.00 to go to the carnival."

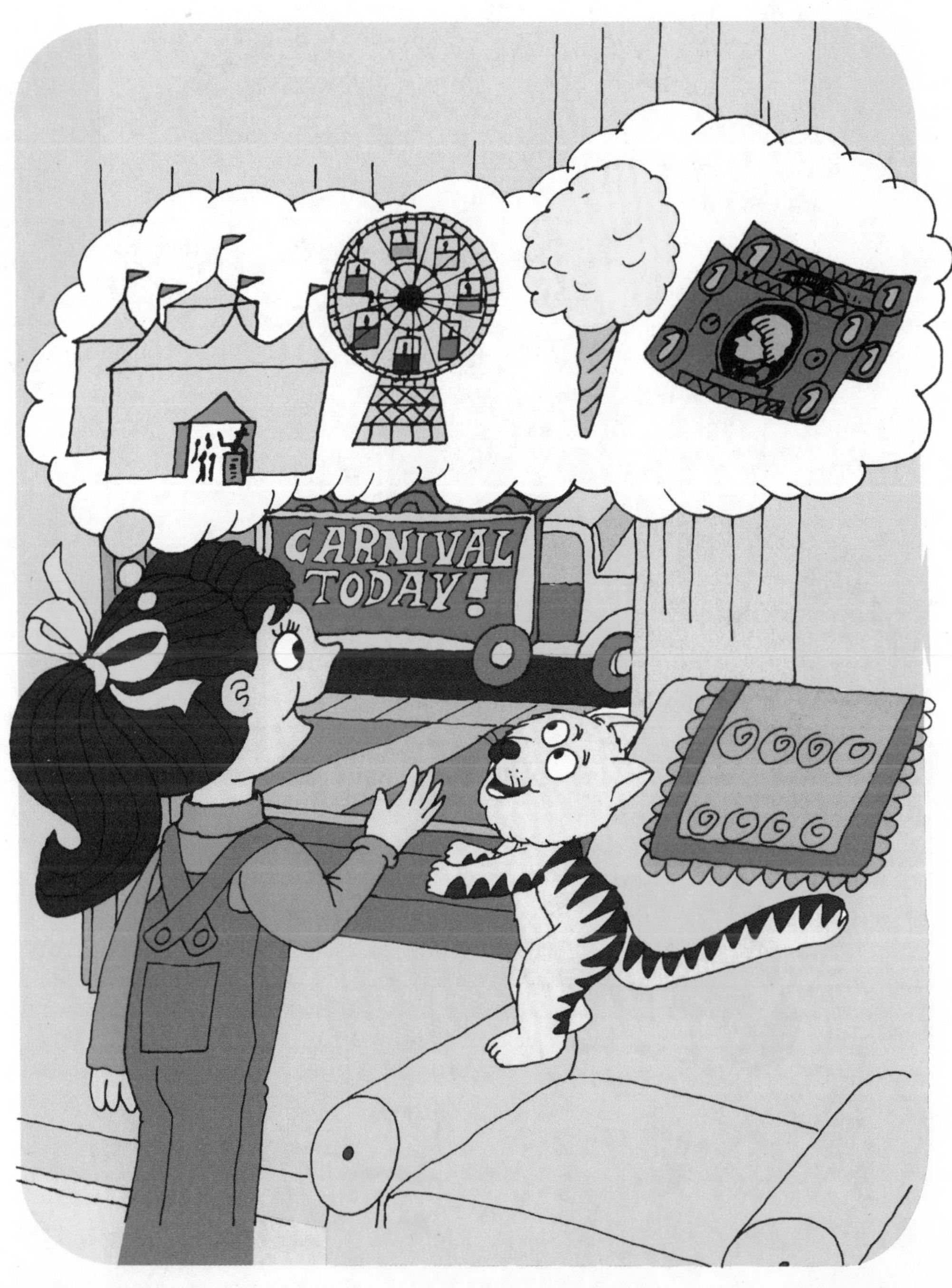


**Skills:** Can you find the word **carnival** in the picture?

# Vocabulary and Math Skill Builder

Lil looked in her piggy bank.
Lil saw 2 quarters and 5 dimes.
That was not enough money for the carnival!

1 quarter is 25¢ 

= 25¢

25¢ + 25¢ = 50¢

1 dime is 10¢ 

= 10¢

10¢ + 10¢ + 10¢ + 10¢ + 10¢ = 50¢

1 dollar is 100¢ 

= $1.00

= 

50¢ + 50¢ = $1.00

# Vocabulary and Math Skill Builder

Lil thought and thought.
She thought about where she could get money.

Lil sat and sat.
She sat and thought about how to get money for the carnival.

**Skills:** Can you think of a word that rhymes with sat?
Can you think of more?

# Vocabulary and Math Skill Builder

All this thinking and sitting made Lil hungry.
Lil got a glass of lemonade and a cookie.

**Skills:** Can you find the word **cookies** in the picture?

Then she had an idea.
She could sell lemonade.

**Skills:** Can you find the word **lemonade** in the picture?

## Vocabulary and Math Skill Builder

Lil went to the store.
Lil got a carton of lemonade. It cost 50¢.
Lil got a box of cups. It cost 50¢.

Skills: Point to a sign that says 50¢.

## Vocabulary and Math Skill Builder

Lil had just enough money.

## Vocabulary and Math Skill Builder

Lil set up a table up outside her house.

## Vocabulary and Math Skill Builder

Lil made a sign that read:



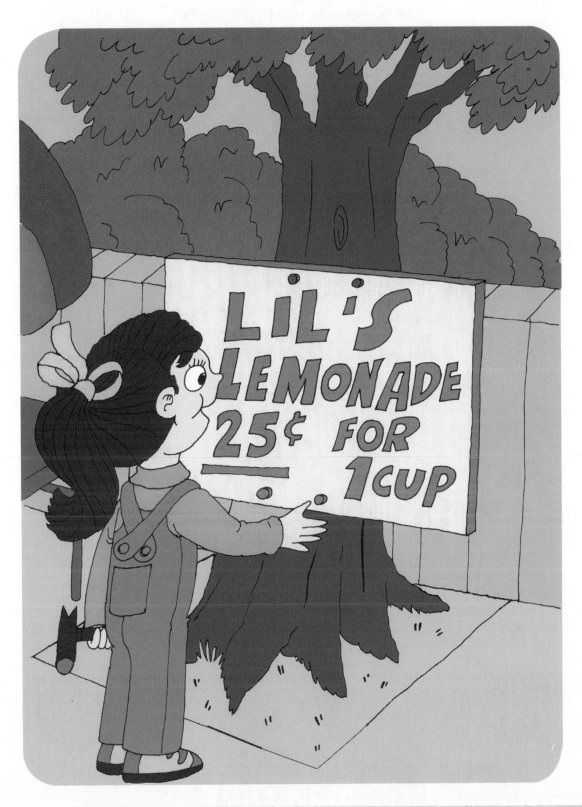

**Skills:** Can you find the word **cup** in the picture?

## Vocabulary and Math Skill Builder

Lil sat and sat.
Mrs. Gray and her dog came by.
"I'll have a cup," said Mrs. Gray.
She gave Lil 2 dimes and 1 nickel.

1 dime = 10¢

1 nickel = 5¢

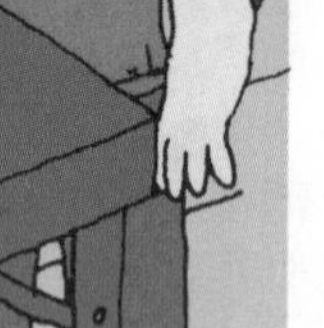

 = 5¢

10¢ + 10¢ + 5¢ = 25¢

   = 

# Vocabulary and Math Skill Builder

Lil and Bill sat and sat.
Tommy and Sue came by.

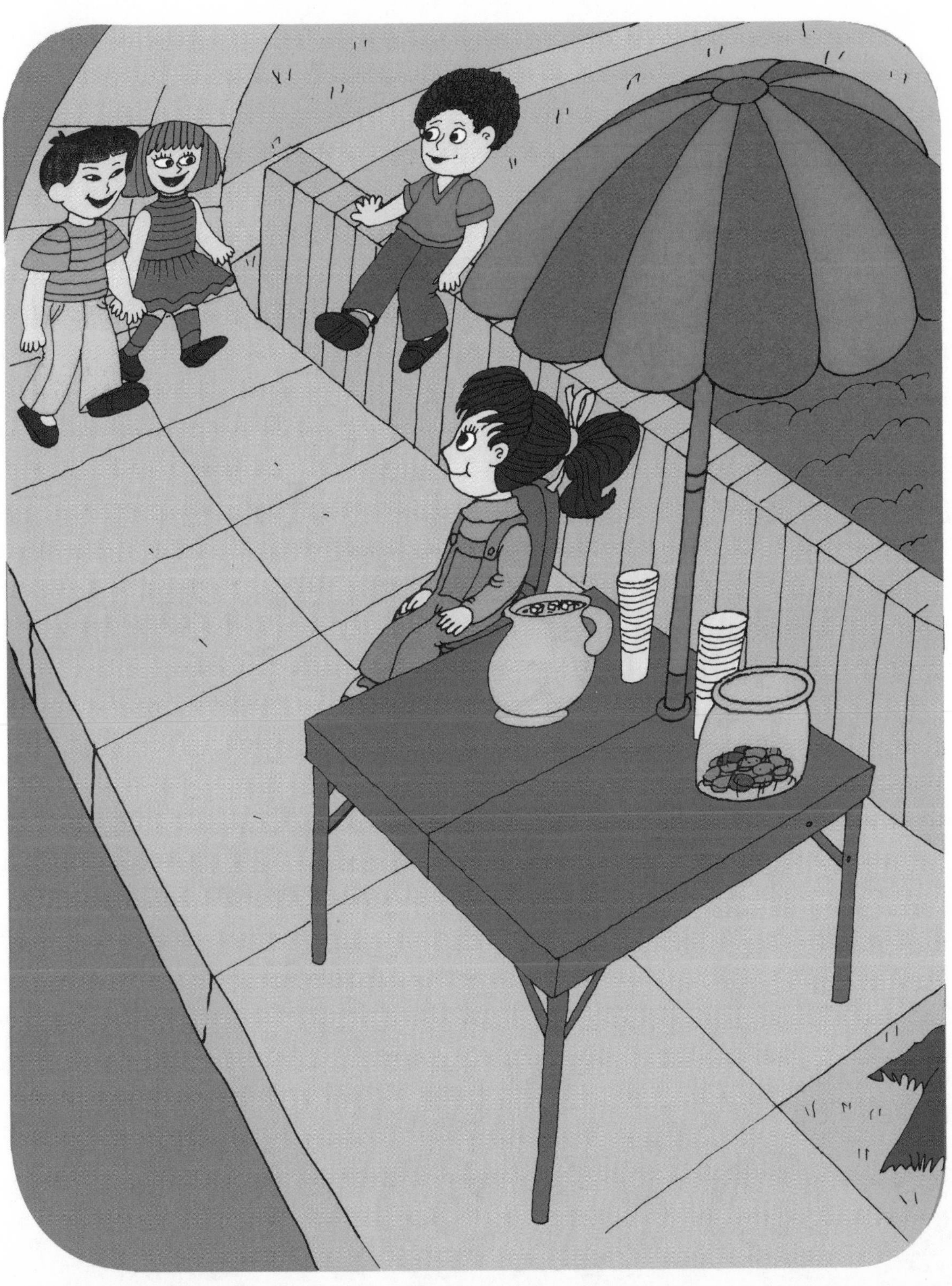

**Skills:** What is the same about the names Lil and Bill?
What is different?

## Vocabulary and Math Skill Builder

"Can I have a cup?" asked Tommy.
He gave Lil 1 dime and 3 nickels. Was that enough?

1 dime =10¢
1 nickel = 5¢

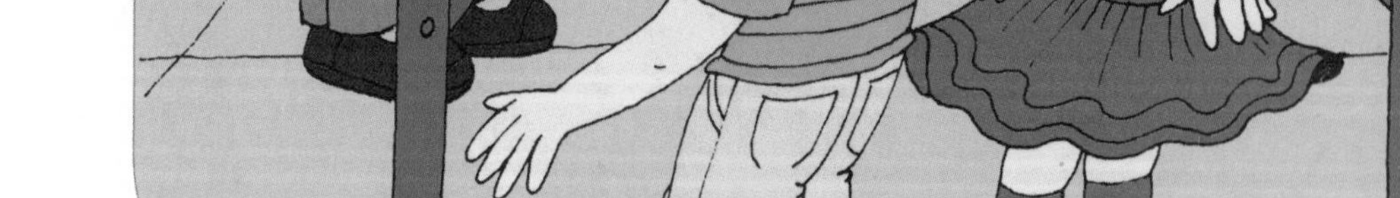

    = 

10¢ + 5¢ + 5¢ + 5¢ = 25¢

# Vocabulary and Math Skill Builder

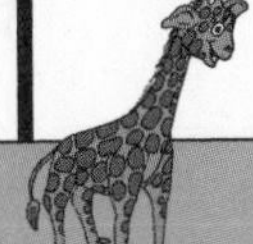

"I want a cup, too," said Sue.
She gave Lil one quarter.

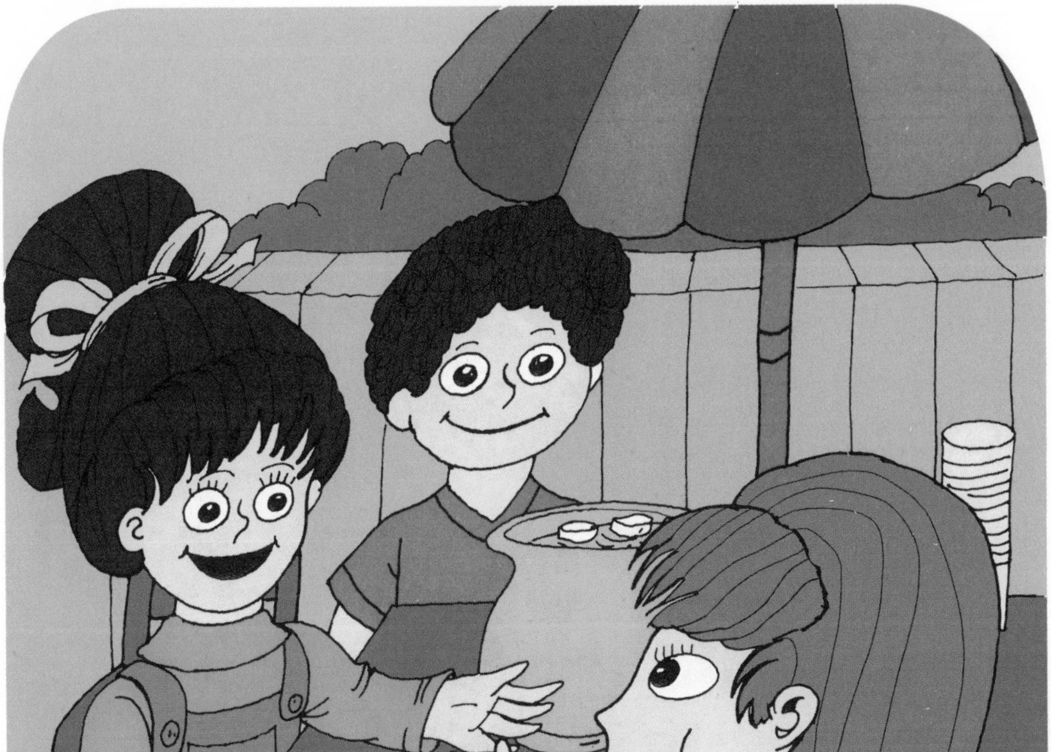

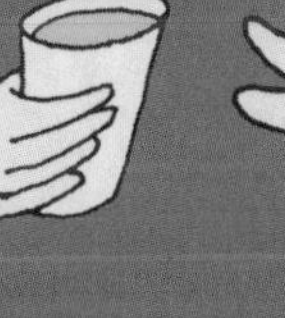

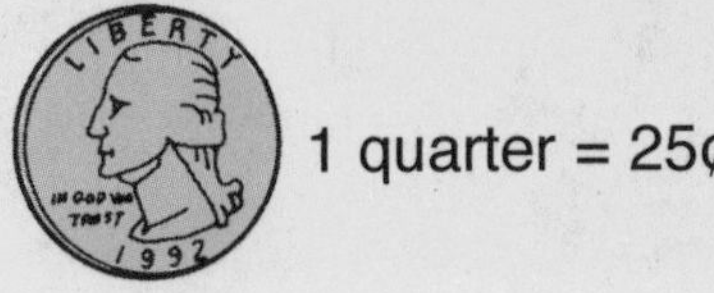

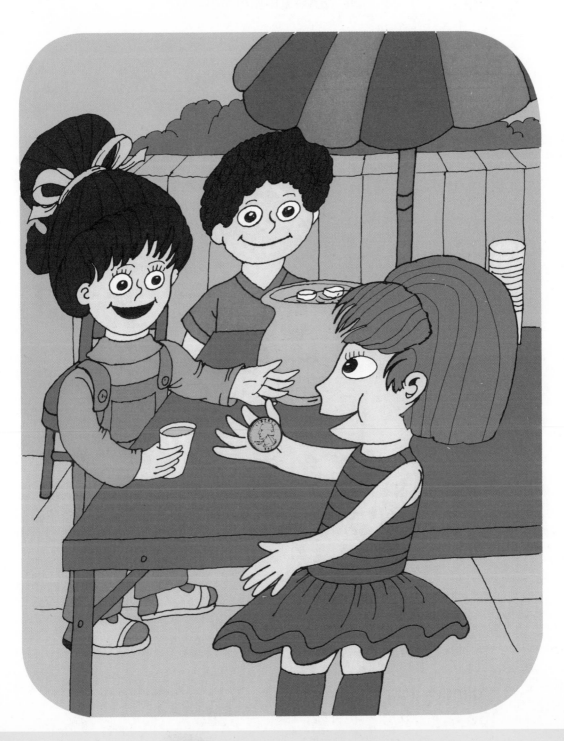

1 quarter = 25¢

# Vocabulary and Math Skill Builder

Mr. Stephens was driving by.
He stopped when he saw Lil's sign.
He gave Lil 3 dimes.

1 dime = 10¢

10¢ + 10¢ + 10¢ = 30¢

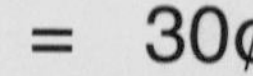

   =  

# Vocabulary and Math Skill Builder

"The lemonade is only 25¢," said Lil.
"I will give you 5¢ back."

30¢ – 25¢ = 5¢

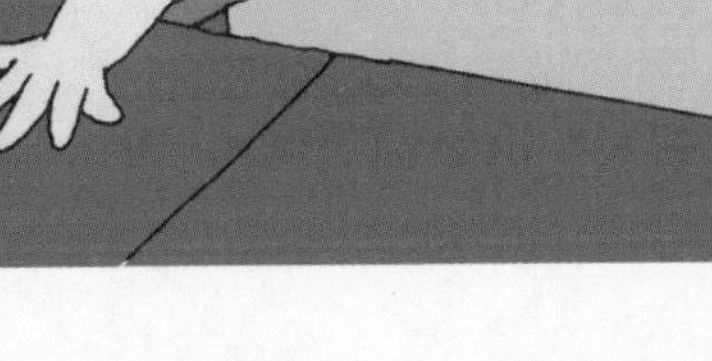

## Vocabulary and Math Skill Builder

Bill looked into the pitcher.
It was half empty already!
Lil counted the money she earned from her neighbors:

25¢ from Mrs. Gray
25¢ from Tommy
25¢ from Sue
25¢ from Mr. Stephens.

25¢ + 25¢ + 25¢ + 25¢ = $1.00

# Vocabulary and Math Skill Builder

More thirsty people passed by.
They bought 4 cups of lemonade.

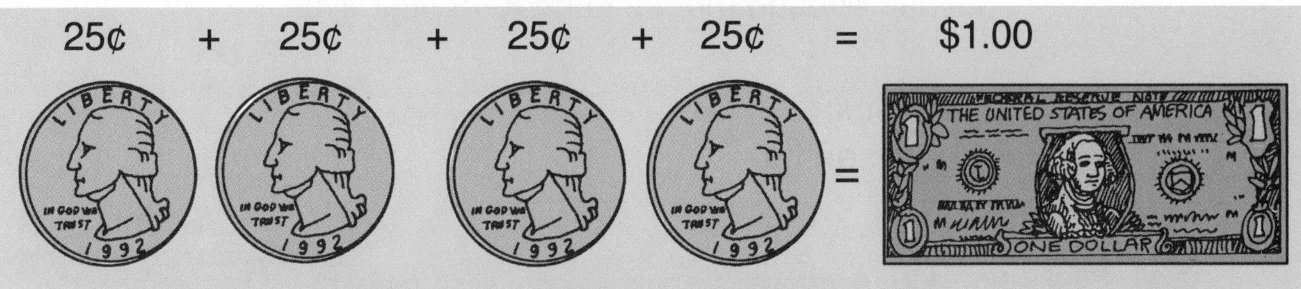

# Vocabulary and Math Skill Builder

Now Lil had no more lemonade.
Lil counted up what she had earned.
Lil had enough money to go to the carnival!

$1.00 from Lil's neighbors
$1.00 from the 4 passersby

| $1.00 | + | $1.00 | = | $2.00 |
|---|---|---|---|---|
|  | |  | = |  |

## Vocabulary and Math Skill Builder

Lil took down her sign.
Lil put away her cups.

# Vocabulary and Math Skill Builder

Lil thought about the carnival.

**Skills:** Can you make smaller words from the letters in the word **carnival?**

# Vocabulary and Math Skill Builder

She thought about her lemonade stand.

**Skills:** Can you make smaller words from the letters in the word **lemonade?**

# Vocabulary and Math Skill Builder

Lil had fun selling lemonade.
Bill had fun selling lemonade.
Lil wanted to sell more lemonade.

**Skills:** How many times do you see the word **fun** on this page?

## Vocabulary and Math Skill Builder

Lil had an idea.
Lil took her $2.00 to the store.
Lil got more lemonade.
Lil got some cookies, too.

# Vocabulary and Math Skill Builder

The lemonade cost 50¢.
The cookies cost $1.50.
Did Lil have enough money?

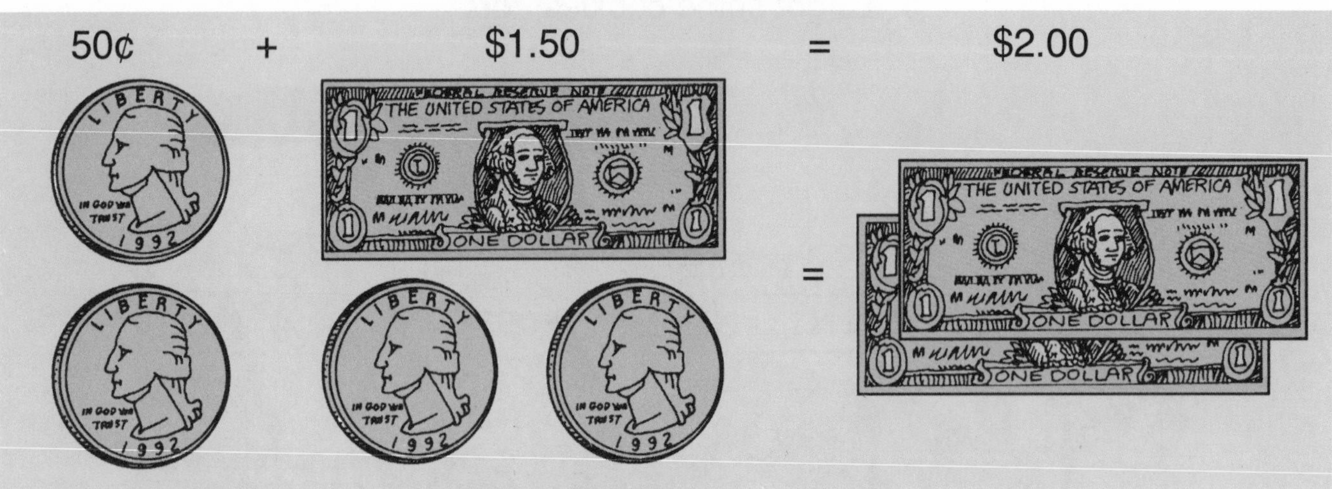


Lil had just enough money.

## Vocabulary and Math Skill Builder

Lil changed her sign.

# Vocabulary and Math Skill Builder

Lil sat at her lemonade stand.
Lil thought about the carnival.

"Next year I will go to the carnival."
"Next year I will have more money."
"But maybe next year...

...it will be called Lil's Carnival!"

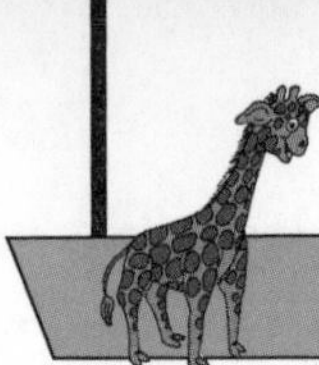

## Vocabulary and Math Skill Builder

**Here are some money math activities to try.**

Make rubbings of different coins. Put a coin under a piece of white paper. Rub the side of a crayon or pencil over the paper. Watch carefully as the image of the coin is visible on the paper. Encourage the child to notice the details on each coin.

Play “Toss and Tell” using a variety of coins. Take a handful of coins. Toss several of them onto a table. Encourage the child to calculate the amount of money shown.

Go to the market. Give the child a short shopping list and some money. Help the child determine how much each product will cost.

Help the child create and run a lemonade stand. There is no better way to learn about money than using it in the real world.

**Here are some vocabulary and language ideas to try.**

Make a double set of flash cards using simple words from the story. Lay the cards in rows face down on a table. Play concentration with the child. Each player turns over a pair of cards. Players keep the cards that match. The player with the most cards wins.

Encourage the child to act out the story. The child can play all the characters or just one person. Encourage the child to use the dialogue from the story.

Have the child to draw a picture from the story. Then encourage the child to label everything in the picture. The child may find some of the words for labels in the story.

Help the child find words that are easy to rhyme and make word families. Choose a word like Lil. Encourage the child to make a list of words that rhyme with Lil, such as fill, hill, will, still, and so on.

# Excellent!

## Give yourself a star!

# Phonics Skills I

## Phonics Skills I

Initial consonant: b

Print the letters and words.

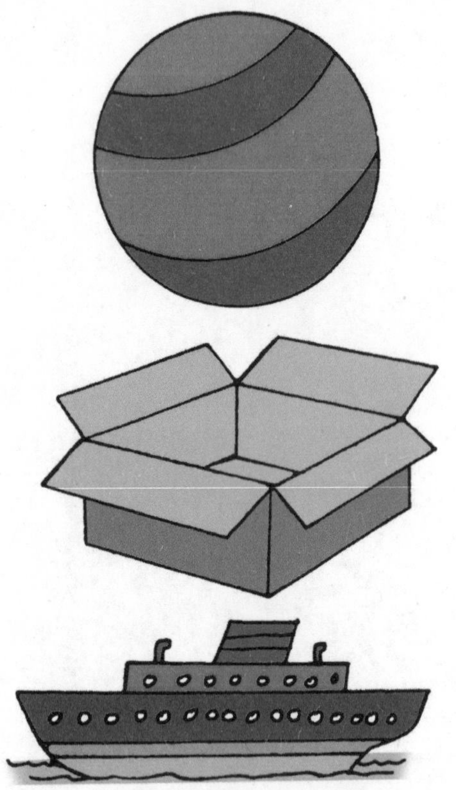

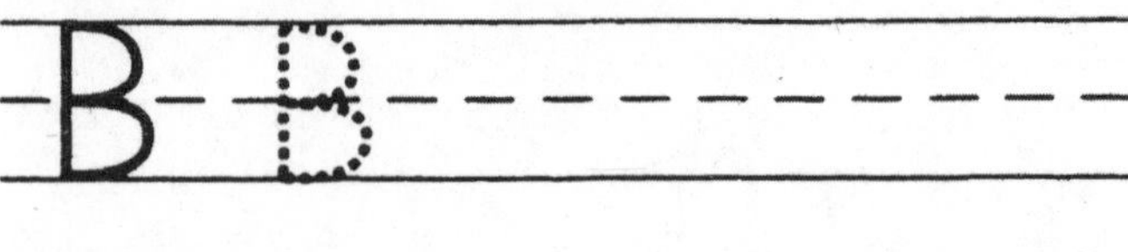


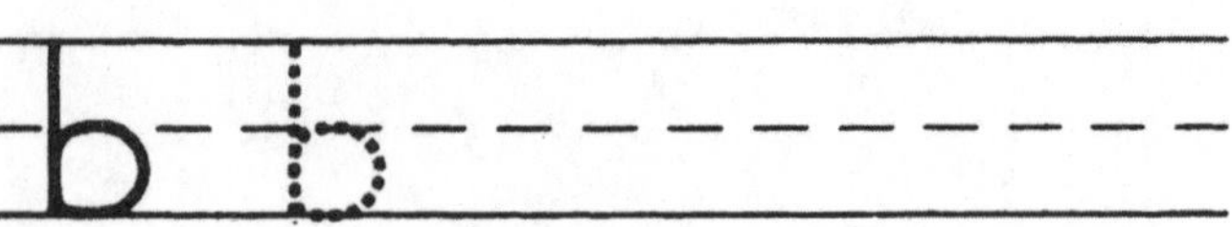


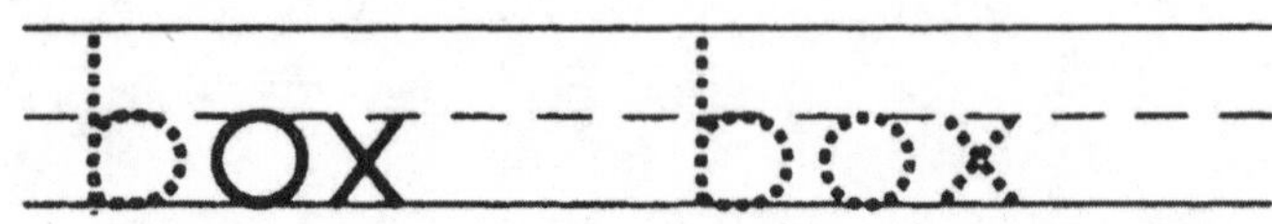


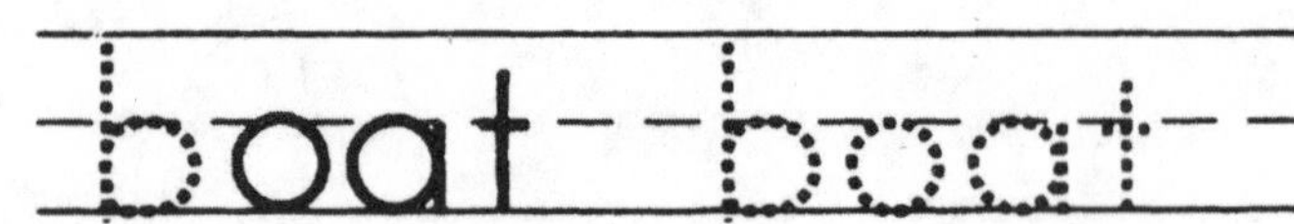


Finish the pictures. Finish the words.

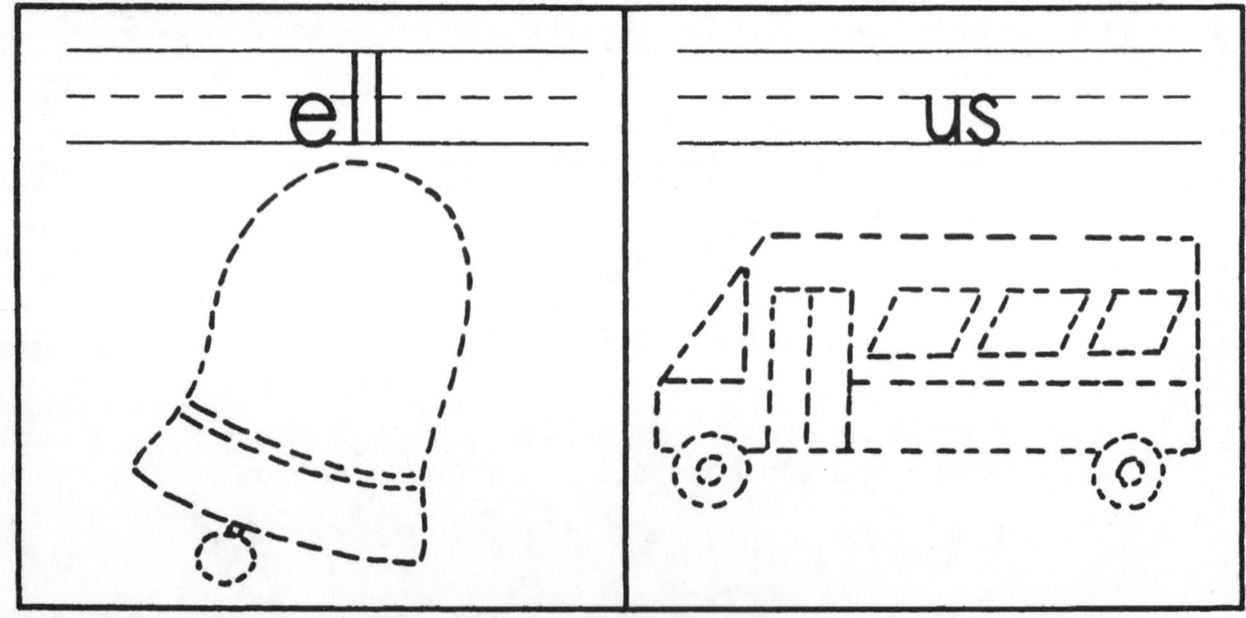


**Skills:** Recognition of the initial consonant "b"; Writing letters and words; Association between sounds, symbols, and words

# Phonics Skills I

Initial consonant: f

Print the letters and words.

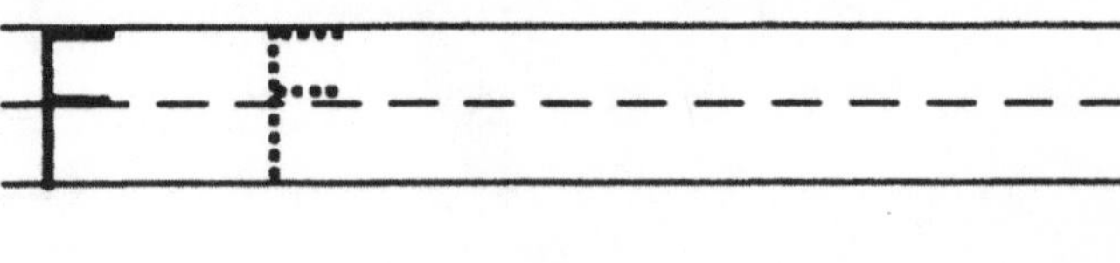


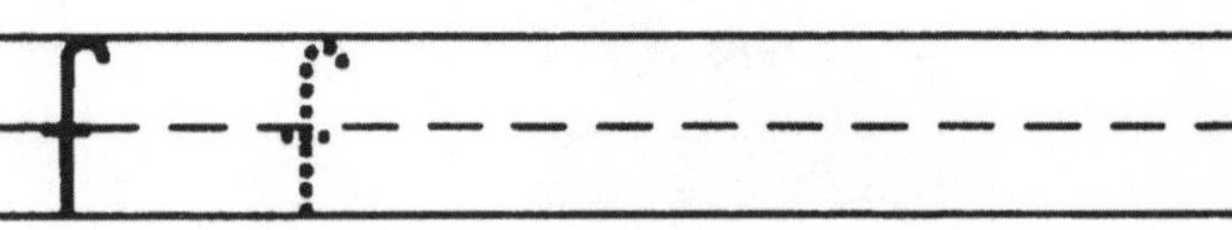


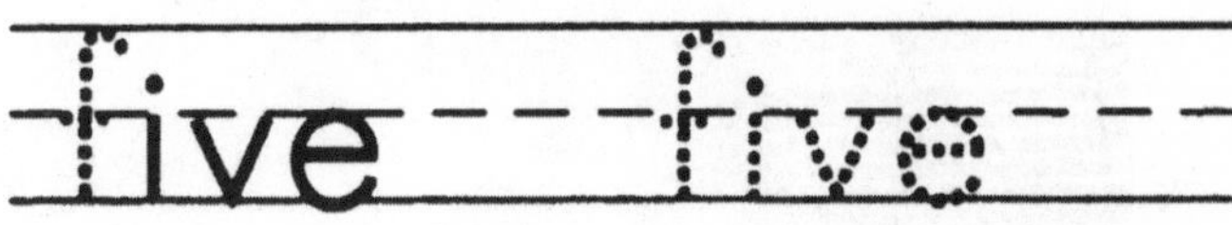


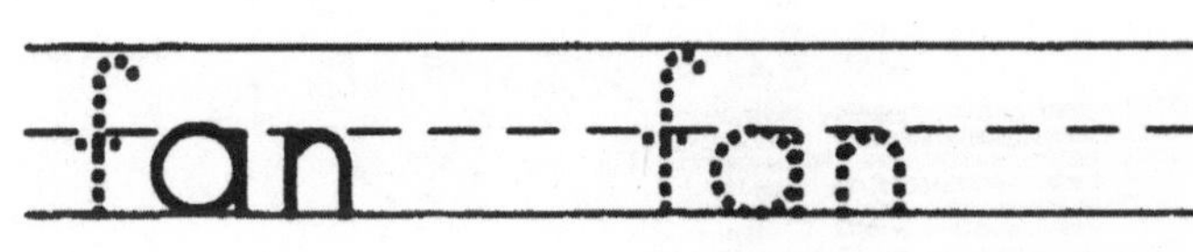


Finish the pictures. Finish the words.

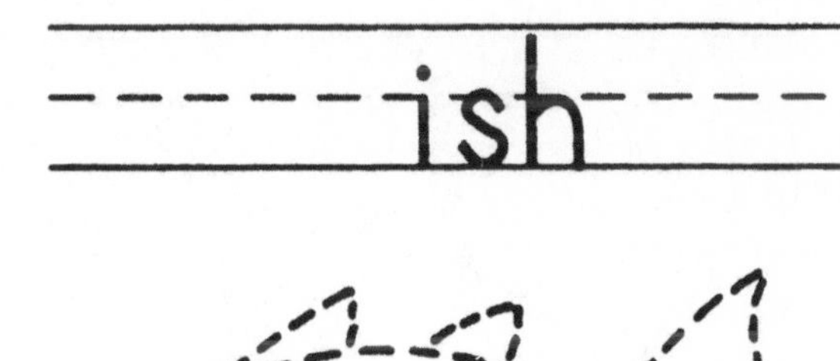


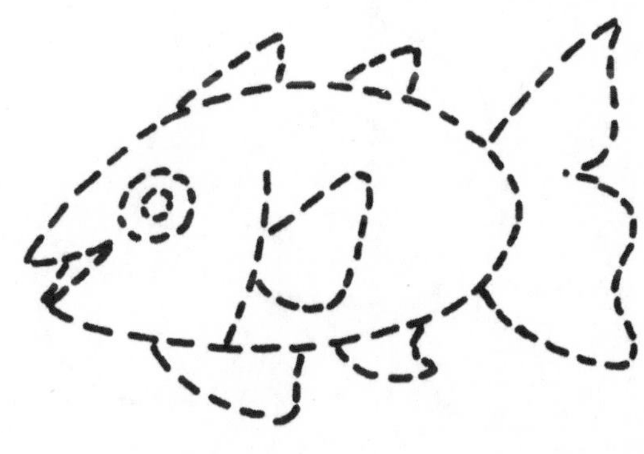

**Skills:** Recognition of the initial consonant "f"; Writing letters and words; Association between sounds, symbols, and words

# Phonics Skills I

Initial consonant: g

Print the letters and words.

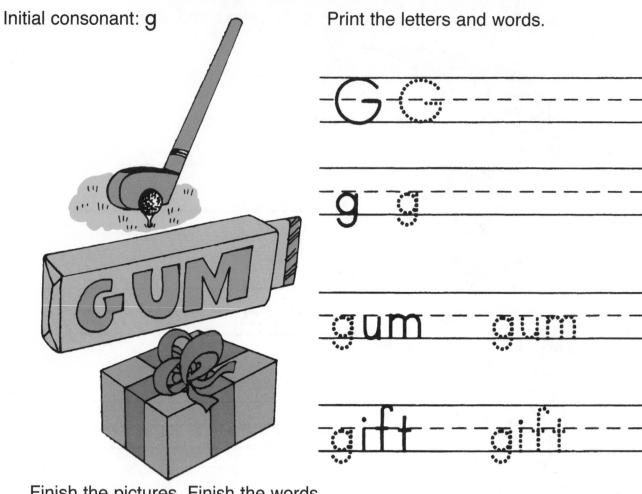

G G

g g

gum gum

gift gift

Finish the pictures. Finish the words.

**Skills:** Recognition of the initial consonant "g"; Writing letters and words; Association between sounds, symbols, and words

# Phonics Skills I

Initial consonant: k

Print the letters and words.

Finish the pictures. Finish the words.

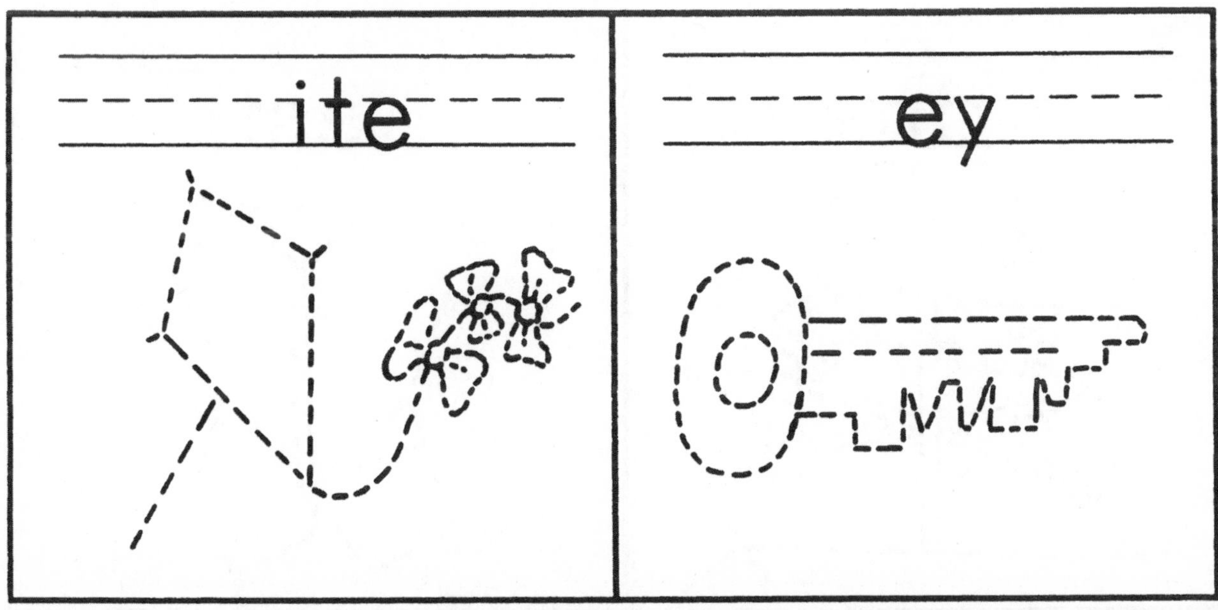


**Skills:** Recognition of the initial consonant "k"; Writing letters and words; Association between sounds, symbols, and words

# Phonics Skills I

Initial consonant: v

Print the letters and words.

V V

v v

van van

vase vase

Finish the pictures. Finish the words.

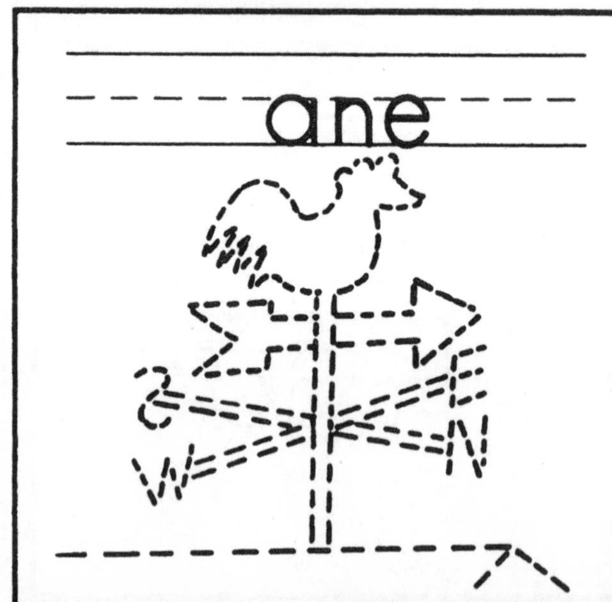


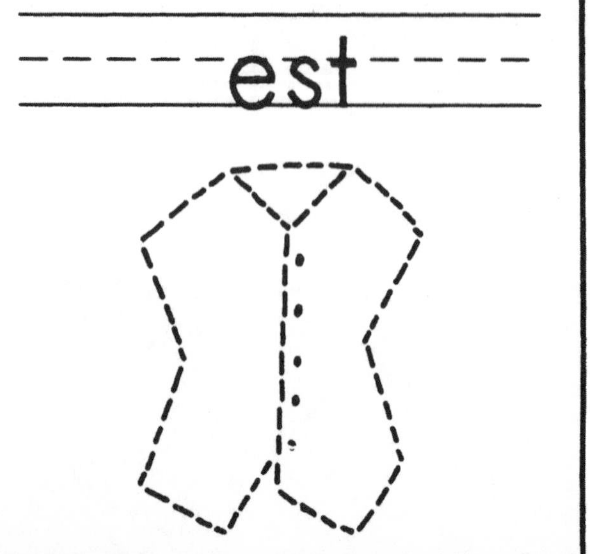


**Skills:** Recognition of the initial consonant "v"; Writing letters and words; Association between sounds, symbols, and words

# Phonics Skills I

Initial consonant: C

Print the letters and words.

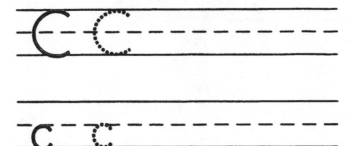

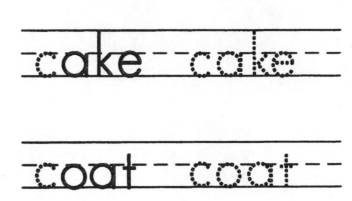

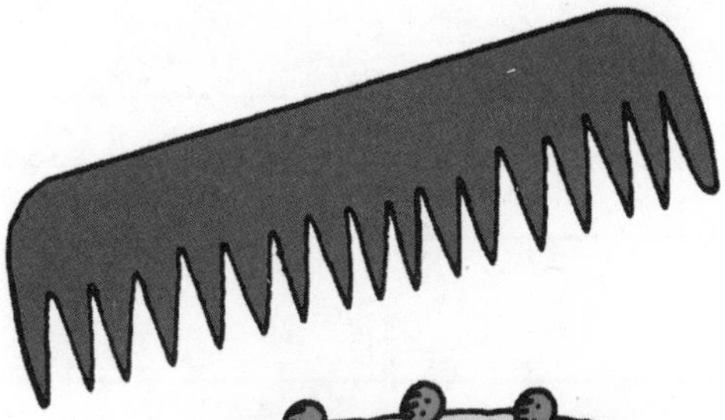

C C

c c

cake cake

coat coat

Finish the pictures. Finish the words.

**Skills:** Recognition of the initial consonant "c"; Writing letters and words; Association between sounds, symbols, and words

# Phonics Skills I

Initial consonant: h

Print the letters and words.

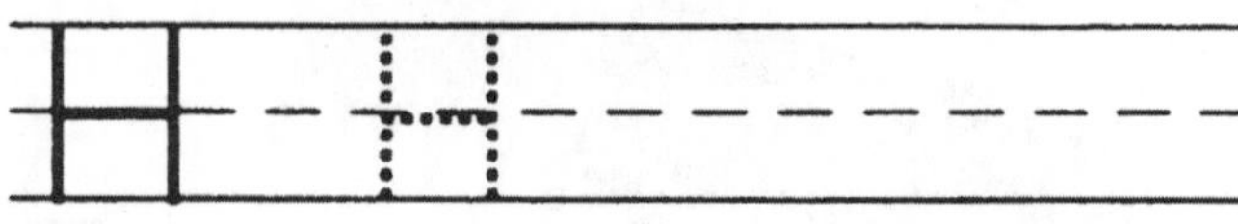


h h

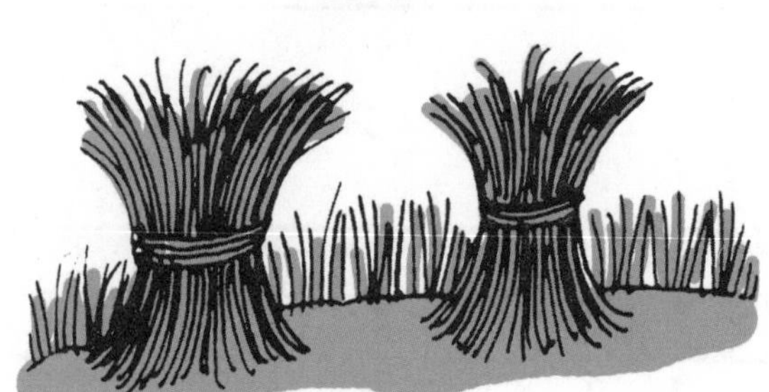

hay hay

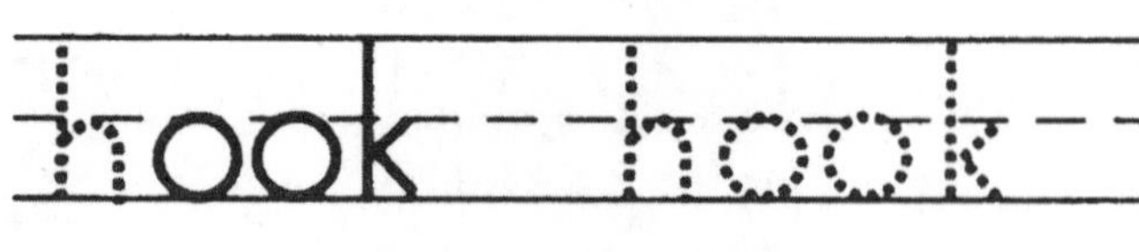


Finish the pictures. Finish the words.

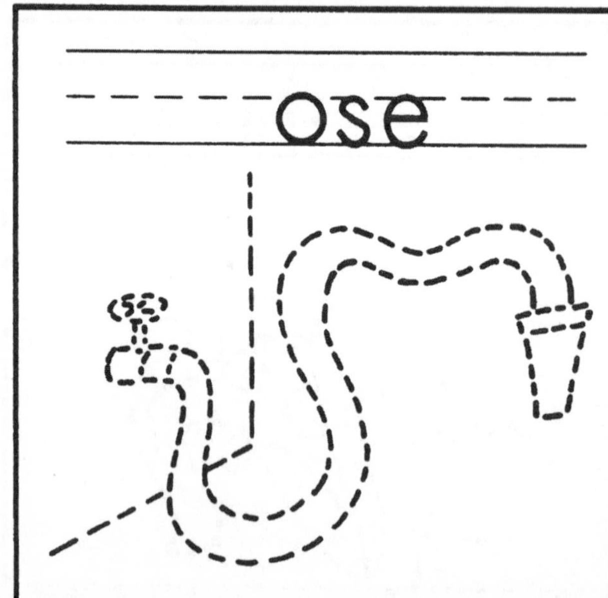


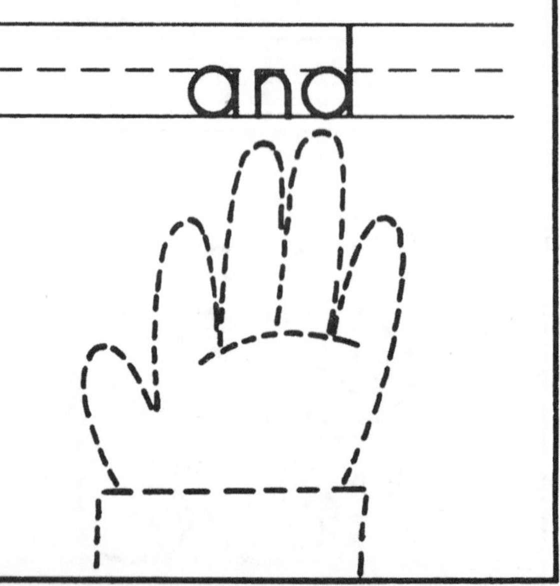


**Skills:** Recognition of the initial consonant "h"; Writing letters and words; Association between sounds, symbols, and words

# Phonics Skills I

Initial consonant: m

Print the letters and words.

M M

m m

mask mask

man man

Finish the pictures. Finish the words.

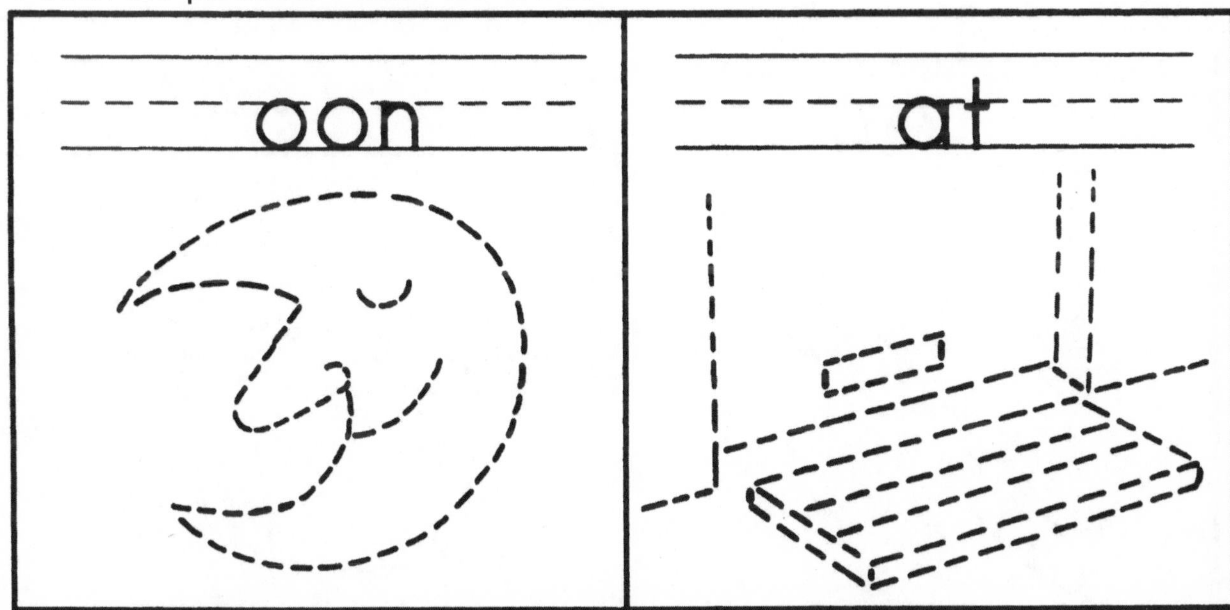


**Skills:** Recognition of the initial consonant "m"; Writing letters and words; Association between sounds, symbols, and words

# Phonics Skills 1

Initial consonant: p

Print the letters and words.

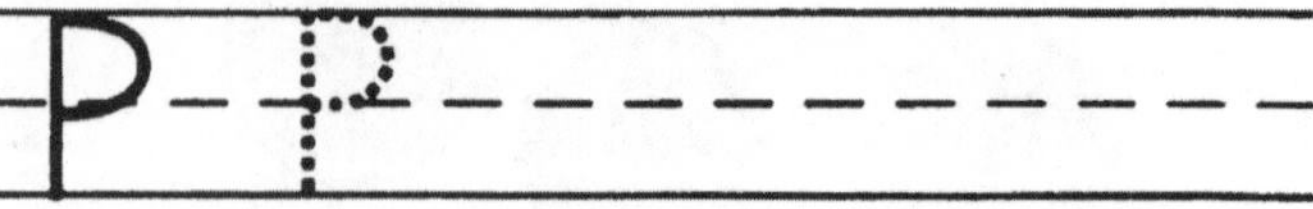

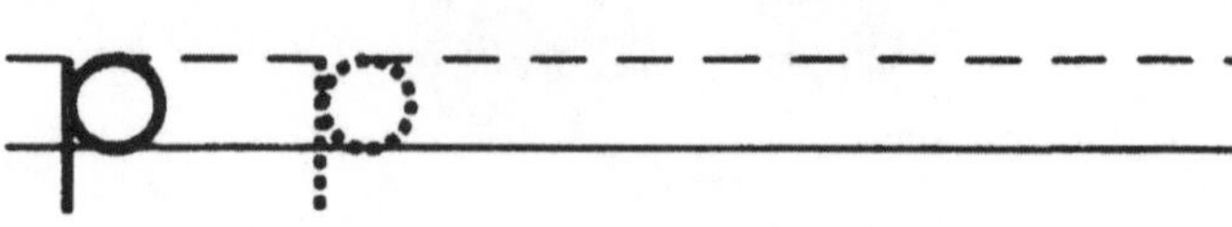

pan pan

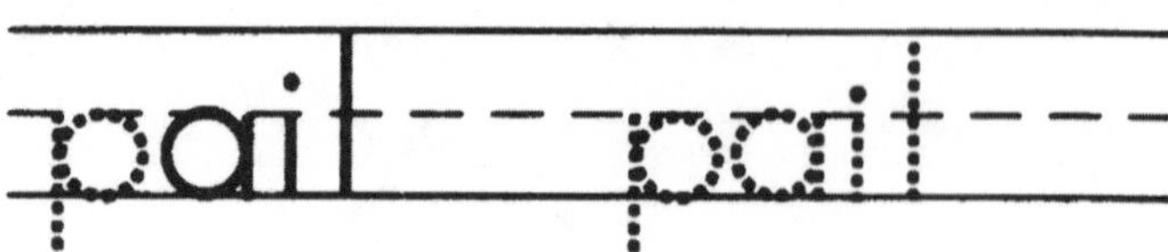

Finish the pictures. Finish the words.

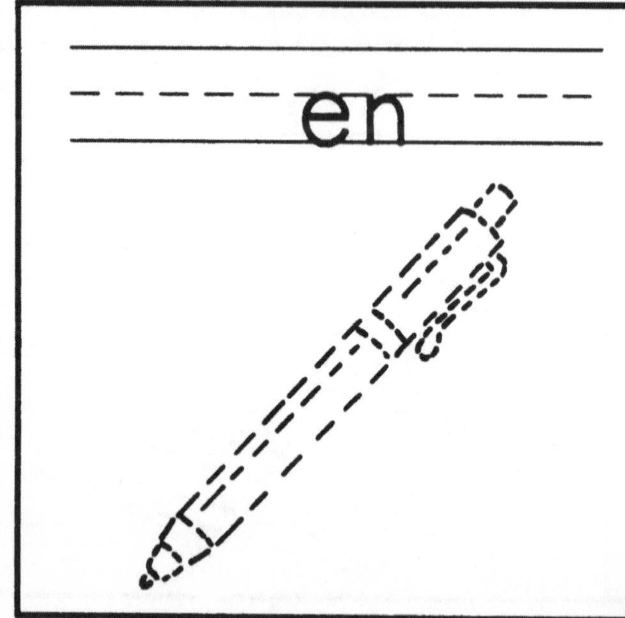

en

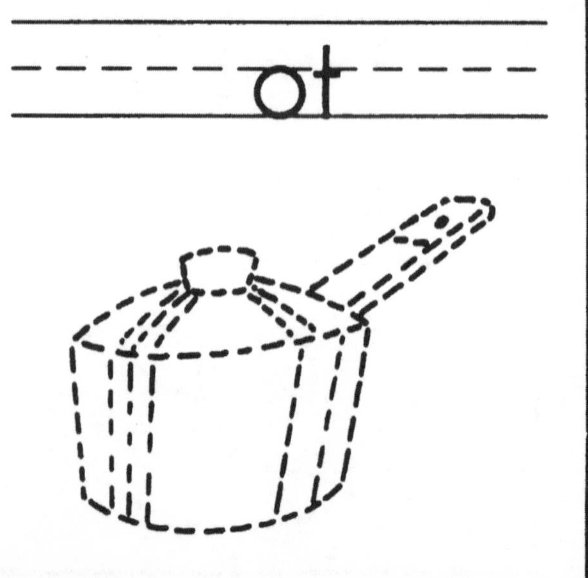

ot

**Skills:** Recognition of the initial consonant "p"; Writing letters and words; Association between sounds, symbols, and words

# Phonics Skills I

Initial consonant: y

Print the letters and words.

Y Y

y y

yo-yo yo-yo

yawn yawn

Finish the pictures. Finish the words.

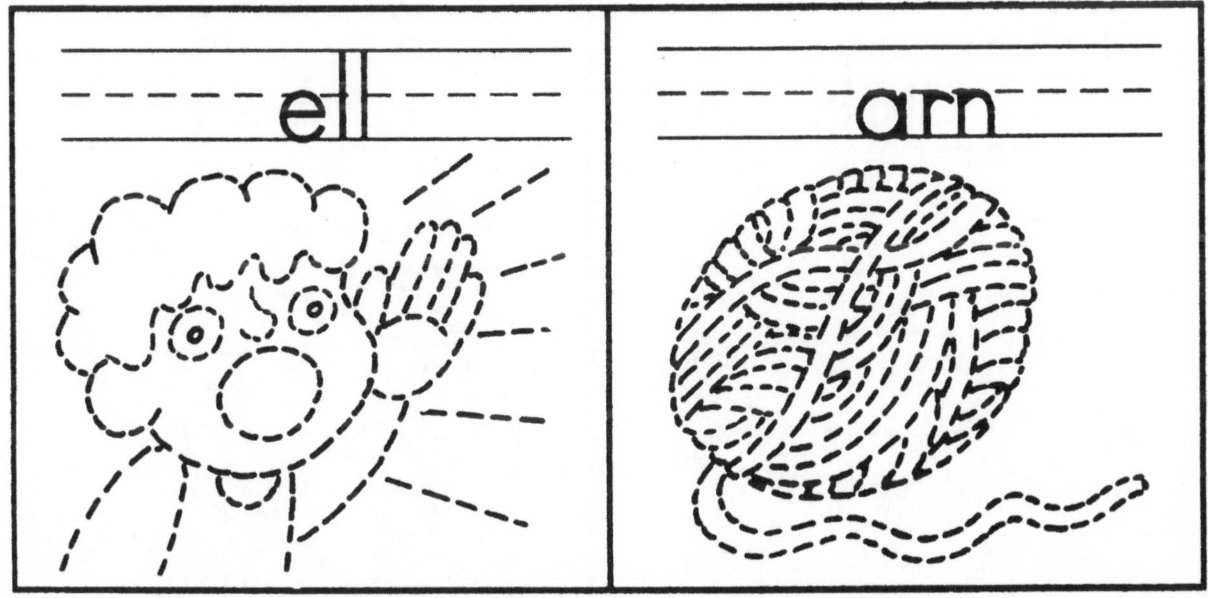


**Skills:** Recognition of the initial consonant "y"; Writing letters and words; Association between sounds, symbols, and words

# Phonics Skills I

Initial consonant: d

Print the letters and words.

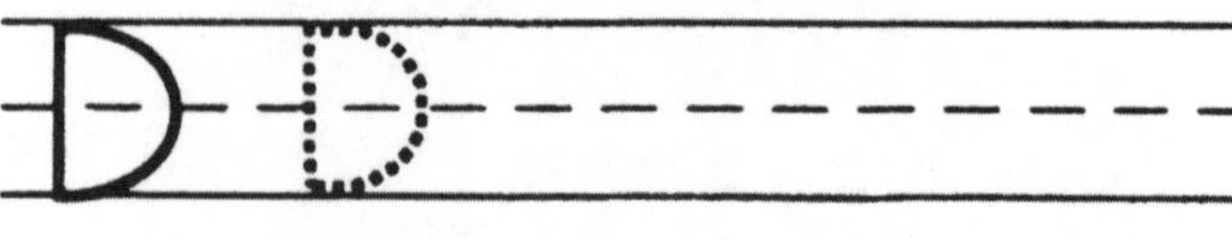


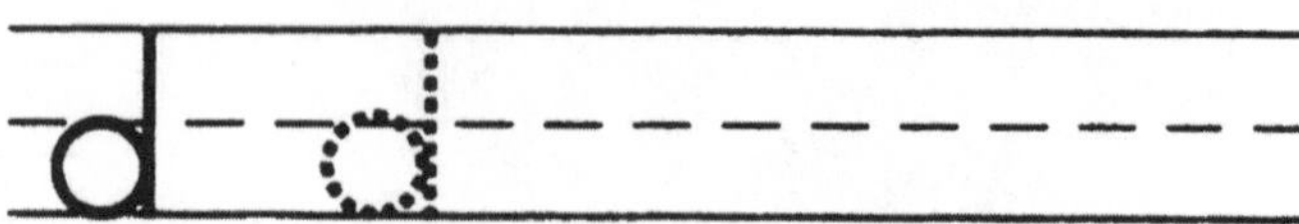


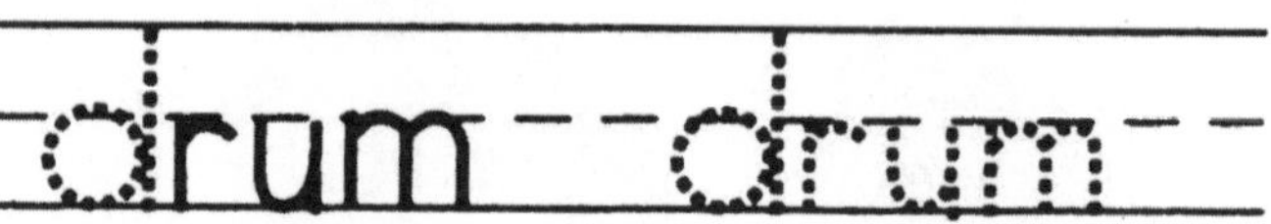


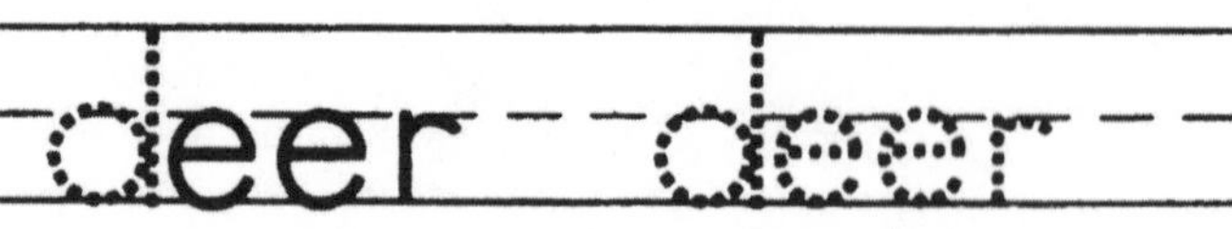


Finish the pictures. Finish the words.

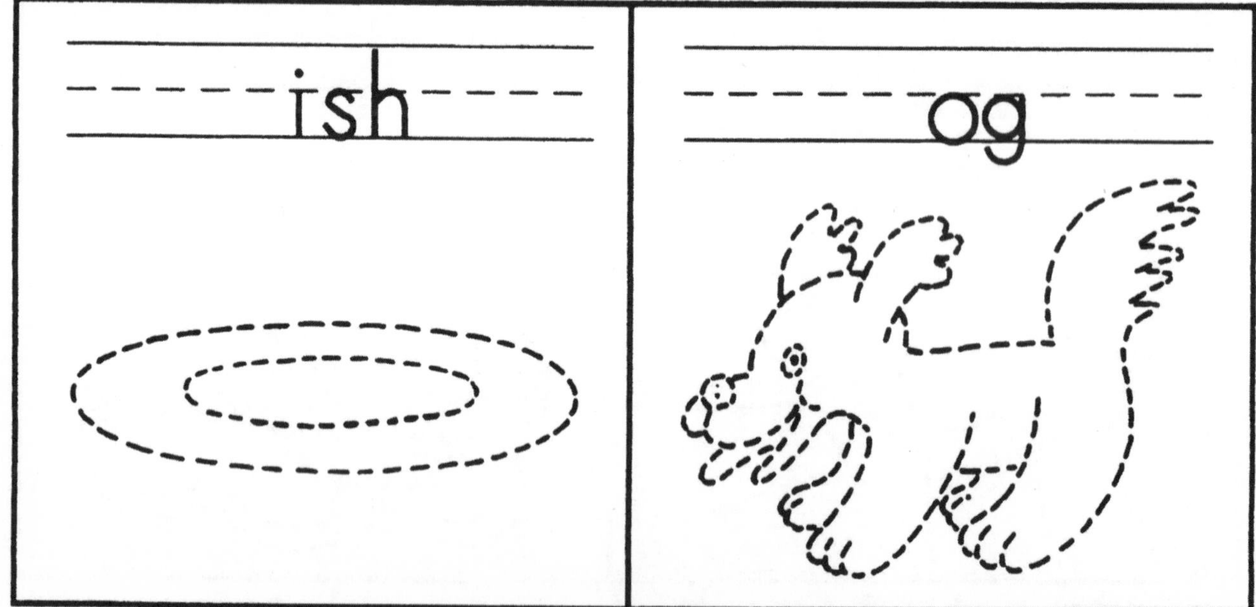


**Skills:** Recognition of the initial consonant "d"; Writing letters and words; Association between sounds, symbols, and words

# Phonics Skills I

Initial consonant: j

Print the letters and words.

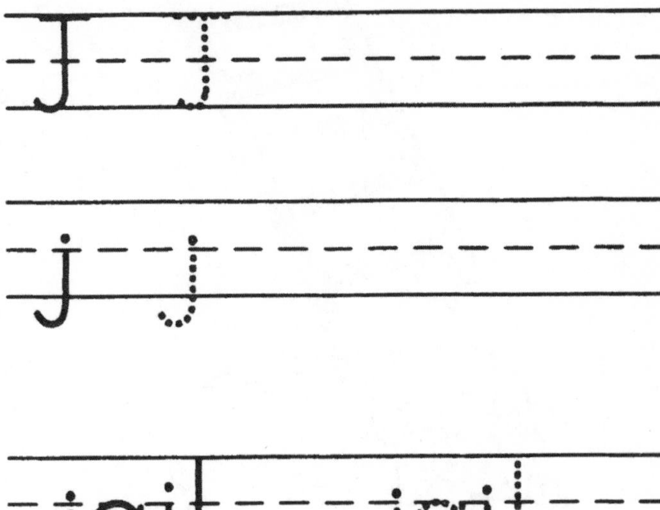


Finish the pictures. Finish the words.

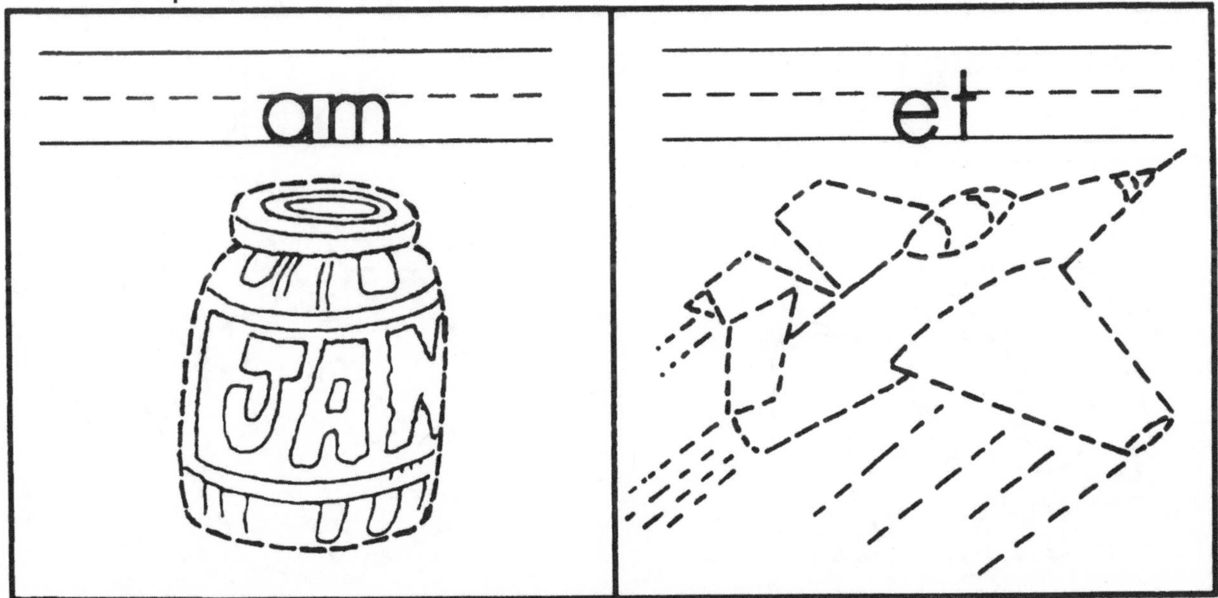


**Skills:** Recognition of the initial consonant "j"; Writing letters and words; Association between sounds, symbols, and words

# Phonics Skills I

Initial consonant: l

Print the letters and words.

L L

l l

lamb lamb

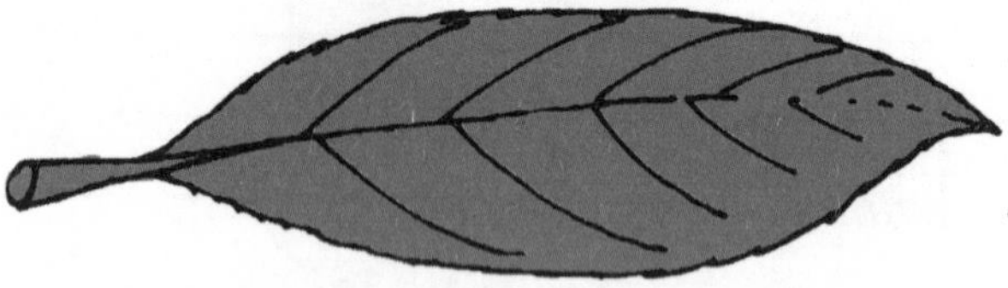

leaf leaf

Finish the pictures. Finish the words.

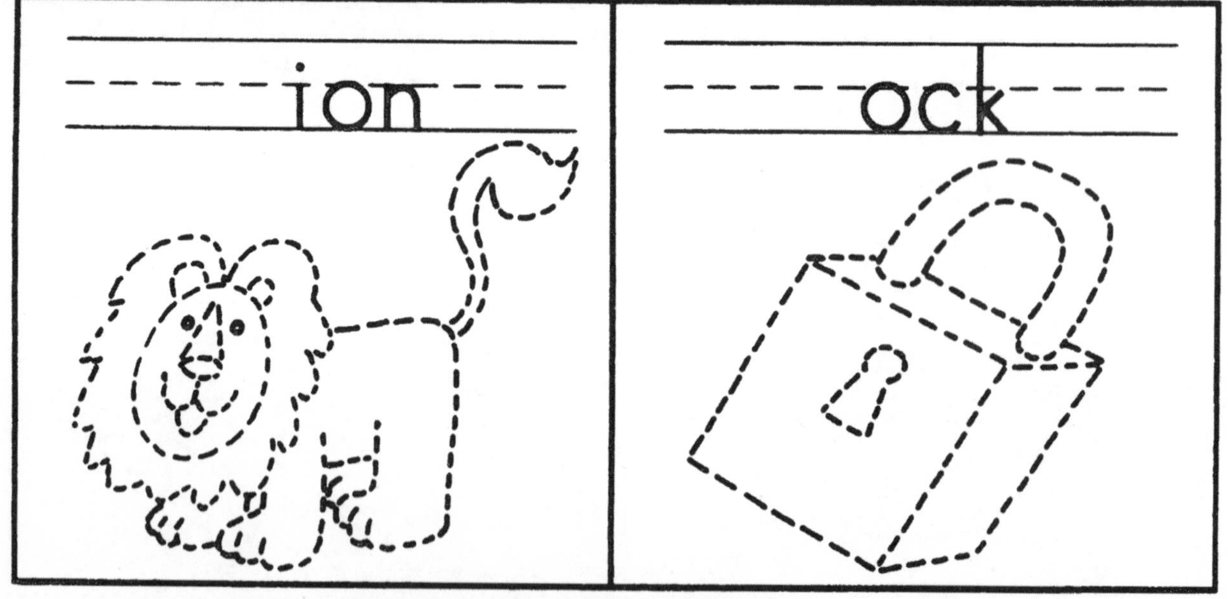


**Skills:** Recognition of the initial consonant "l"; Writing letters and words; Association between sounds, symbols, and words

# Phonics Skills I

Initial consonant: **w**

Print the letters and words.

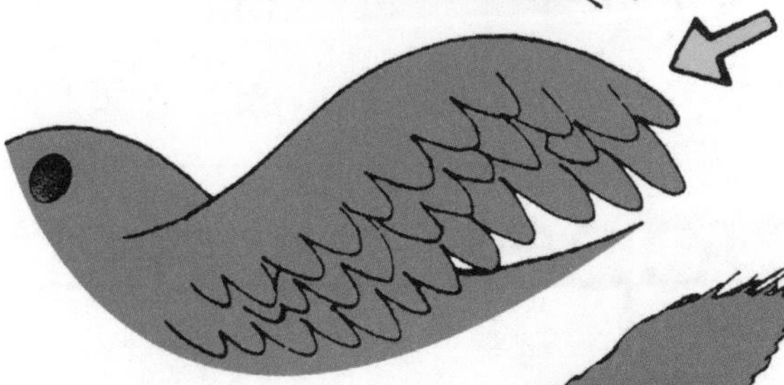

W W

w w

wing wing

wolf wolf

Finish the pictures. Finish the words.

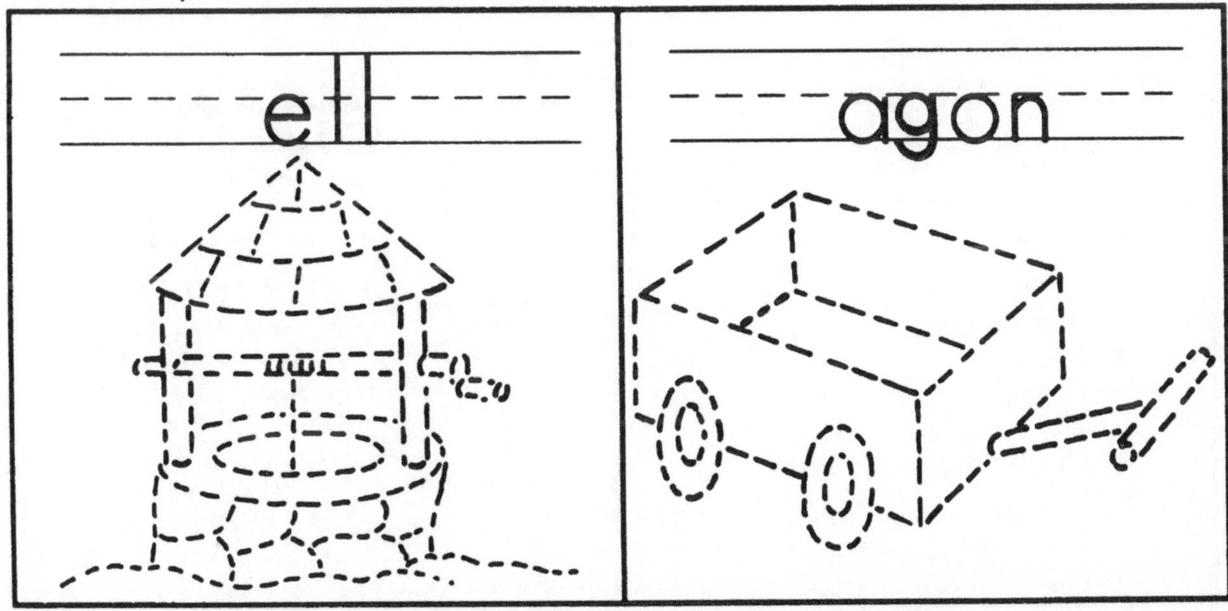


**Skills:** Recognition of the initial consonant "w"; Writing letters and words; Association between sounds, symbols, and words

# Phonics Skills I

Initial consonant: **z**

Print the letters and words.

Z Z

z z

zipper zipper

zoo zoo

Finish the pictures. Finish the words.

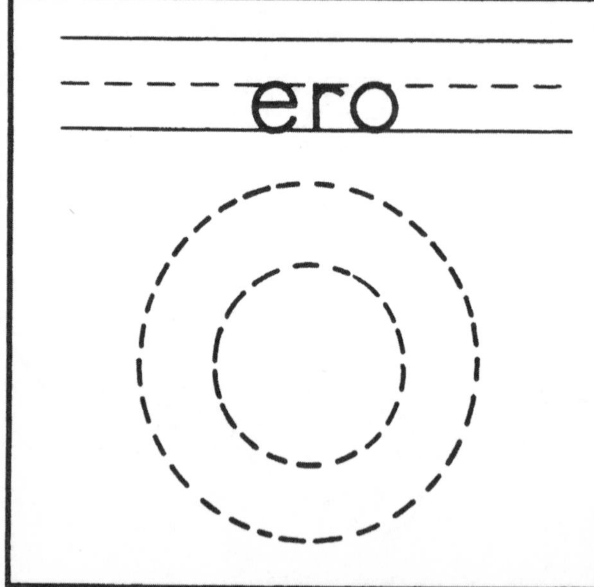

ero

ebra

**Skills:** Recognition of the initial consonant "z"; Writing letters and words; Association between sounds, symbols, and words

# Phonics Skills I

Initial consonant: **n**

Print the letters and words.

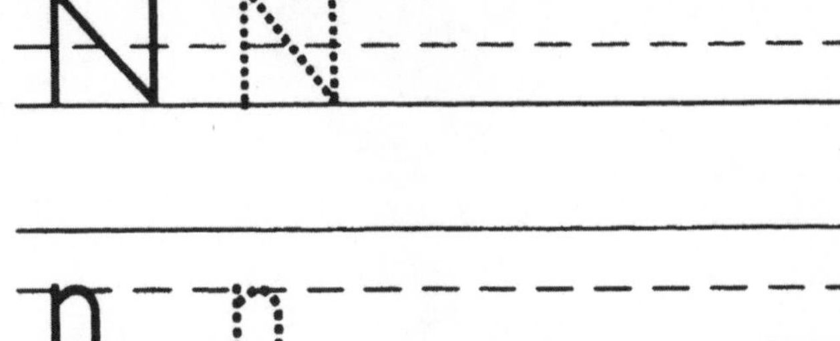

nail nail

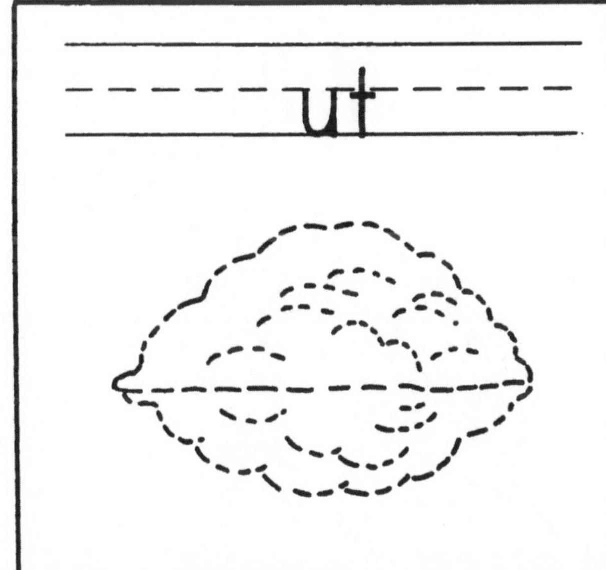

nest nest

Finish the pictures. Finish the words.

| ut | eedle |
|---|---|

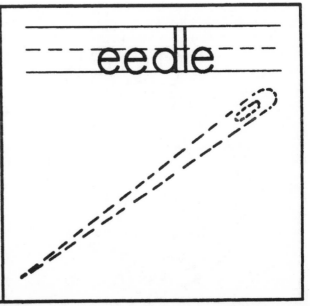

Skills: Recognition of the initial consonant "n"; Writing letters and words; Association between sounds, symbols, and words

# Phonics Skills I

Initial consonant: q

Print the letters and words.

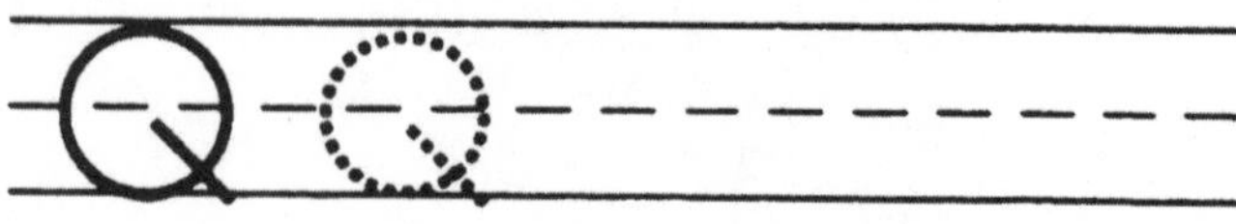


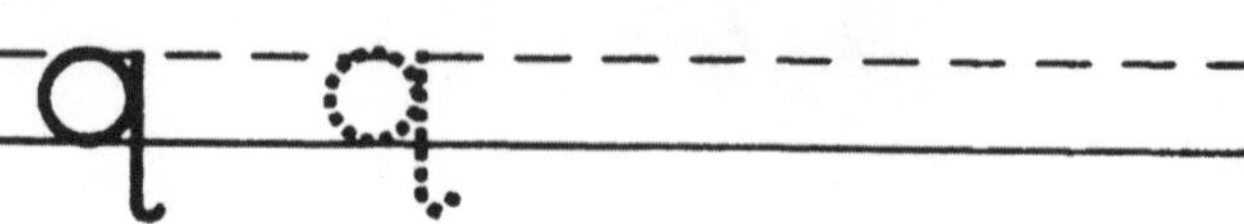


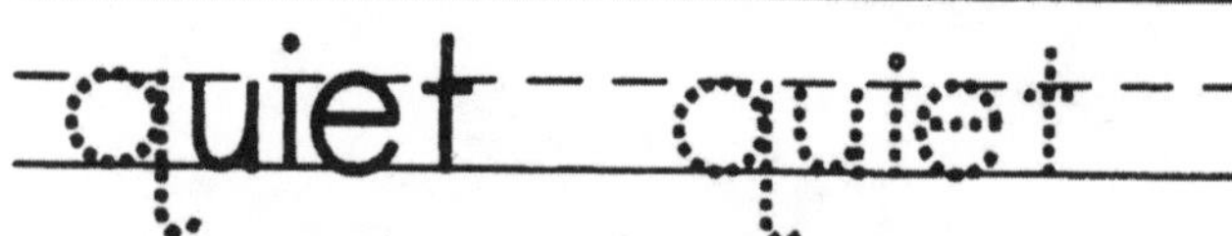


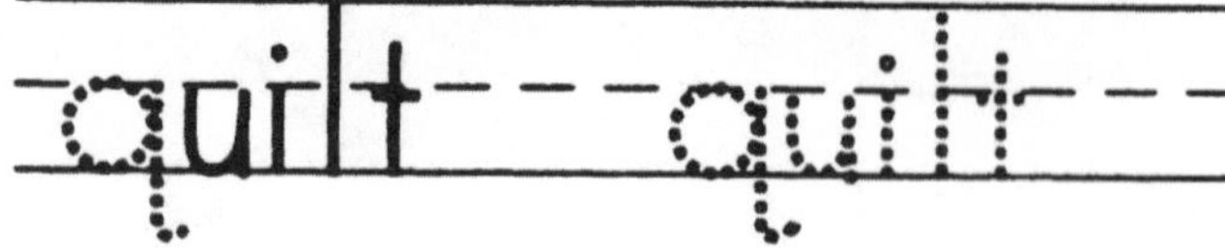


Finish the pictures. Finish the words.

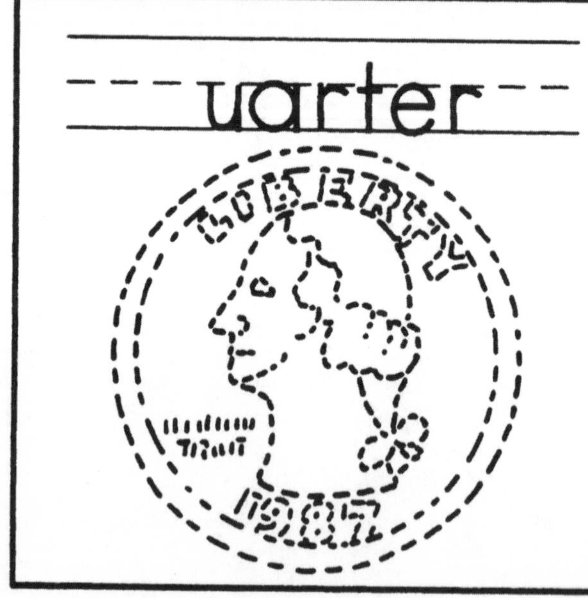


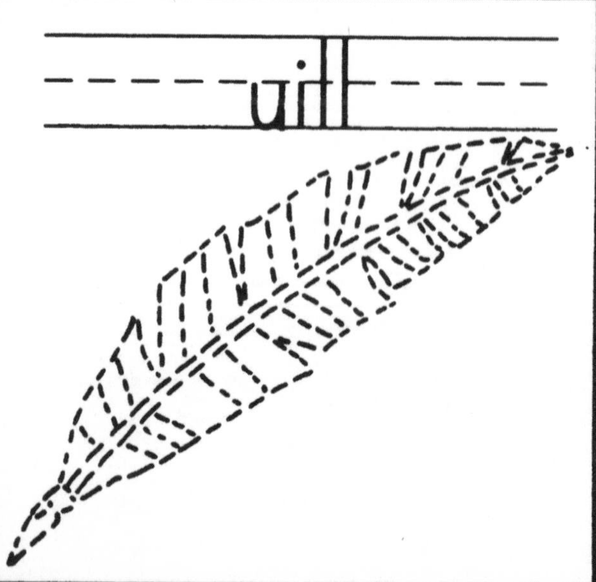


**Skills:** Recognition of the initial consonant "q"; Writing letters and words; Association between sounds, symbols, and words

# Phonics Skills I

Initial consonant: r

Print the letters and words.

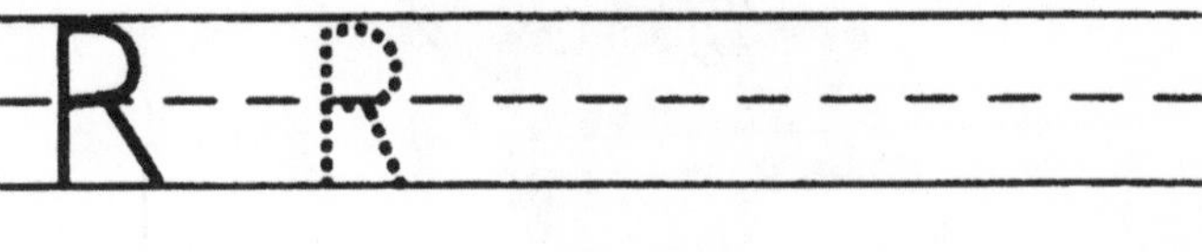


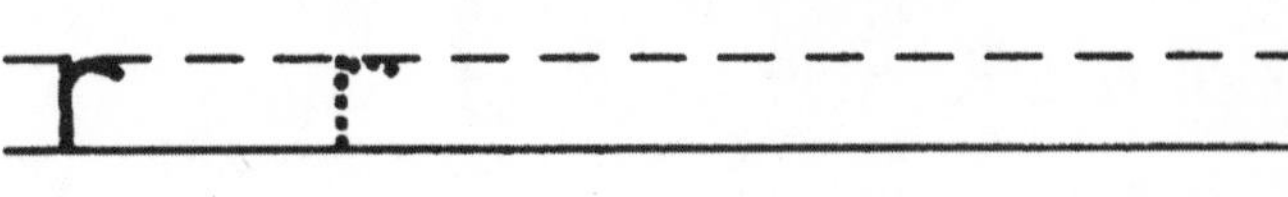


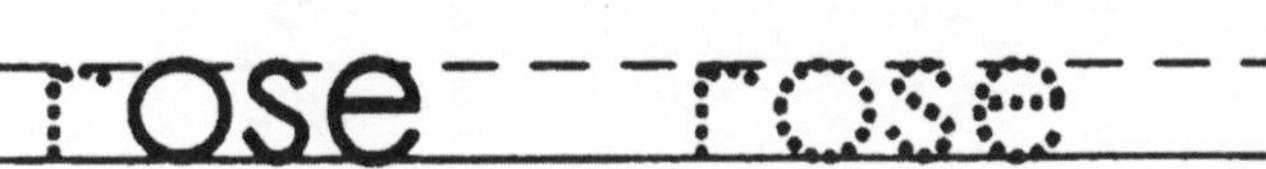


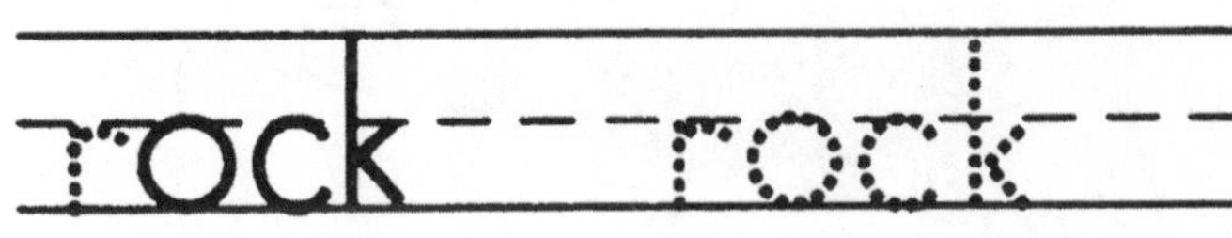


Finish the pictures. Finish the words.

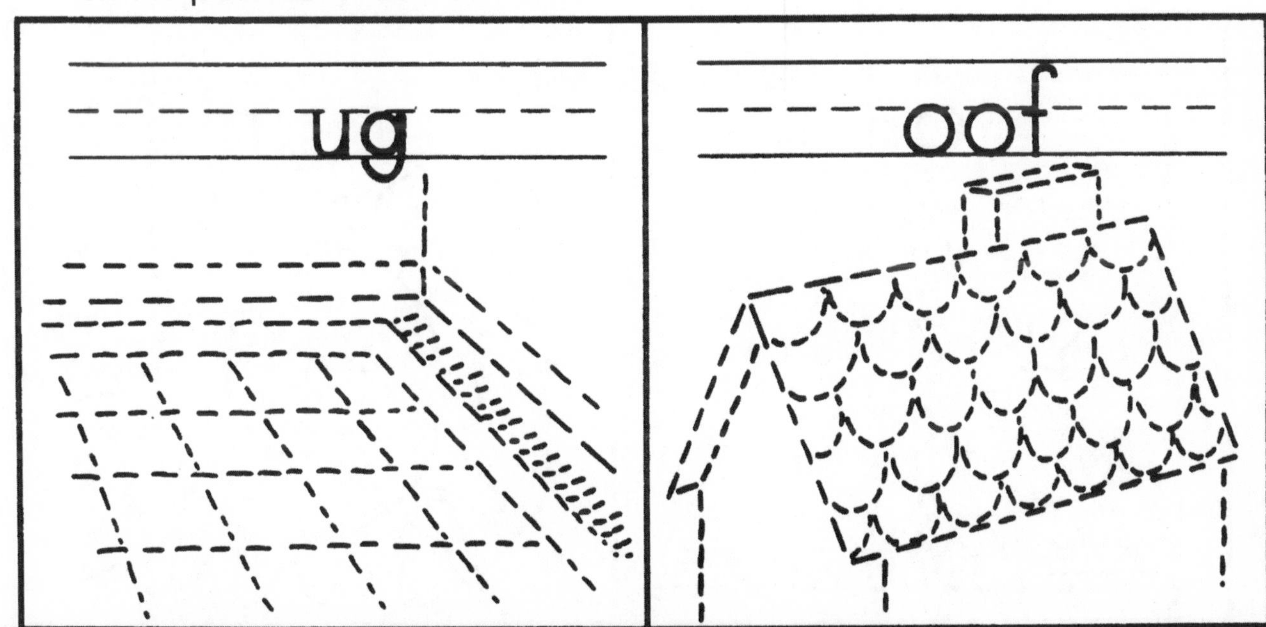


**Skills:** Recognition of the initial consonant "r"; Writing letters and words; Association between sounds, symbols, and words

# Phonics Skills I

Initial consonant: s

Print the letters and words.

S S

s s

soap soap

saw saw

Finish the pictures. Finish the words.

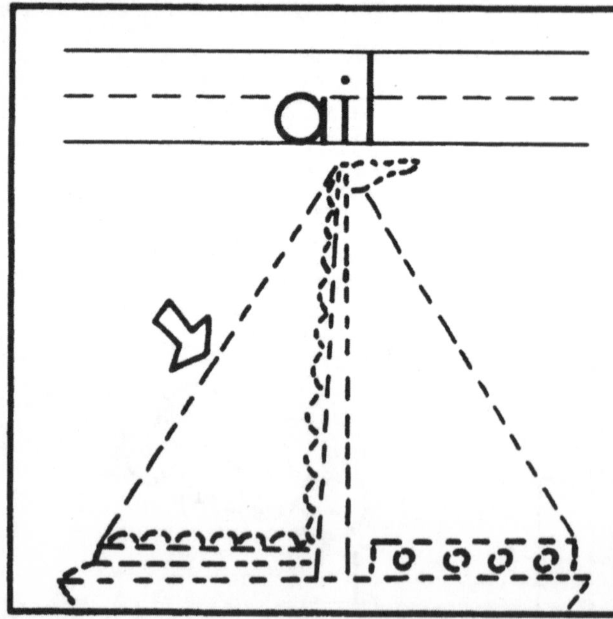

**Skills:** Recognition of the initial consonant "s"; Writing letters and words; Association between sounds, symbols, and words

# Phonics Skills I

Initial consonant: t

Print the letters and words.

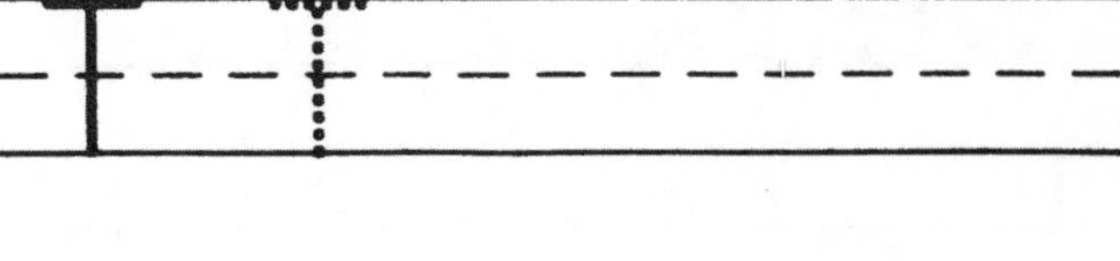


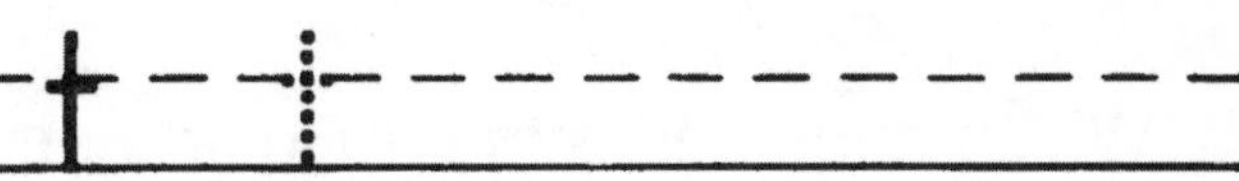


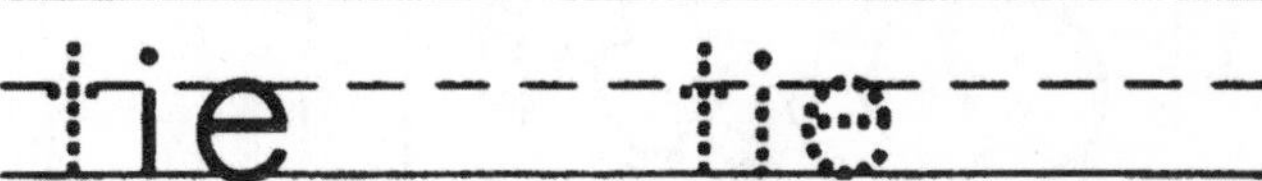


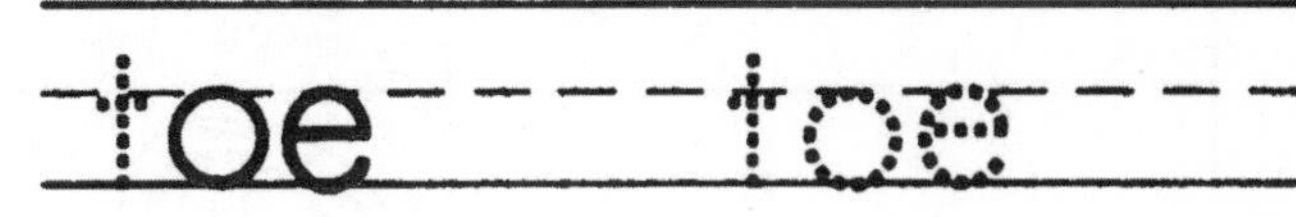


Finish the pictures. Finish the words.

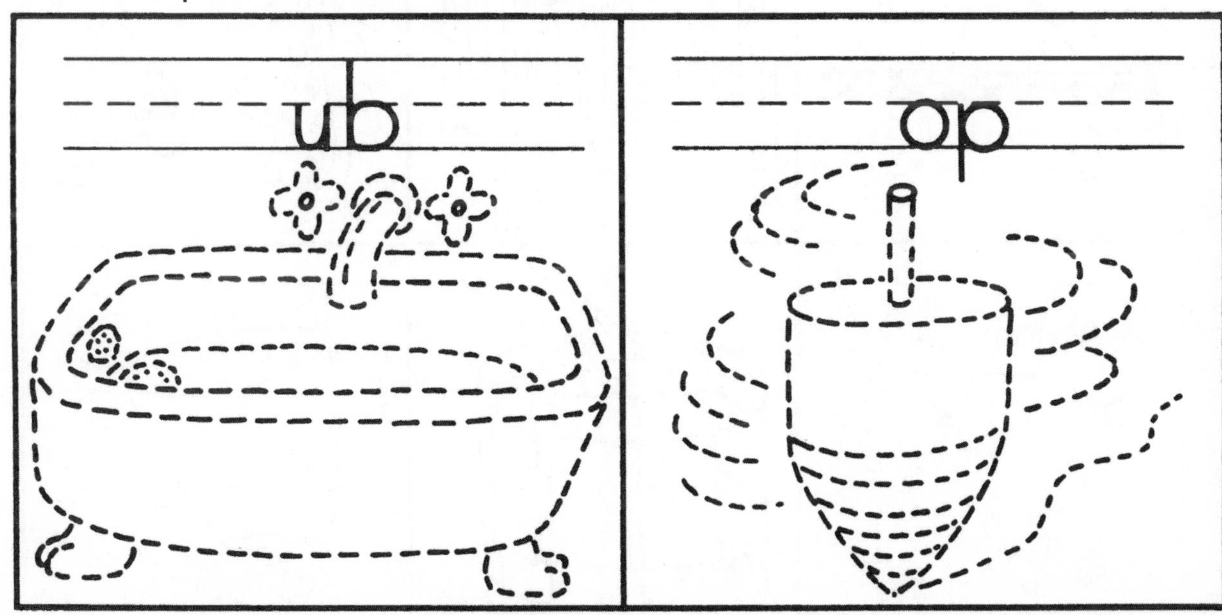


**Skills:** Recognition of the initial consonant "t"; Writing letters and words; Association between sounds, symbols, and words

# Phonics Skills I

Final consonant: b

web

b b

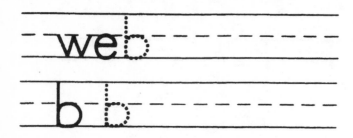

Which ones end with b? Color them red. Color the other pictures blue.

**Skills:** Recognition of the final consonant "b"; Auditory discrimination; Writing the letter "b"; Sound/symbol association

# Phonics Skills I

Final consonant: f

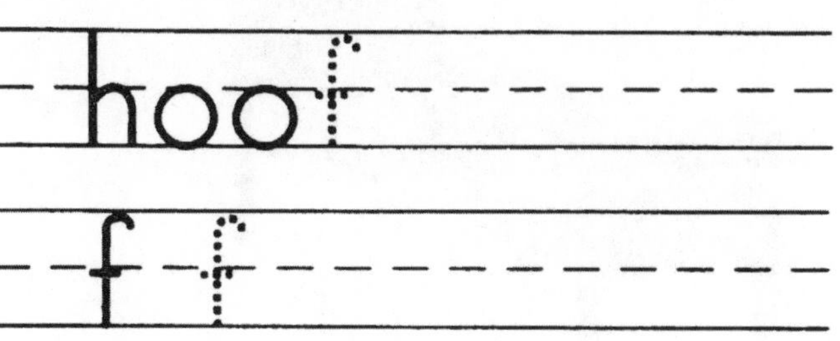

Which ones end with f? Color them red. Color the other pictures blue.

Skills: Recognition of the final consonant "f"; Auditory discrimination; Writing the letter "f"; Sound/symbol association

# Phonics Skills I

Final consonant: d

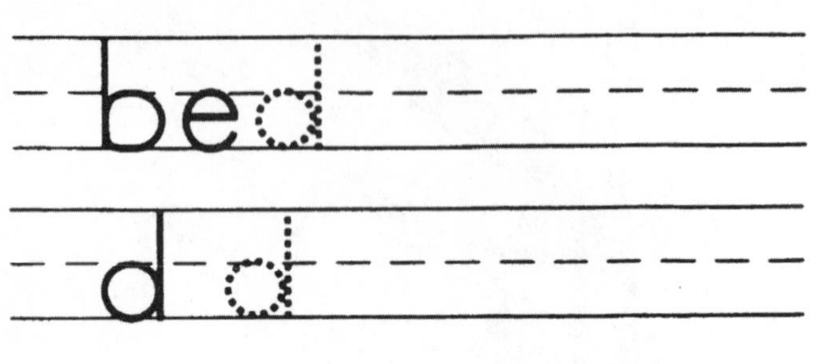


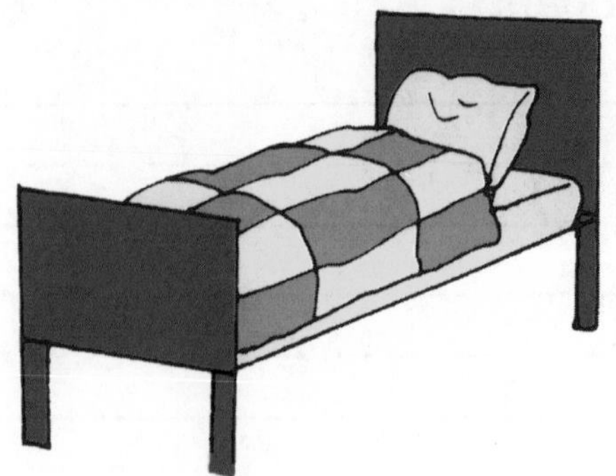

Which ones end with d? Color them purple. Color the other pictures orange.

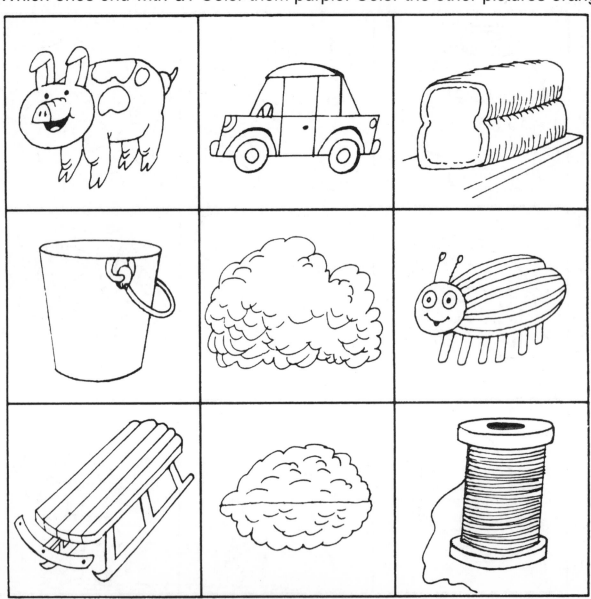

**Skills:** Recognition of the final consonant "d"; Auditory discrimination; Writing the letter "d"; Sound/symbol association

Final consonant: g

bug

g g

Which ones end with g? Color them brown. Color the other pictures blue.

Skills: Recognition of the final consonant "g"; Auditory discrimination; Writing the letter "g"; Sound/symbol association

# Phonics Skills I

Final consonant: k

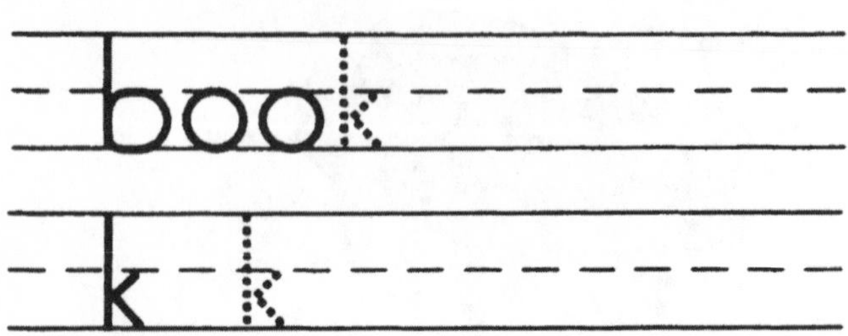

Which ones end with k? Color them red. Color the other pictures green.

Skills: Recognition of the final consonant "k"; Auditory discrimination; Writing the letter "k"; Sound/symbol association

# Phonics Skills I

Final consonant: **m**

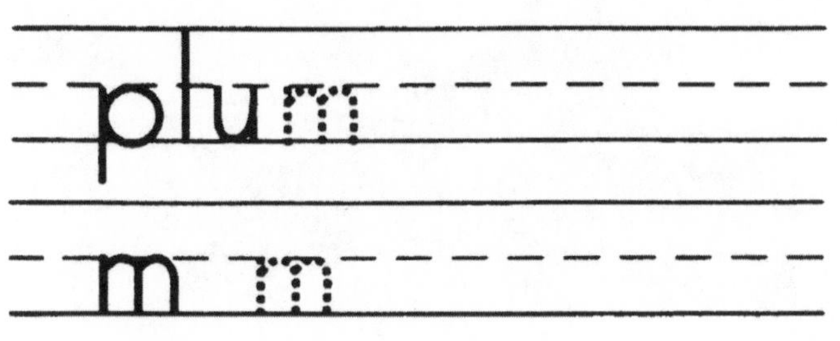

Which ones end with **m**? Color them green. Color the other pictures yellow.

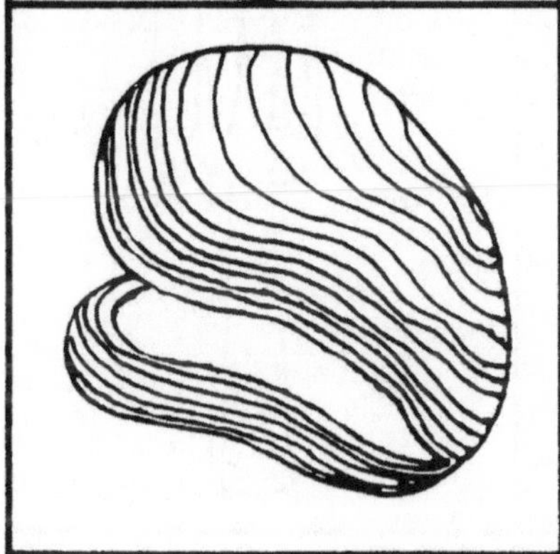

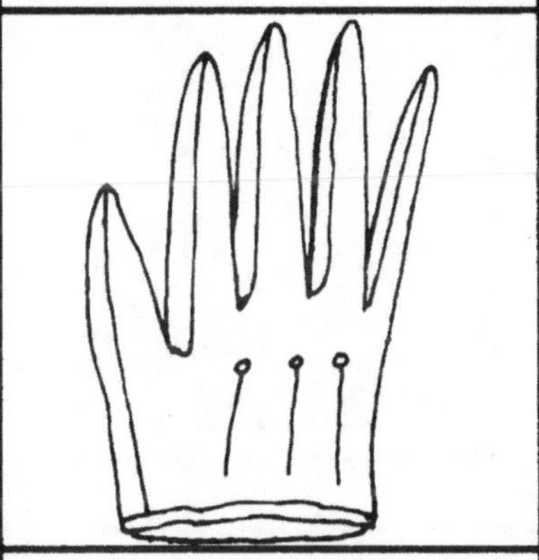

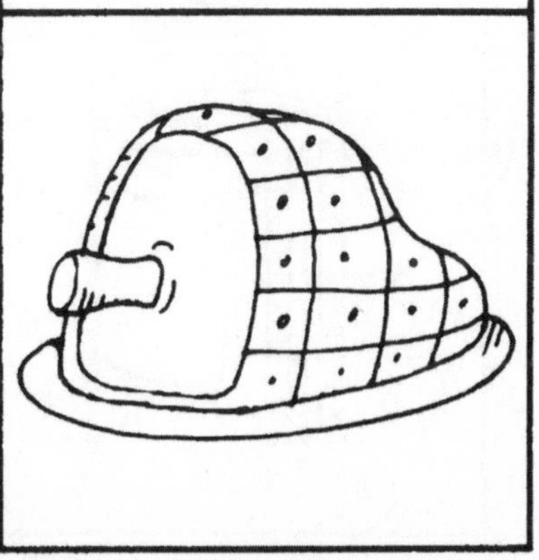

**Skills:** Recognition of the final consonant "m"; Auditory discrimination; Writing the letter "m"; Sound/symbol association

# Phonics Skills I

Final consonant: l

sea

l

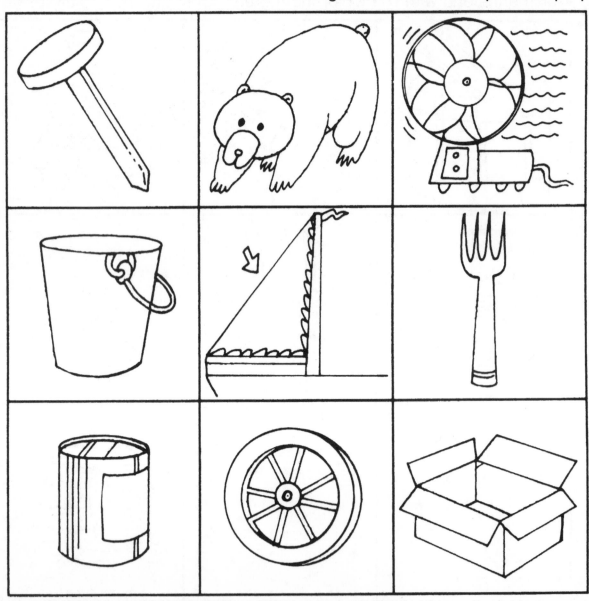

Which ones end with l? Color them orange. Color the other pictures purple.

**Skills:** Recognition of the final consonant "l"; Auditory discrimination; Writing the letter "l"; Sound/symbol association

# Phonics Skills I

Final consonant: **n**

moon

n n

Which ones end with **n**? Color them brown. Color the other pictures blue.

10

**Skills:** Recognition of the final consonant "n"; Auditory discrimination; Writing the letter "n"; Sound/symbol association

# Phonics Skills I

Final consonant: p

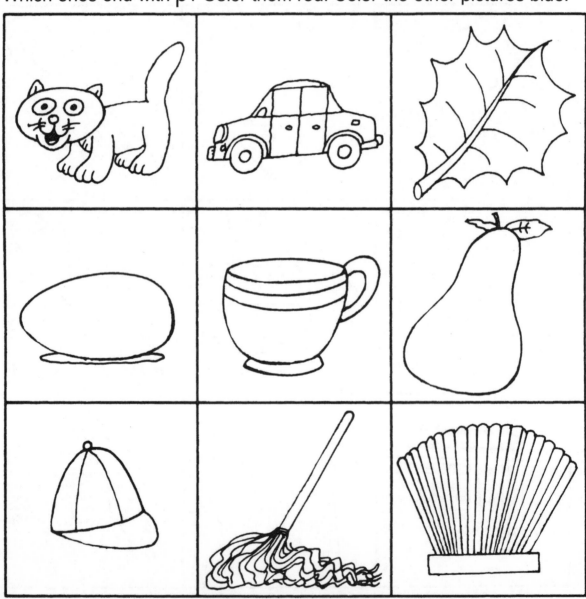


Which ones end with p? Color them red. Color the other pictures blue.

**Skills:** Recognition of the final consonant "p"; Auditory discrimination; Writing the letter "p"; Sound/symbol association

# Phonics Skills I

Final consonant: r

car

r r

Which ones end with r? Color them yellow. Color the other pictures green.

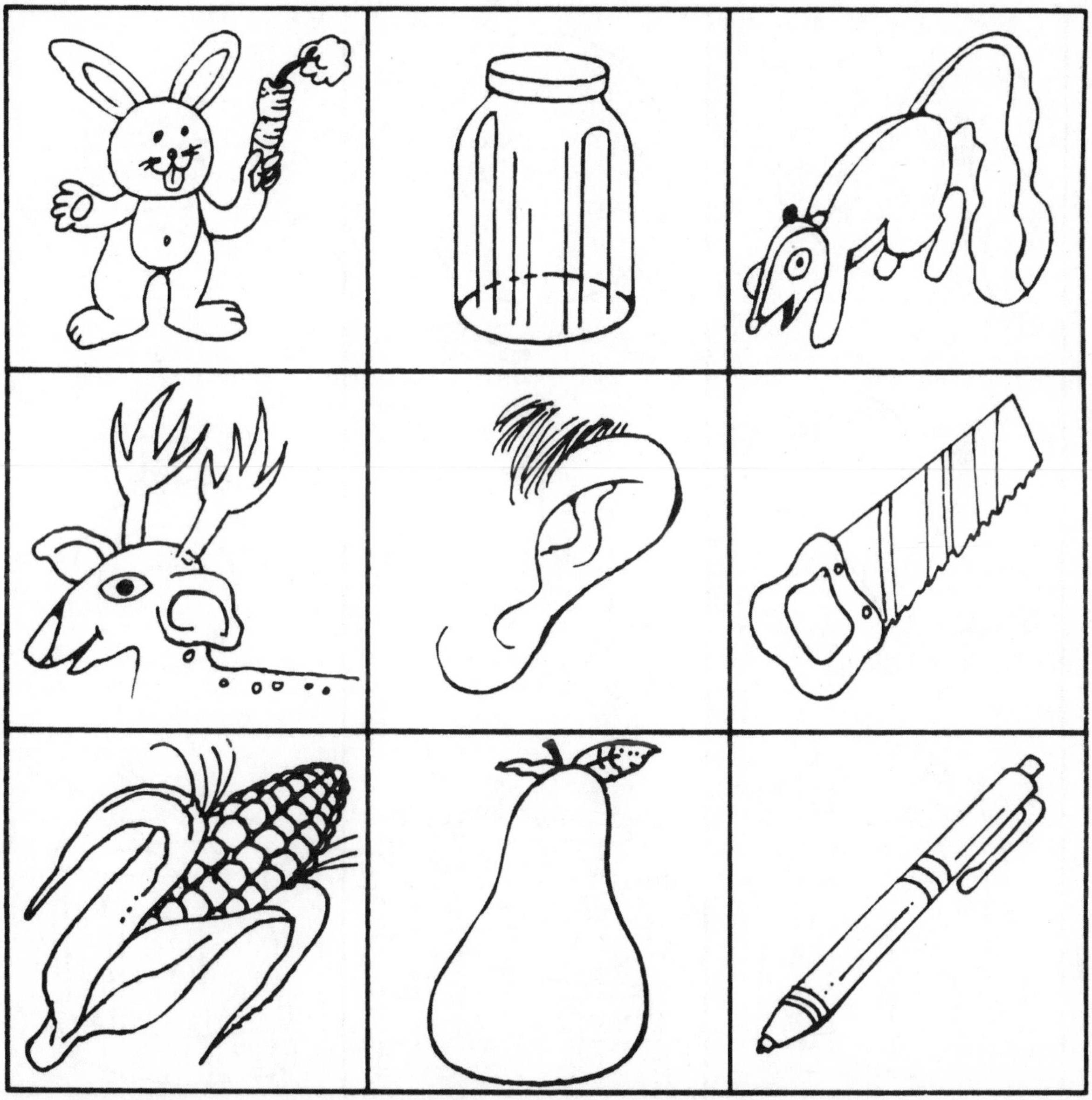

**Skills:** Recognition of the final consonant "r"; Auditory discrimination; Writing the letter "r"; Sound/symbol association

Final consonant: t

bat

t t

Which ones end with t? Color them purple. Color the other pictures orange.

**Skills:** Recognition of the final consonant "t"; Auditory discrimination; Writing the letter "t"; Sound/symbol association

# Good Job!

Give
yourself
a star!

# Phonics Skills II

# Phonics Skills II

Short vowel : a

Print the letters and words.

Finish the pictures. Finish the words.

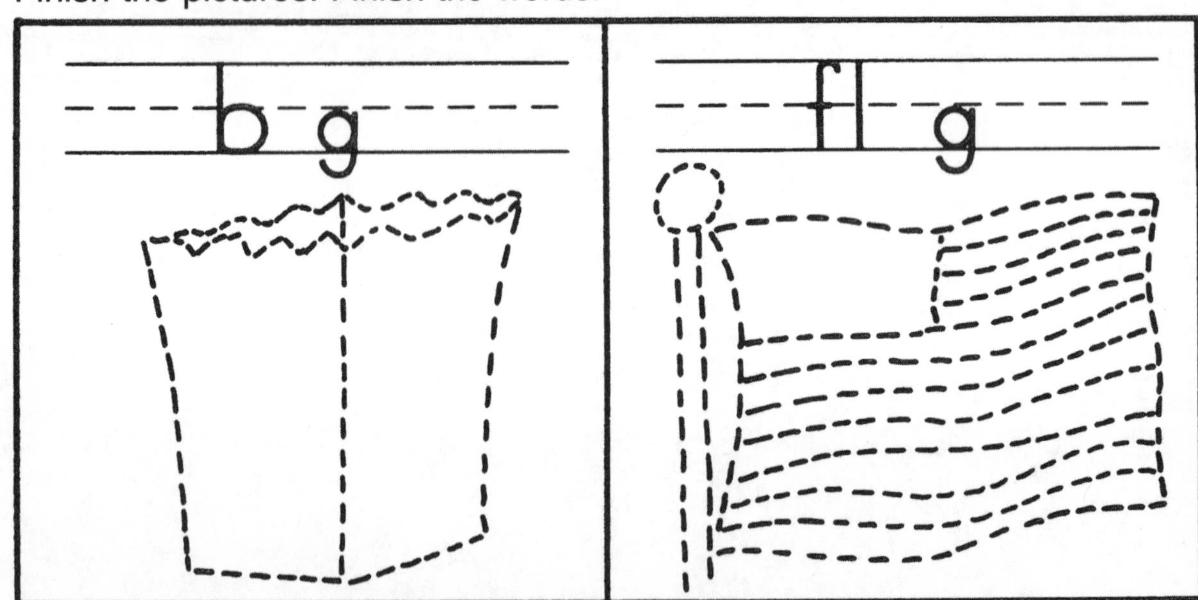


**Skills:** Recognition of the short vowel "a"; Writing letters and words; Association between sounds, symbols, and words

# Phonics Skills II

Short vowel : e

Print the letters and words.

Finish the pictures. Finish the words.

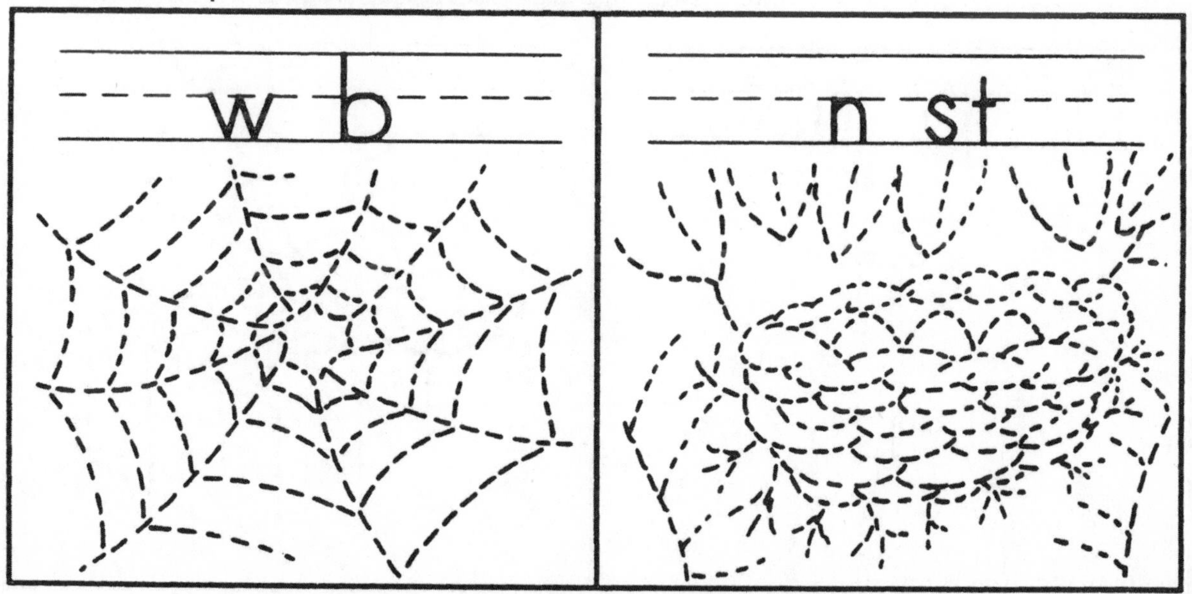


Skills: Recognition of the short vowel "e"; Writing letters and words; Association between sounds, symbols, and words

# Phonics Skills II

Short vowel : i

Print the letters and words.

Finish the pictures. Finish the words.

**Skills:** Recognition of the short vowel "i"; Writing letters and words; Association between sounds, symbols, and words

# Phonics Skills II

Short vowel : o

Print the letters and words.

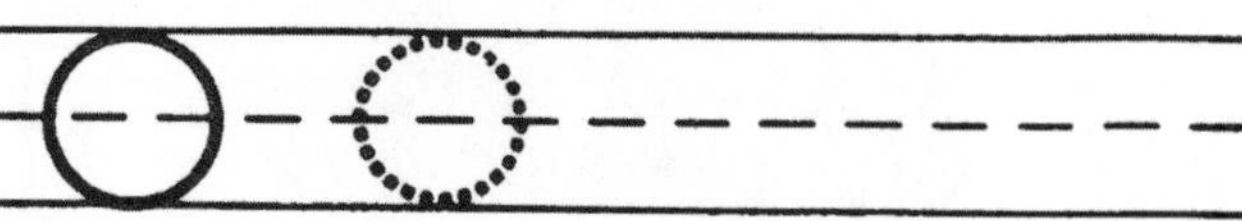


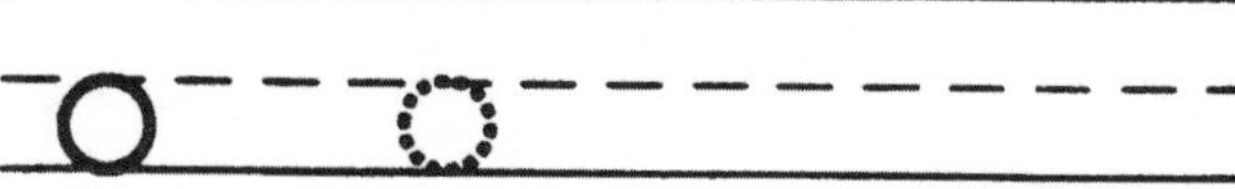


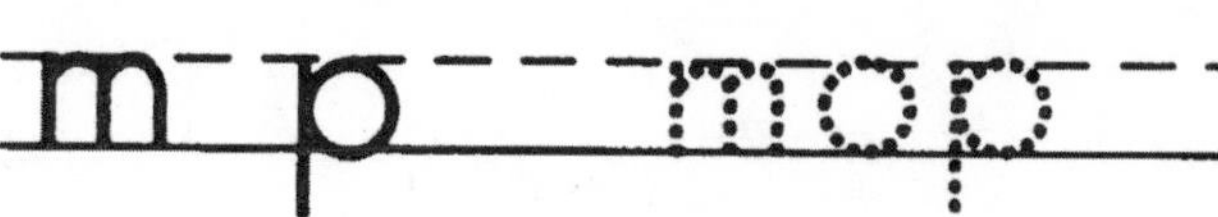


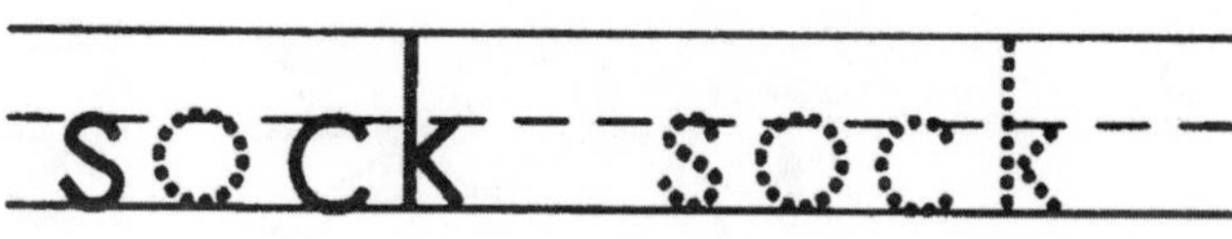


Finish the pictures. Finish the words.

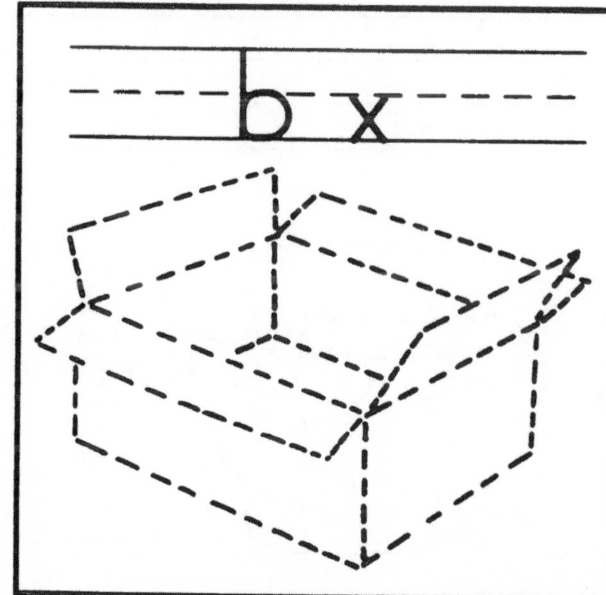


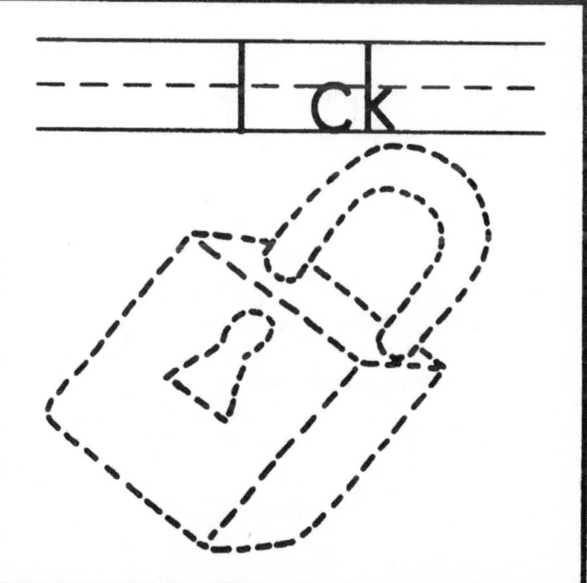


**Skills:** Recognition of the short vowel "o"; Writing letters and words; Association between sounds, symbols, and words

Short vowel : u

Print the letters and words.

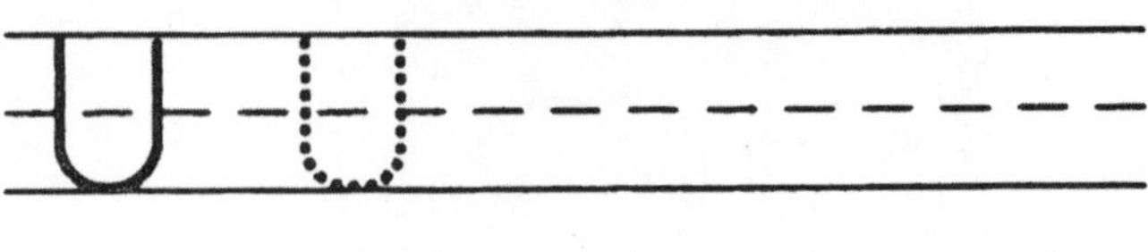


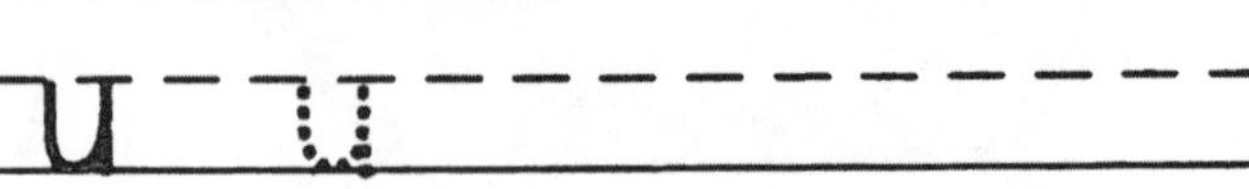


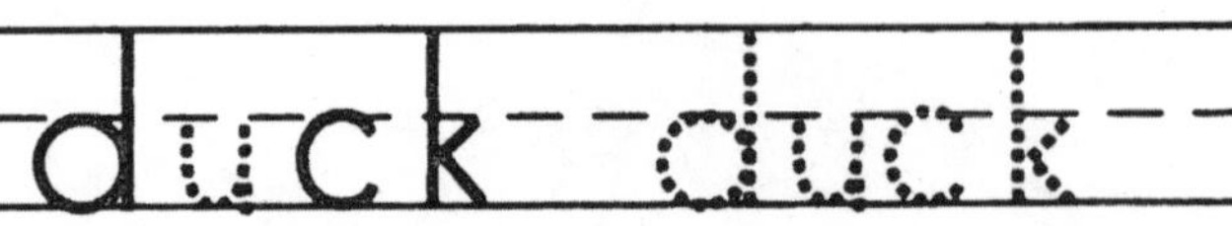


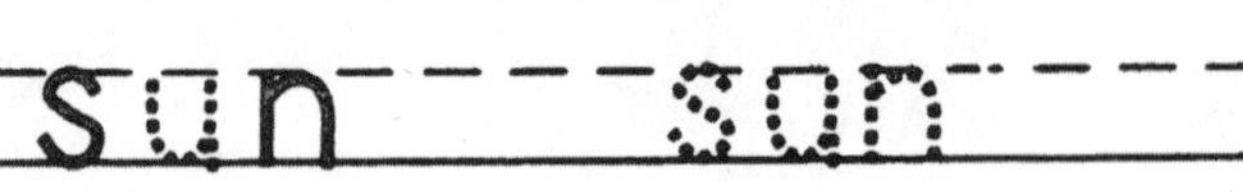


Finish the pictures. Finish the words.

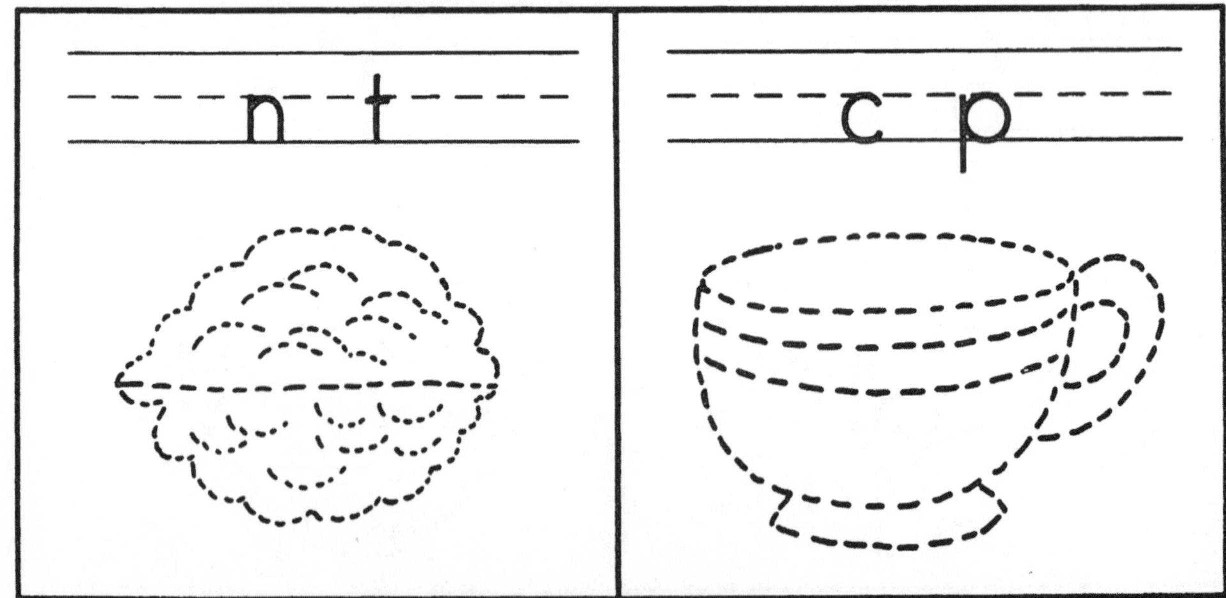


**Skills:** Recognition of the short vowel "u"; Writing letters and words; Association between sounds, symbols, and words

# Phonics Skills II

Long vowel : $\bar{a}$

Print the letters and words.

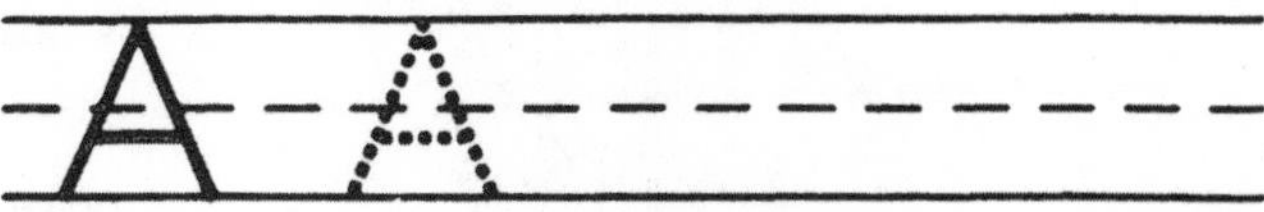

A A

a a

vase vase

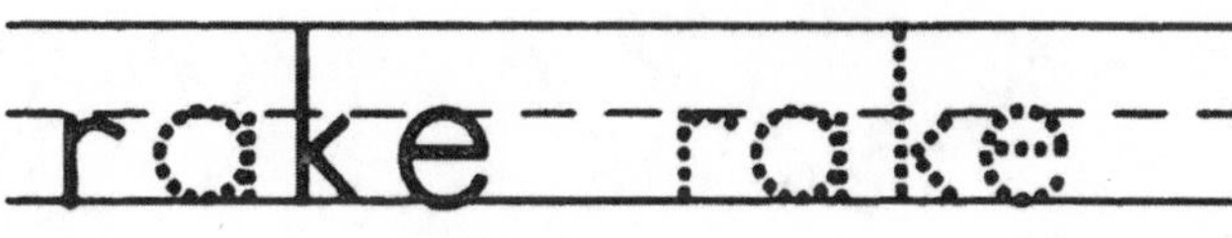

rake rake

Finish the pictures. Finish the words.

sn ke

c ne

Skills: Recognition of the long vowel "a"; Writing letters and words; Association between sounds, symbols, and words

## Phonics Skills II

Long vowel : $\bar{e}$

Print the letters and words.

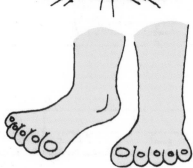

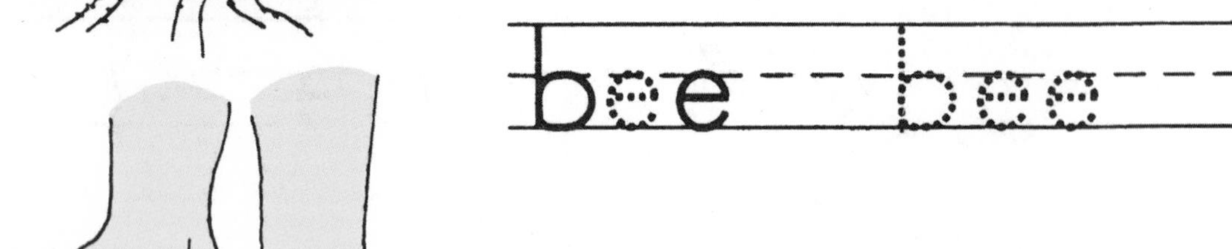


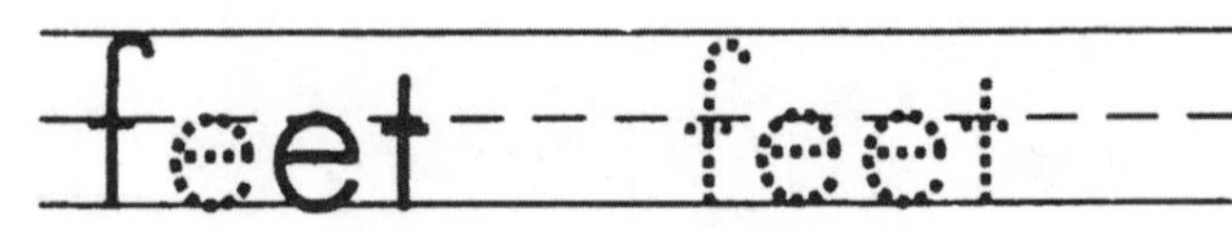


Finish the pictures. Finish the words.

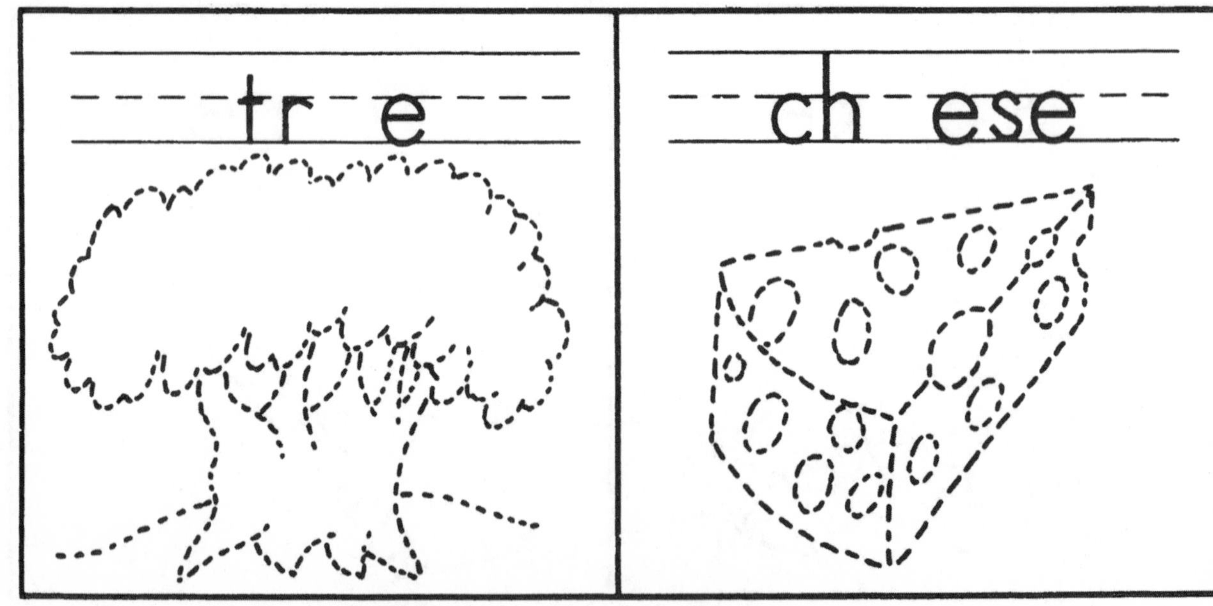


**Skills:** Recognition of the long vowel "e"; Writing letters and words; Association between sounds, symbols, and words

# Phonics Skills II

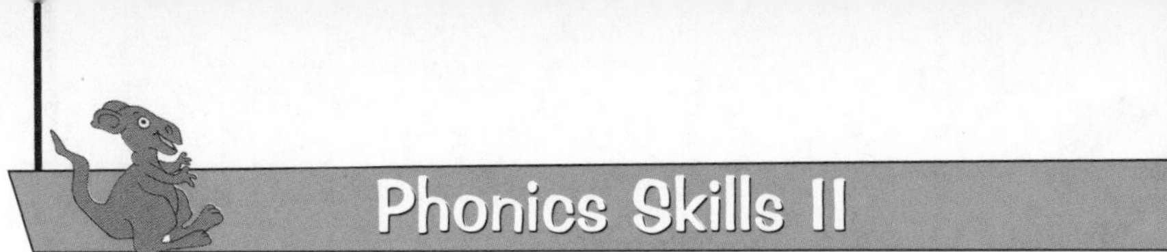

Long vowel : ī

Print the letters and words.

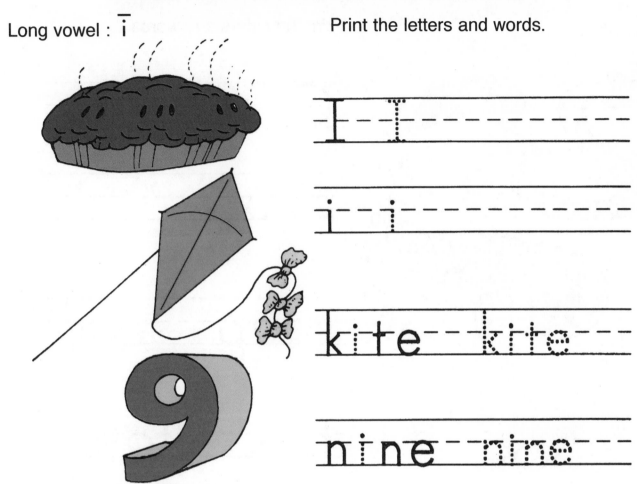

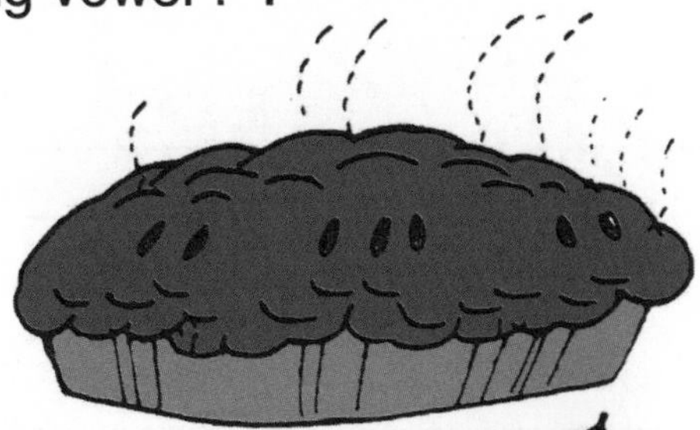

I I

i i

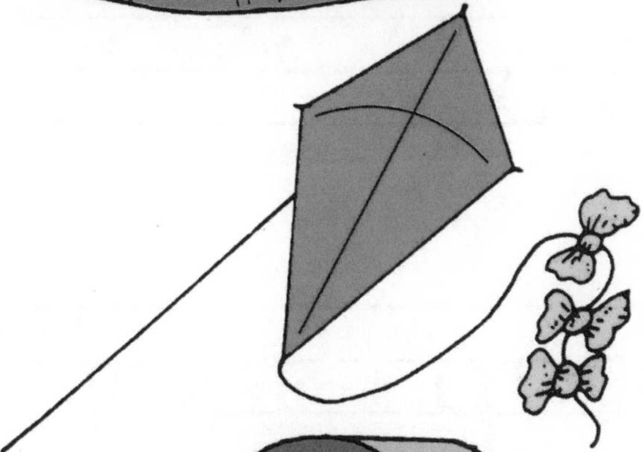

kite kite

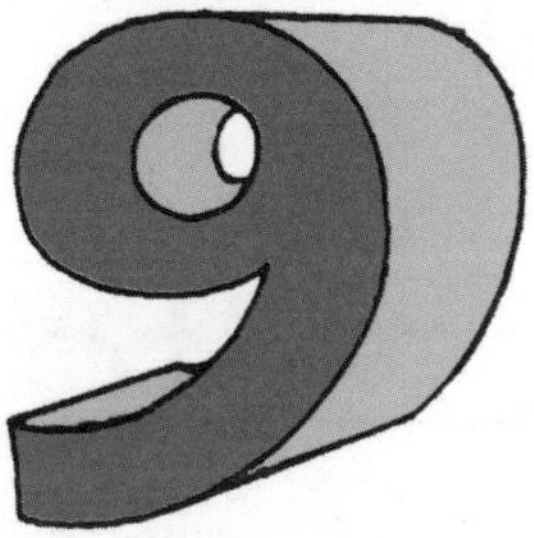

nine nine

Finish the pictures. Finish the words.

| t e | h ve |
|---|---|
|  |  |

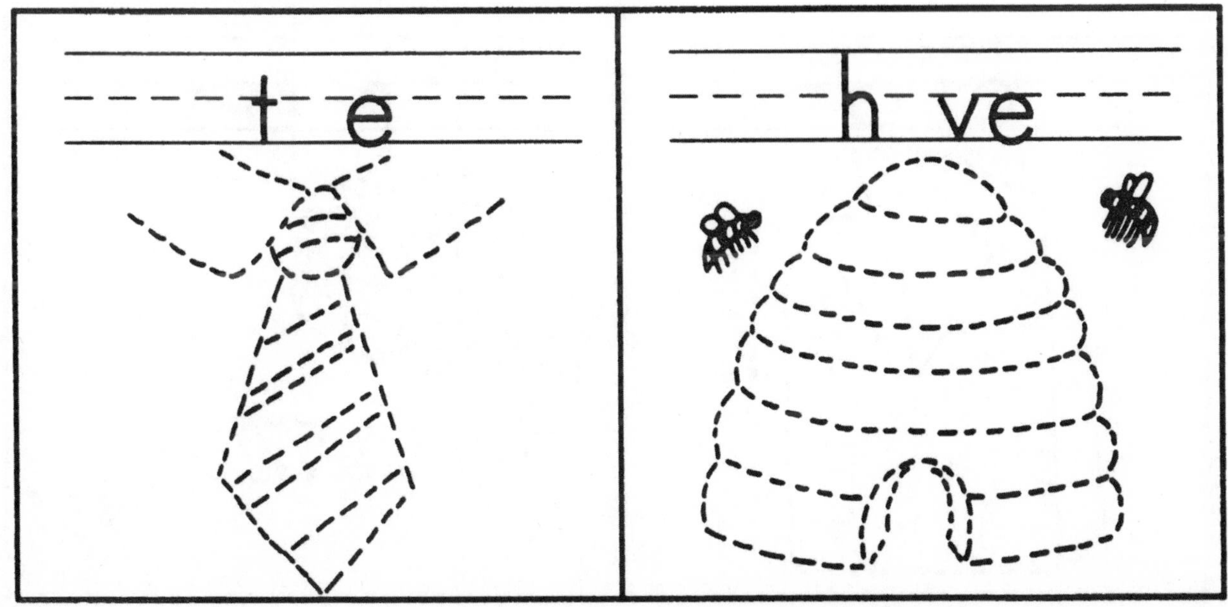

**Skills:** Recognition of the long vowel "i"; Writing letters and words; Association between sounds, symbols, and words

# Phonics Skills II

Long vowel : $\bar{o}$

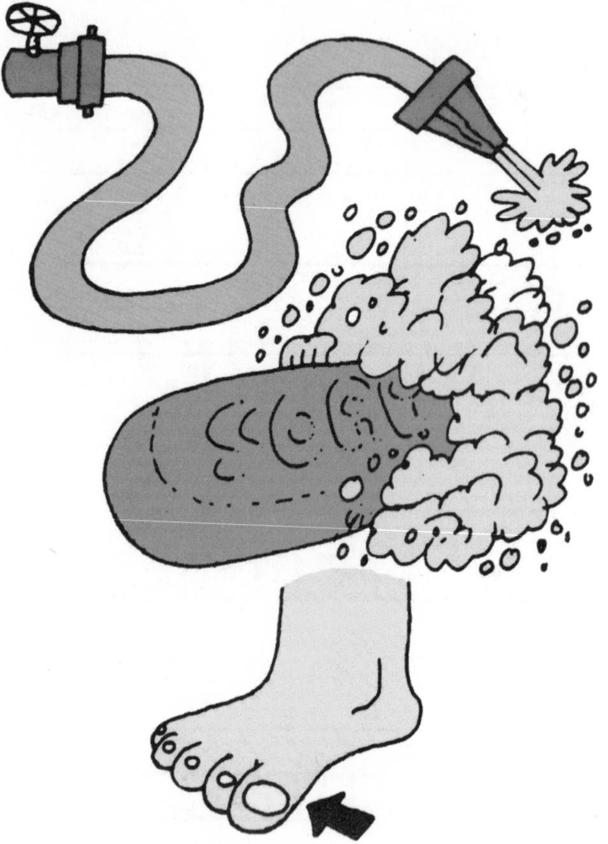

Print the letters and words.

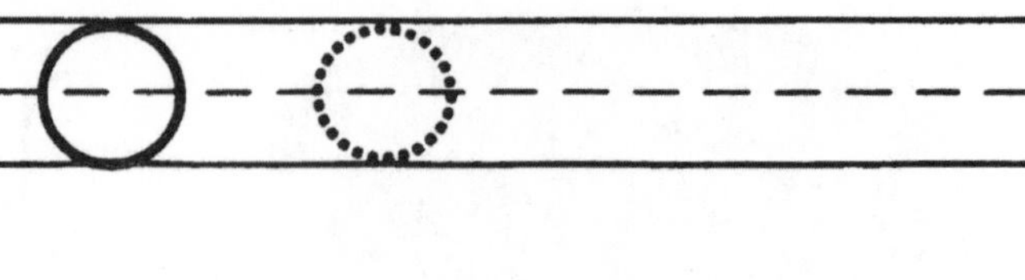

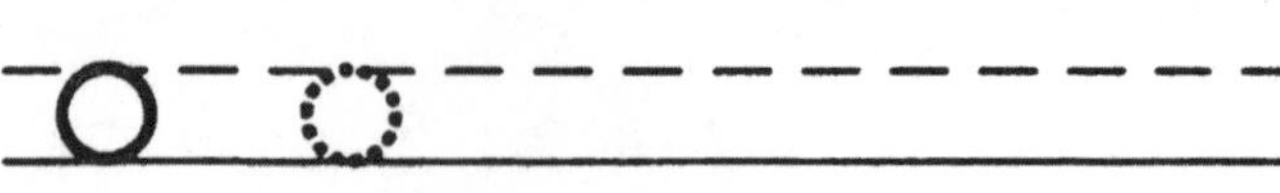

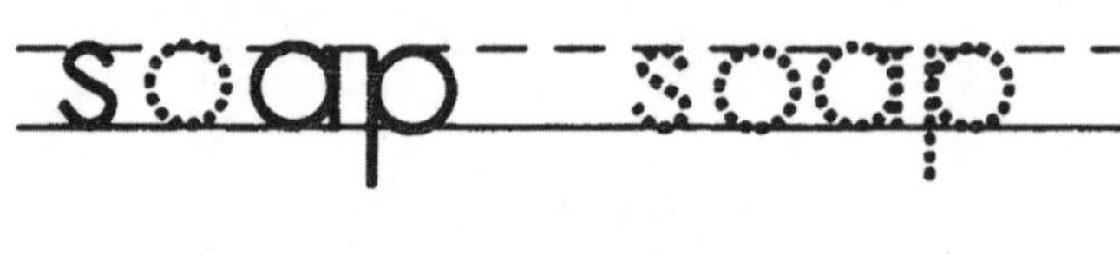


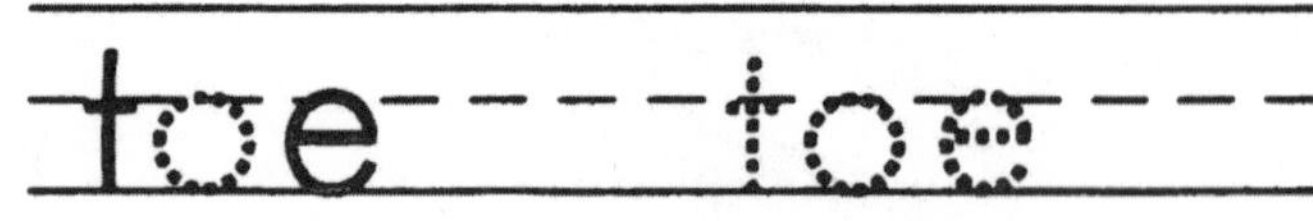


Finish the picture. Finish the word.

c at

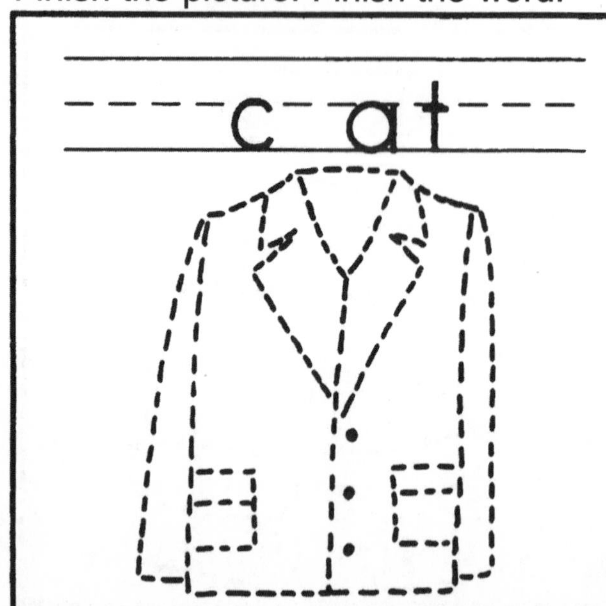

r pe

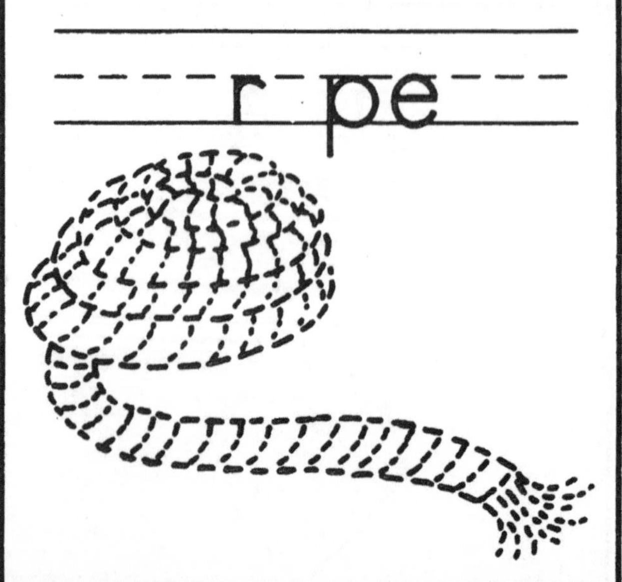

**Skills:** Recognition of the long vowel "o"; Writing letters and words; Association between sounds, symbols, and words

# Phonics Skills II

Long vowel : $\bar{u}$

Print the letters and words.

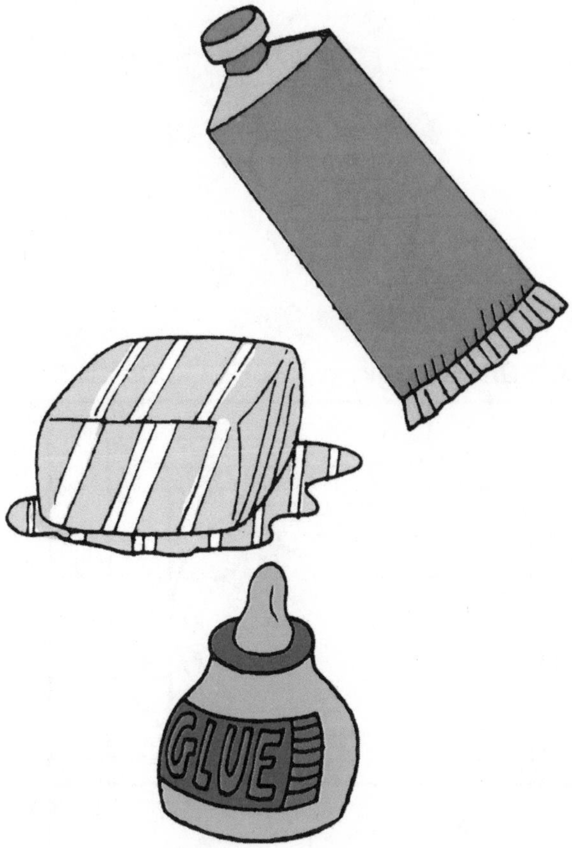

U U

u u

icecube icecube

glue glue

Finish the picture. Finish the word.

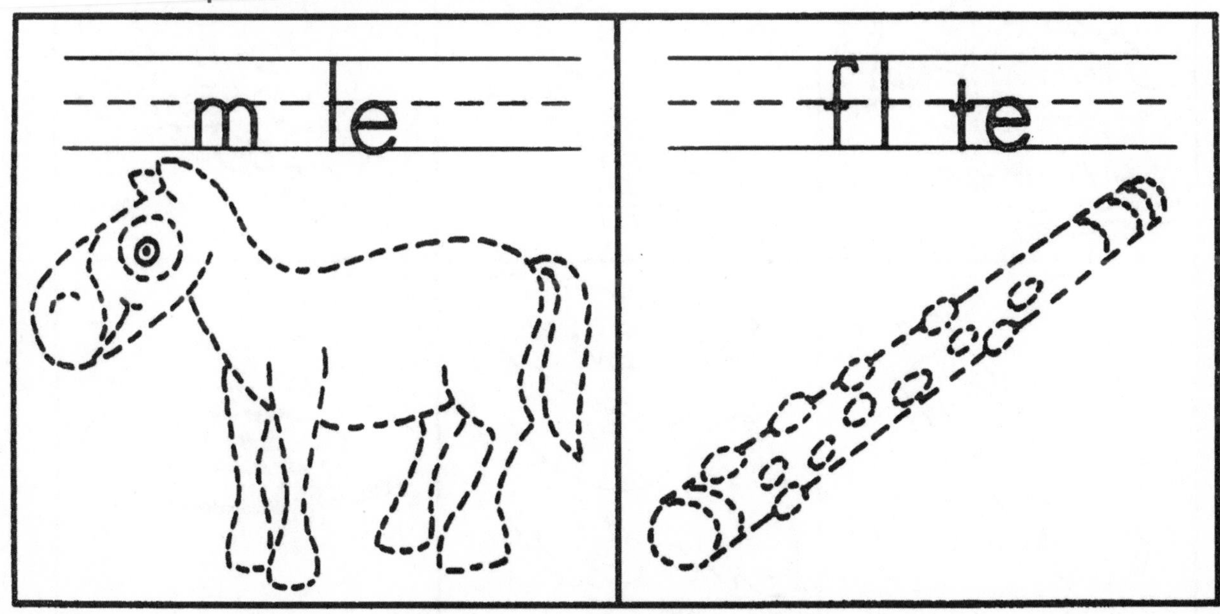


Skills: Recognition of the long vowel "u"; Writing letters and words; Association between sounds, symbols, and words

# Phonics Skills II

Initial consonant blends: **cl, cr**

cl

cr

Which ones begin with **cl**? Color them red. Which ones begin with **cr**? Color them blue.

**Skills:** Understanding that some consonants can be blended together; Sound/symbol association

Initial consonant blends: **bl, br**

bl

br

Which ones begin with **bl**? Color them red. Which ones begin with **br**? Color them blue.

**Skills:** Understanding that some consonants can be blended together; Sound/symbol association

# Phonics Skills II

Initial consonant blends: **dr, tr**

Which ones begin with **dr**? Color them red. Which ones begin with **tr**? Color them blue.

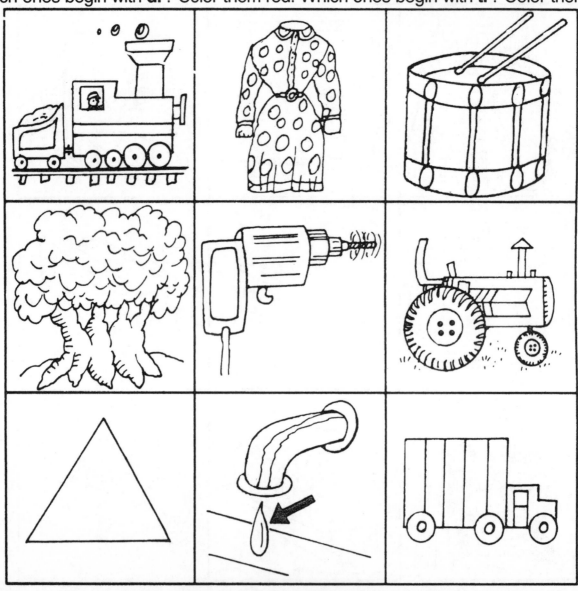

**Skills:** Understanding that some consonants can be blended together; Sound/symbol association

# Phonics Skills II

Initial consonant blends: **sk, sl**

sk

sl

Which ones begin with **sk**? Color them red. Which ones begin with **sl**? Color them blue.

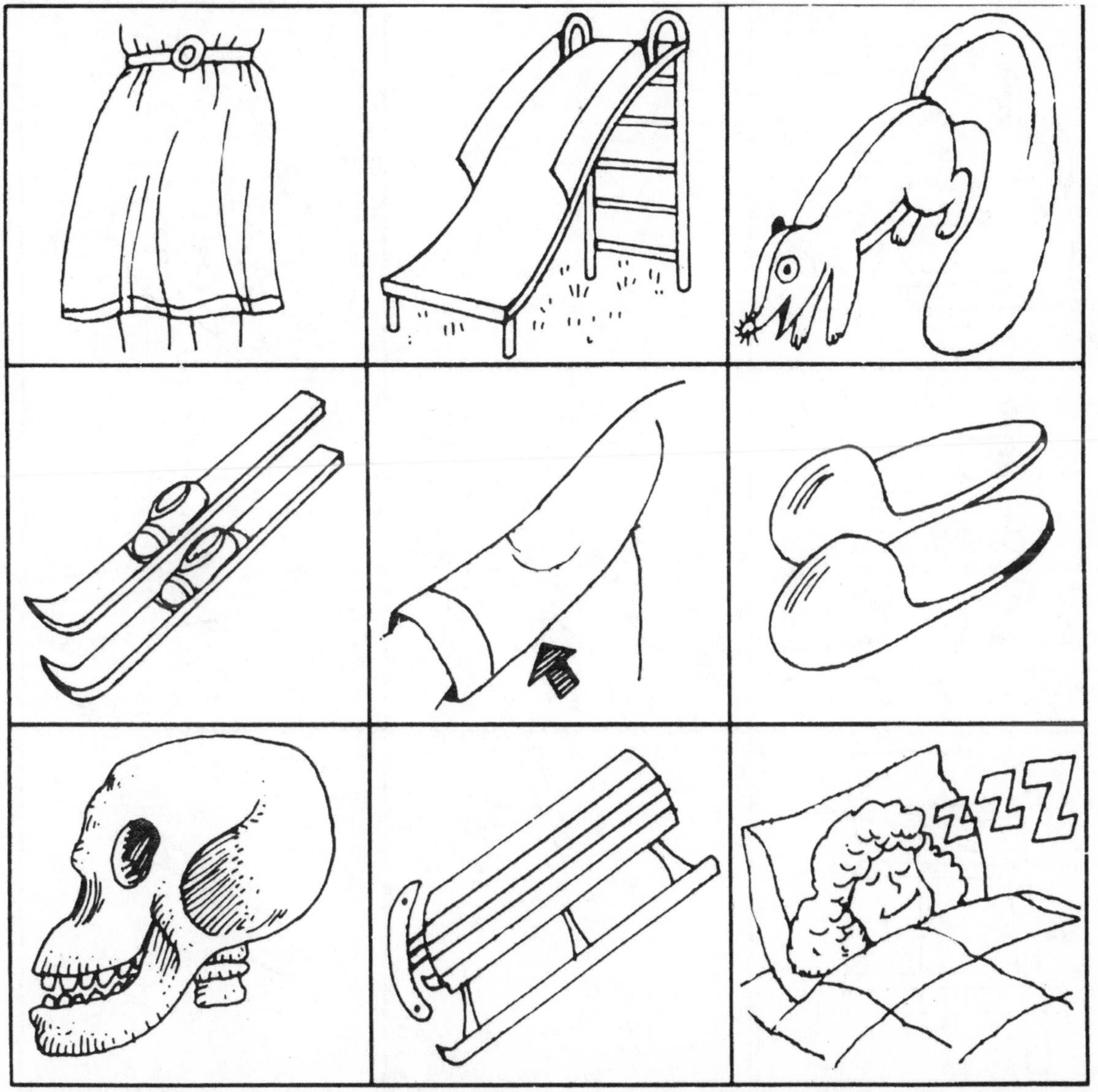

**Skills:** Understanding that some consonants can be blended together; Sound/symbol association

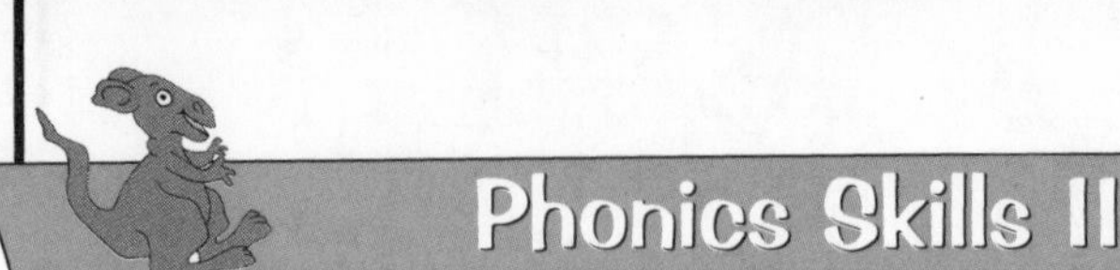

Initial consonant blends: **st, sp**

Which ones begin with **st**? Color them red. Which ones begin with **sp**? Color them blue.

**Skills:** Understanding that some consonants can be blended together; Sound/symbol association

Initial consonant blends: **gr, gl**

gr

gl

Which ones begin with **gr**? Color them red. Which ones begin with **gl**? Color them blue.

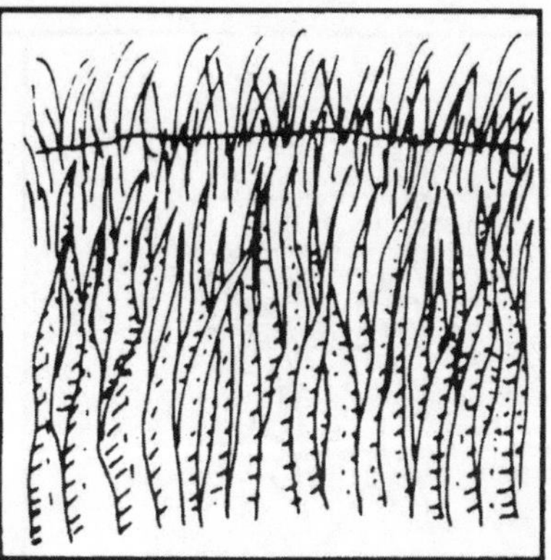

GLUE

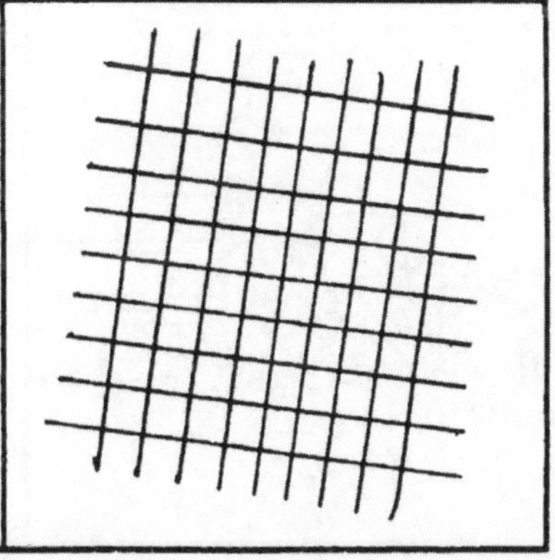

**Skills:** Understanding that some consonants can be blended together; Sound/symbol association

Initial consonant blends: **pl, pr**

pl

pr

Which ones begin with **pl**? Color them red. Which ones begin with **pr**? Color them blue.

**Skills:** Understanding that some consonants can be blended together; Sound/symbol association

Initial consonant blends: **sn, sw**

sn

sw

Which ones begin with **sn**? Color them red. Which ones begin with **sw**? Color them blue.

**Skills:** Understanding that some consonants can be blended together; Sound/symbol association

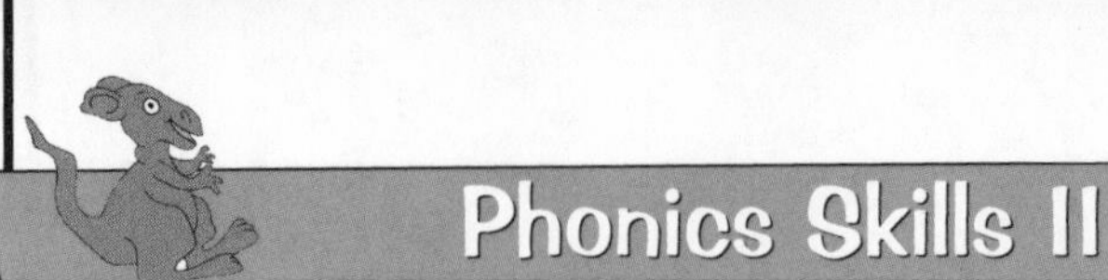


Initial consonant blends: **fr, fl**

fr

fl

Which ones begin with **fr**? Color them red. Which ones begin with **fl**? Color them blue.

**Skills:** Understanding that some consonants can be blended together; Sound/symbol association

# Phonics Skills II

Consonant digraph: **sh**

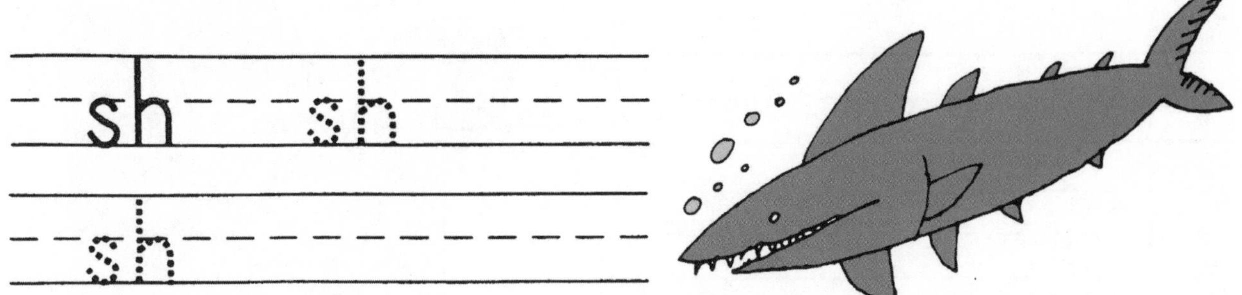


Which ones begin with **sh**? Color them orange. Color the other pictures purple.

Skills: Recognizing and understanding consonant digraphs; Sound/symbol association

Consonant digraph: **th**

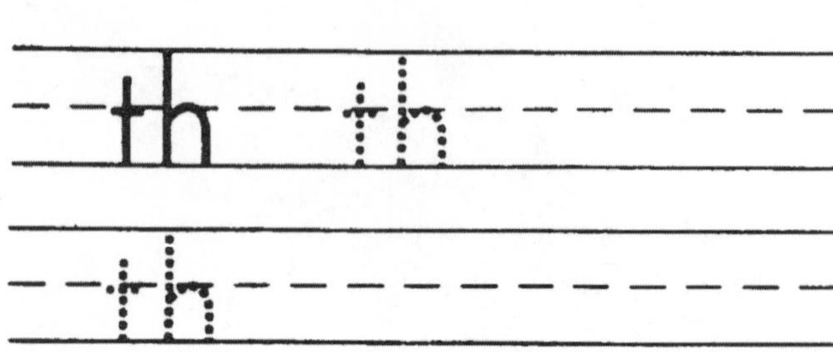


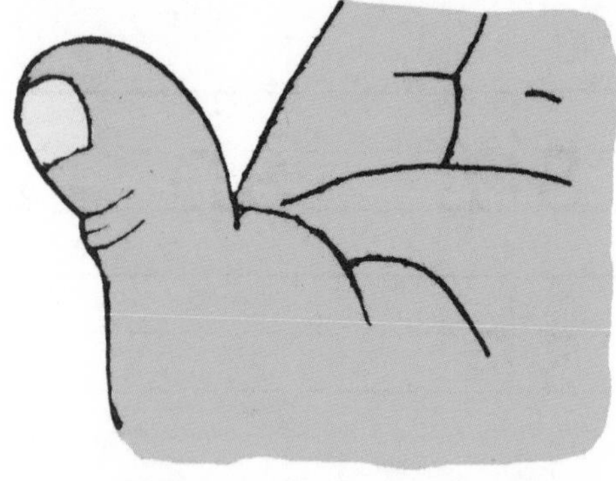

Which ones begin with **th**? Color them brown. Color the other pictures green.

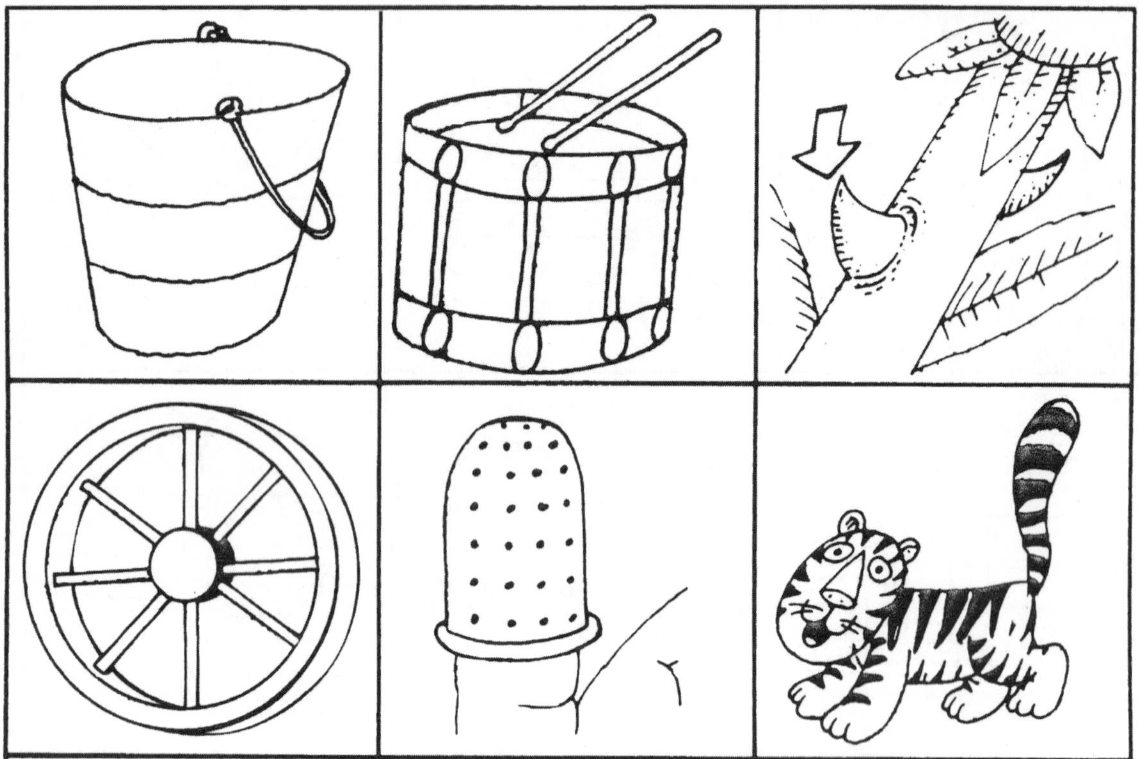

**Skills:** Recognizing and understanding consonant digraphs; Sound/symbol association

Consonant digraph: **wh**

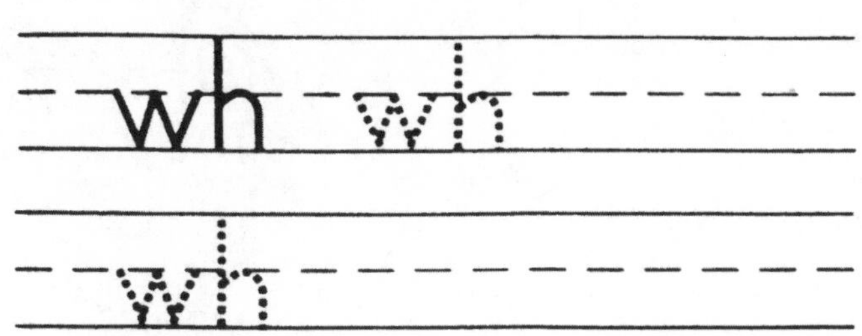


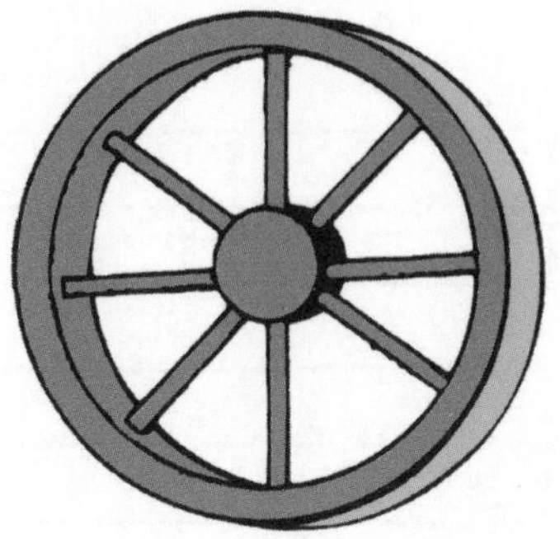

Which ones begin with **wh**? Color them red. Color the other pictures blue.

**Skills:** Recognizing and understanding consonant digraphs; Sound/symbol association

Consonant digraph: **ch**

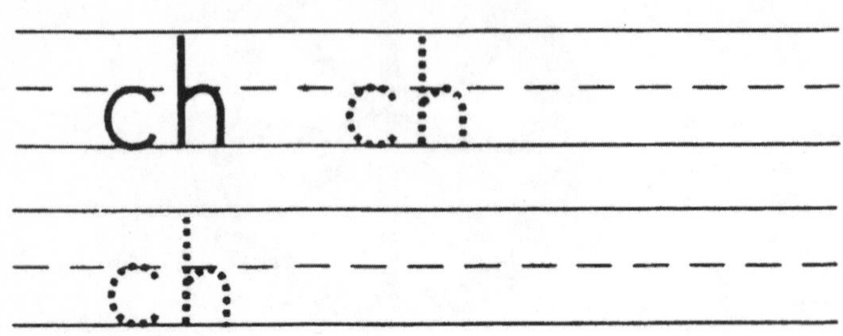

Which ones begin with **ch**? Color them brown. Color the other pictures red.

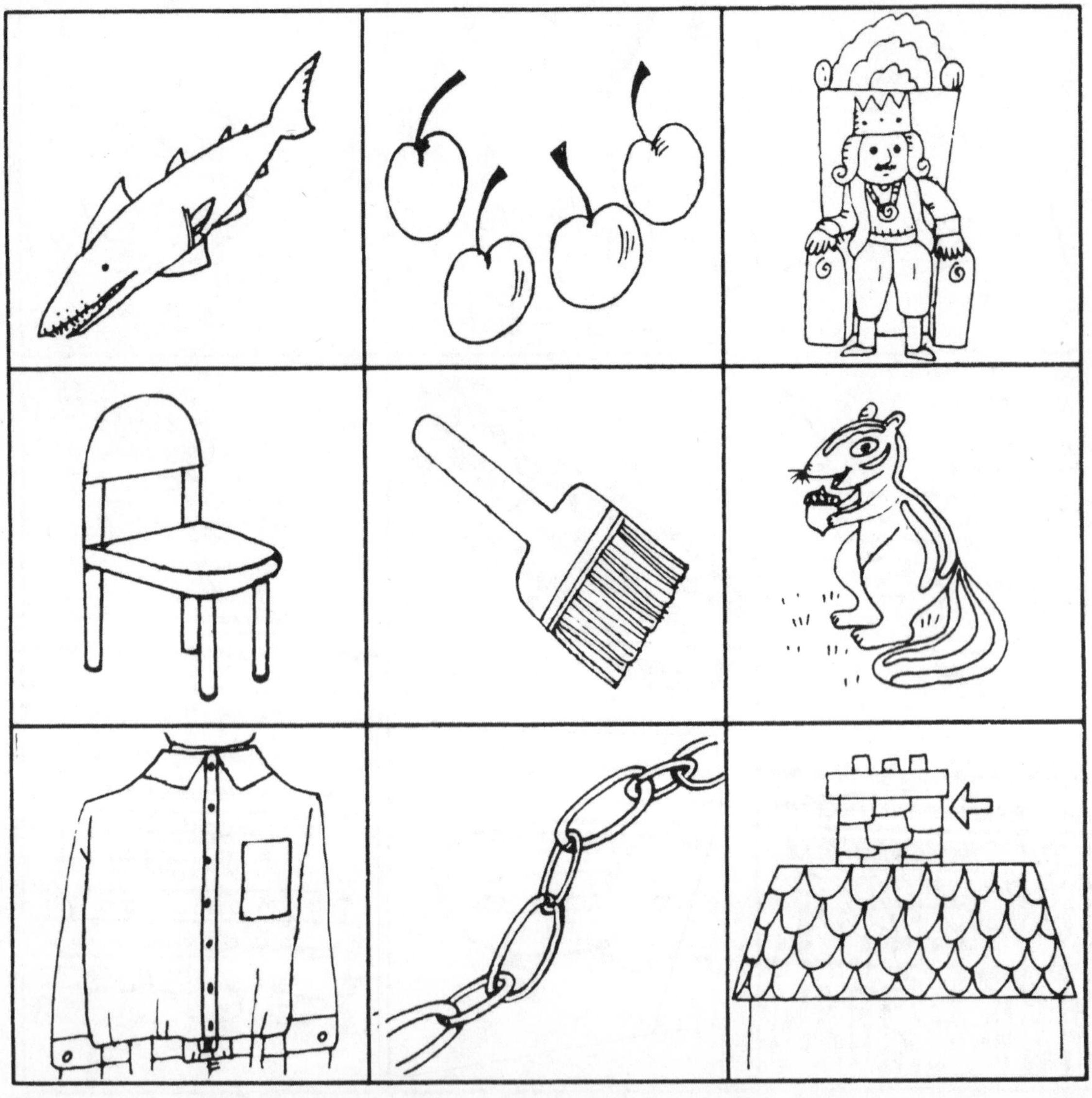

**Skills:** Recognizing and understanding consonant digraphs; Sound/symbol association

# Good Job!

## Give yourself a star!

# Putting Words Together

# Putting Words Together

The word **and** connects other words.

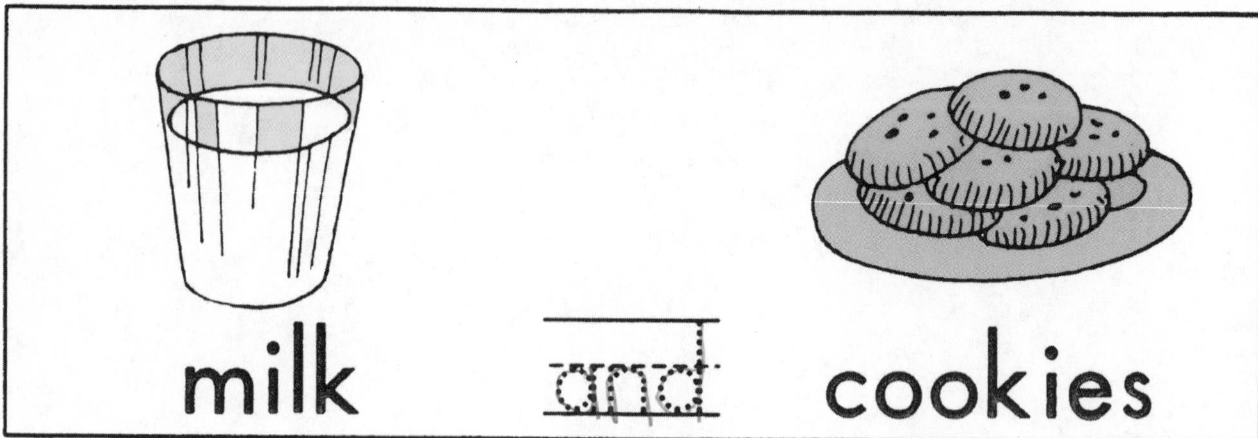


Trace the word **and**. Then name the things that go together.

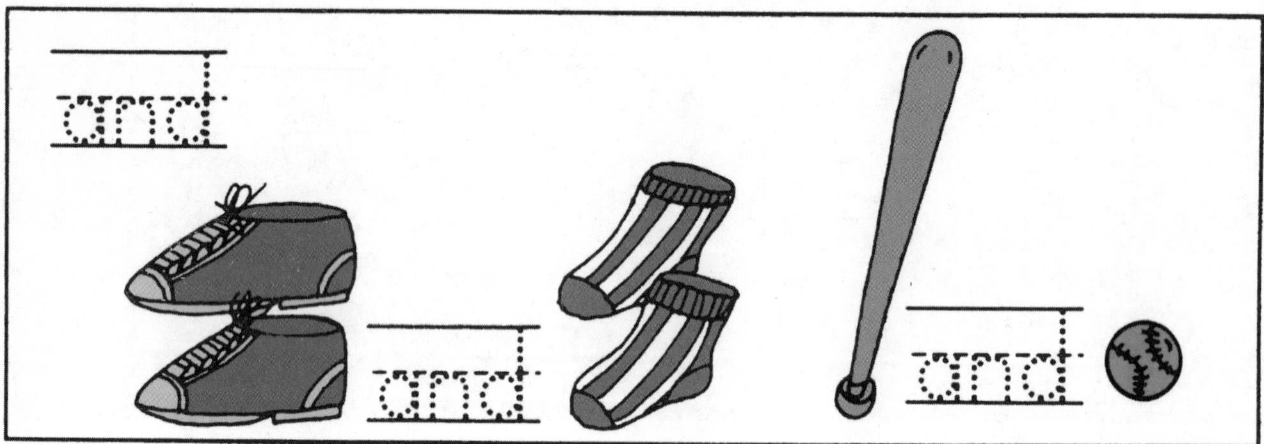


Draw two other things that go together. Then write the word **and**.

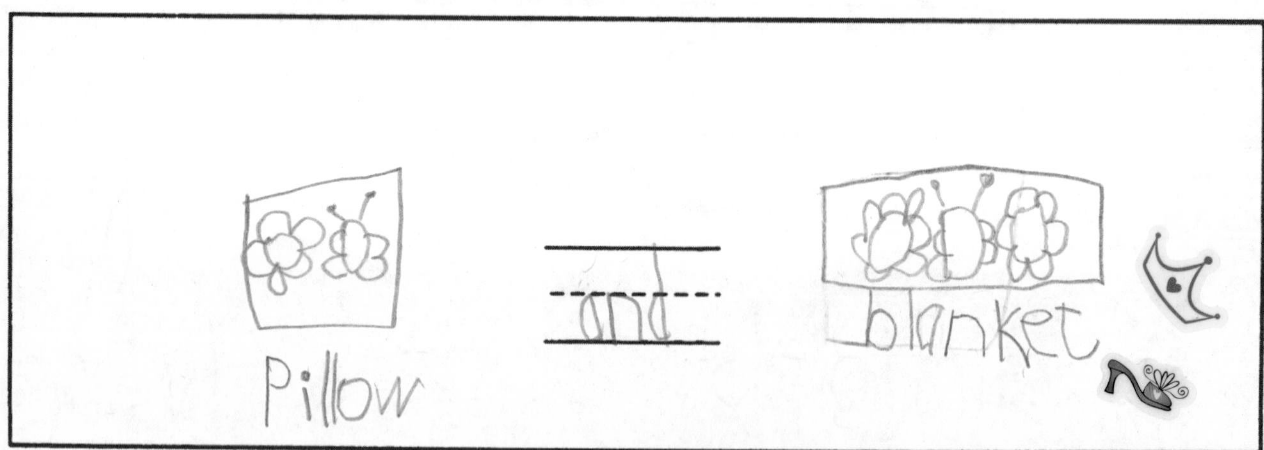


**Skills:** Spelling, writing and using sight vocabulary

# Putting Words Together

Trace and read the words.

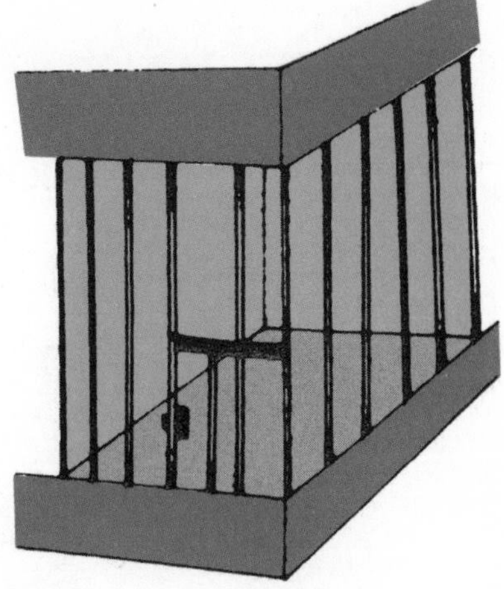

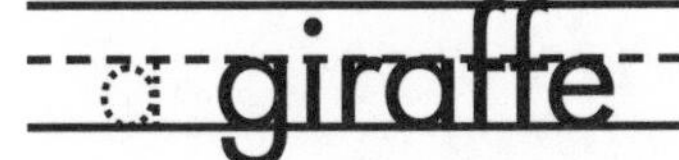

a giraffe

an elephant

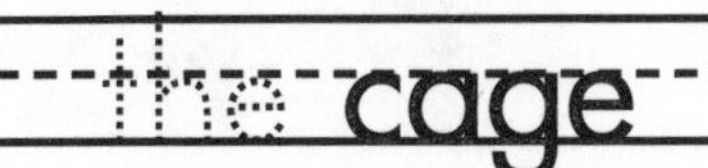

the cage

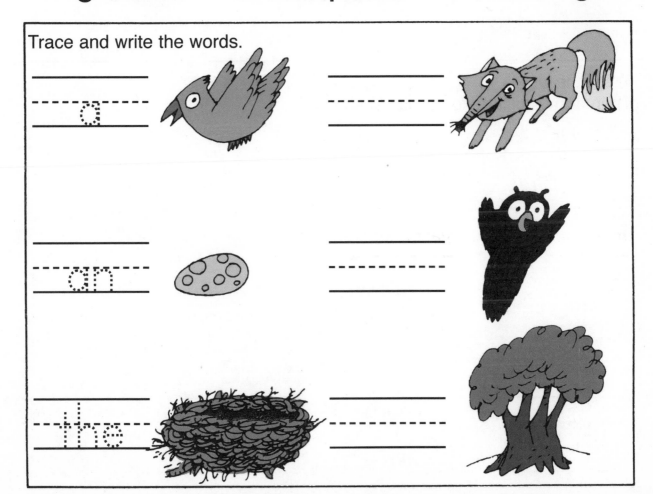

Trace and write the words.

a

an

the

**Skills:** Spelling, writing and using sight vocabulary

# Putting Words Together

Read the words.

Trace the words.
Then draw a picture to go with each word.

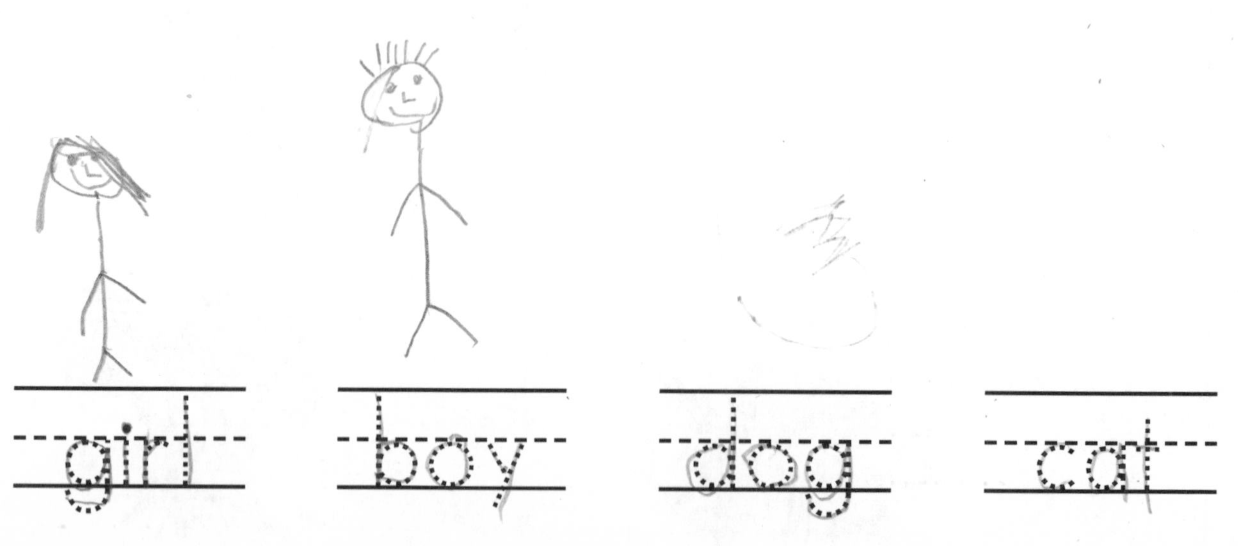


Skills: Spelling, writing and using sight vocabulary

## Putting Words Together

Read the words.

mother son father

Look at who won each medal.
Write the names of the winners.

mother

1ST PLACE

2ND PLACE

3RD PLACE

**Skills:** Spelling, writing and using sight vocabulary

# Putting Words Together

Read the words.

pig cow duck

Connect the dots.
Write the name of each animal.

**Skills:** Spelling, writing and using sight vocabulary

# Putting Words Together

Trace the words.

Look at each picture and the list of words.
Then draw a line from each word to the matching picture.

sit

go

play

read

MENU

**Skills:** Spelling and using sight vocabulary

# Putting Words Together

Trace the words.

Look at each picture and the list of words.
Then draw a line from each word to the matching picture.

sad

happy

old

young

**Skills:** Spelling and using sight vocabulary

# Putting Words Together

Trace the words.

cold hot big little

Look at each picture and the list of words.
Then draw a line from each word to the matching picture.

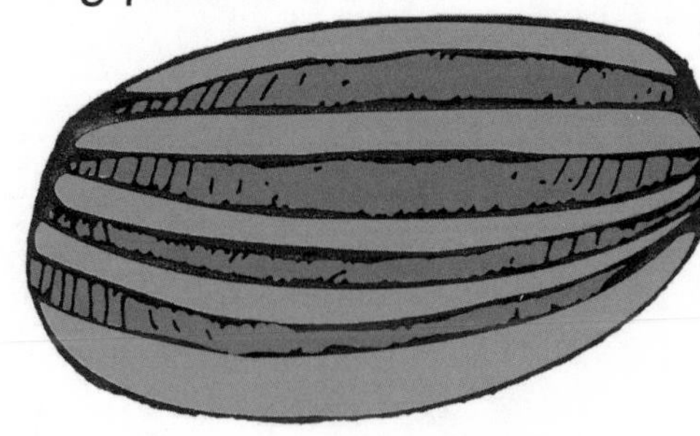

cold

hot

big

little

**Skills:** Spelling and using sight vocabulary

# Putting Words Together

Read the words.

Trace each word.
Then draw a line from each word to the matching picture.

run

jump

fly

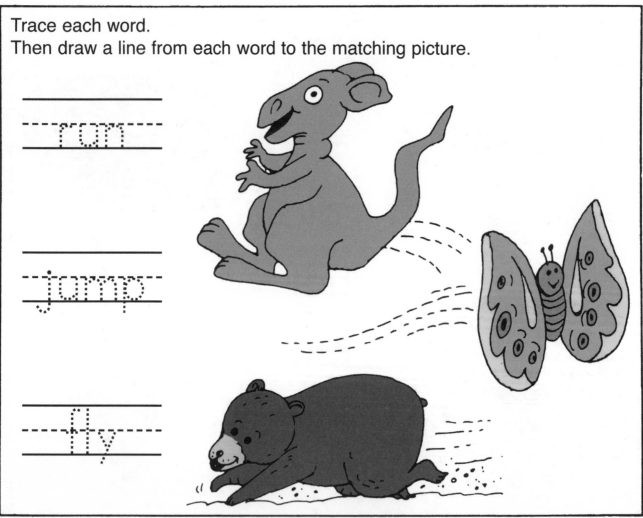

Skills: Spelling, writing and using sight vocabulary

# Putting Words Together

Trace the words.

will can is not

Find the words on the sign on the puzzle.

will
can
is
not

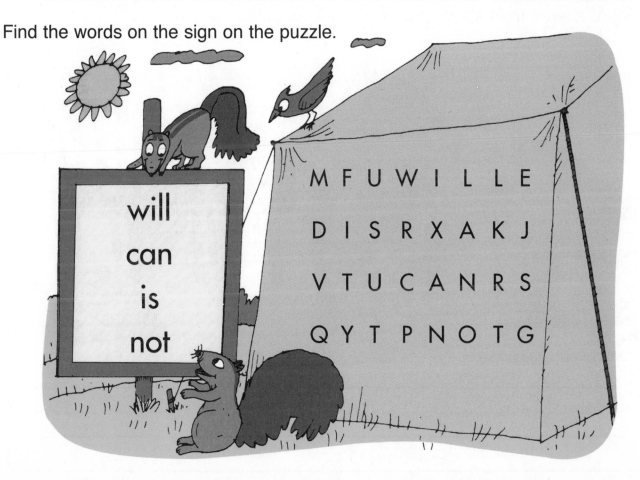

M F U W I L L E
D I S R X A K J
V T U C A N R S
Q Y T P N O T G

**Skills:** Spelling and using sight vocabulary

# Putting Words Together

Read the words.

Look at the pictures below.
Write a word from above on the blank lines below.

# Putting Words Together

Read the words.

Look at the pictures below.
Write a word from above on the blank lines below.

______ ______ ______ ______

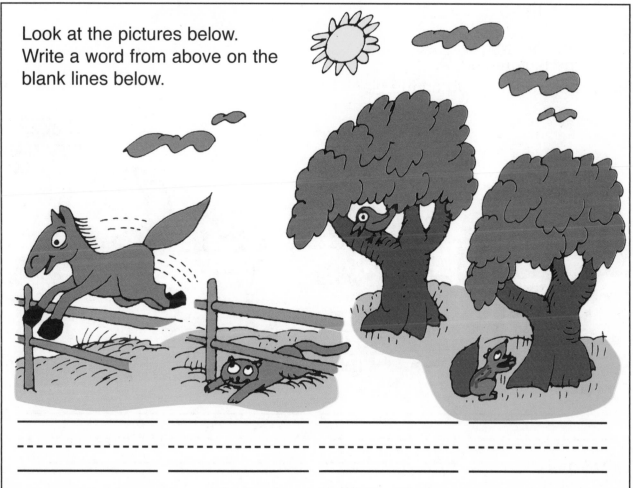

**Skills:** Spelling, writing, and using sight vocabulary

# Putting Words Together

Read the words.

Look at the pictures below.
Write a word from above on the blank lines below.

**Skills:** Spelling, writing, and using sight vocabulary

# Putting Words Together

Read the words.
Look at each picture.
Write the correct word in each blank.

I play ball in the  ______________

The  ______________ has a dog and a bird.

I can read my book at  ______________.

**Skills:** Using spelling words in sentences

# Putting Words Together

Use the words in the box to complete the sentences below.
Then read the sentences.

The ____________ has a car.

The ____________ has a train.

Can I play with your ____________?

The girl is ____________.

**Skills:** Using spelling words in sentences

# Putting Words Together

Use the words in the box to complete the sentences below.
Then read the sentences.

The girl will feed the ____________.

My mother will feed the ____________.

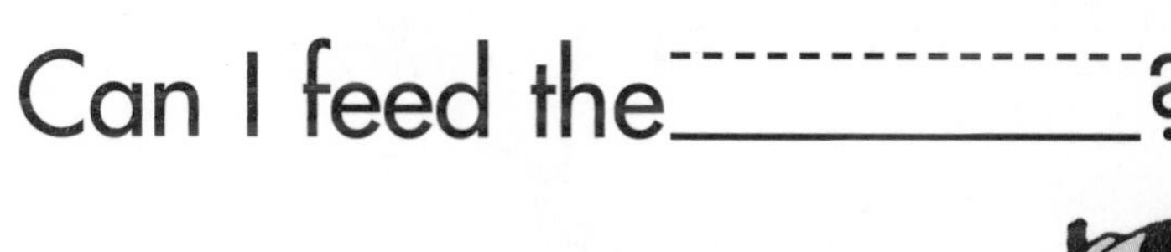

Can I feed the ____________?

The ____________ will come and play.

**Skills:** Using spelling words in sentences

# Putting Words Together

Look at the picture.
Read the sentences.
Circles each sentence that is true.

The elephant is big.

The man has a little hat.

One clown is happy.

One clown is sad.

The dog can jump.

The girl will go up.

**Skills:** Using spelling words in sentences

# Putting Words Together

Read the riddles.
Write the answers on the lines.

I like to eat hay.
I give milk.
Who am I?

I can wag my tail.
I can jump and run.
Who am I?

I can walk.
I can swim and fly.
Who am I?

**Skills:** Using context to answer questions; Spelling words

# Achievement Checklist

Use the checklist below after each session with this book. If your child had trouble with a page, find the problem skill and list the page number in the middle column. You will want to return to it later. If your child successfully completed the pages containing a skill, put a check mark in the "Mastered" column. Your child can watch with pride as the column fills up with skills he or she has mastered.

| BASIC SKILLS | Needs Work | Mastered! |
|---|---|---|
| **HANDWRITING SKILLS** | | |
| Fine motor skills | | |
| Eye/hand coordination | | |
| Forming vertical lines | | |
| Forming diagonal lines | | |
| Forming open curves | | |
| Forming closed curves | | |
| Forming horizontal lines | | |
| Forming upper/lowercase Aa | | |
| Forming upper/lowercase Bb | | |
| Forming upper/lowercase Cc | | |
| Forming upper/lowercase Dd | | |
| Forming upper/lowercase Ee | | |
| Forming upper/lowercase Ff | | |
| Forming upper/lowercase Gg | | |
| Forming upper/lowercase Hh | | |
| Forming upper/lowercase Ii | | |
| Forming upper/lowercase Jj | | |
| Forming upper/lowercase Kk | | |
| Forming upper/lowercase Ll | | |
| Forming upper/lowercase Mm | | |
| Forming upper/lowercase Nn | | |
| Forming upper/lowercase Oo | | |
| Forming upper/lowercase Pp | | |
| Forming upper/lowercase Qq | | |
| Forming upper/lowercase Rr | | |
| Forming upper/lowercase Ss | | |
| Forming upper/lowercase Tt | | |
| Forming upper/lowercase Uu | | |
| Forming upper/lowercase Ww | | |
| Forming upper/lowercase Xx | | |
| Forming upper/lowercase Yy | | |
| Forming upper/lowercase Zz | | |
| **COLORS, SHAPES AND NUMBERS** | | |
| Distinguishing color | | |
| Classification | | |
| Word recognition | | |
| Recognizing and forming shapes | | |
| Symmetry | | |
| Identifying sets and their corresponding numerals | | |
| Matching | | |
| Forming numerals | | |
| Writing number words | | |

# Achievement Checklist

| BASIC SKILLS | Needs Work | Mastered! |
|---|---|---|
| Classifying and recording information | | |
| Creating sets | | |
| **COUNTING AND MATH SKILLS** | | |
| Counting | | |
| Ordering numbers | | |
| Identifying sets | | |
| Comparing numbers | | |
| Odd and even numbers | | |
| Counting by 2s | | |
| Counting by 5s | | |
| Addition | | |
| Subtraction | | |
| Making comparisons | | |
| **MEASURING** | | |
| Measuring lengths | | |
| Using non-standard units | | |
| Comparing size | | |
| **TIME AND MONEY** | | |
| Time duration | | |
| Telling time to the hour and half hour | | |
| Showing time to the hour and half hour | | |
| Identifying money amounts | | |
| Understanding the use of money | | |
| **READING READINESS** | | |
| Association/classification | | |
| Logical reasoning | | |
| One-to-one correspondence | | |
| Visual discrimination | | |
| Following directions | | |
| Opposites | | |
| Observing and continuing patterns | | |
| Visual memory | | |
| Sequencing | | |
| **PHONICS SKILLS I** | | |
| Initial conosonants | | |
| Sound/symbol association | | |
| Auditory discrimination | | |
| Final consonants | | |
| **PHONICS SKILLS II** | | |
| Short vowels | | |
| Long vowels | | |
| Writing letters and words | | |
| Consonant blends | | |
| Consonant digraphs | | |
| **PUTTING WORDS TOGETHER** | | |
| Spelling | | |
| Sight vocabulary | | |
| Using words in sentences | | |

***Awarded to***

_______________________________________________

- - - - - - - - - - - - - - - - - - - - - - - - - - - - - - - -

_______________________________________________

***for extraordinary achievement in Getting Ready For Kindergarten Skills***
***on this date,***

_______________ _______________

- - - - - - - - - - -   - - - - - - - - - - -

_______________, _______________

**CONGRATULATIONS!**